SOVEREIGN SELVES

DAVID J. CARLSON

Sovereign Selves

AMERICAN INDIAN
AUTOBIOGRAPHY
AND THE LAW

UNIVERSITY OF ILLINOIS PRESS

URBANA AND CHICAGO

Library of Congress Cataloging-in-Publication Data
Carlson, David J., 1970–
Sovereign selves : American Indian autobiography and
the law / David J. Carlson.
  p.   cm.
Includes bibliographical references and index.
ISBN-13: 978-0-252-07266-6 (ISBN-10: 13 paper : alk. paper)
ISBN-10: 0-252-07266-9 (ISBN-10: 10 paper : alk. paper)
  1. Indians of North America—Politics and government.
  2. Indians of North America—Legal status, laws, etc.—Language.
  3. Indians of North America—Biography.
  4. Autobiography—Indian authors.
  5. Speeches, addresses, etc., Indian—North America.
  6. American literature—Indian authors.
  7. Apess, William, B. 1798.
  8. Eastman, Charles Alexander, 1858–1939.
  I. Title.
  E78.T77C38   2005
  810.9'492'08997—dc22   2005017120

Contents

Acknowledgments

The research for this book was completed in two places over a period of roughly six years. I began this project at Indiana University, Bloomington, but it was at California State University, San Bernardino, that the work before you assumed its final form. I would like to thank the English Department at Indiana University for awarding me fellowship support in 1999–2000, which provided invaluable time for writing and thinking during the initial stages of my research. I would also like to thank the College of Arts and Letters at California State University for granting me a Summer Research Fellowship in 2002 to complete the first draft of the manuscript. The librarians at the Huntington Library in San Marino, California, deserve special thanks for assisting me in sorting through the Ely Parker Papers and other archival materials. I am grateful for their permission to publish excerpts from several pieces in the collection.

I have received helpful feedback on this manuscript, in its various incarnations, from a number of sources. I would like to thank colleagues Paul John Eakin, Jonathan Elmer, Raymond Hedin, and Michael Grossberg at Indiana University for thoughtful readings of the early versions of this study. My colleagues at California State University, San Bernardino have also generously offered their time and talents to help me focus my ideas and clarify their expression. Philip Page, Suzanne Lane, Rong Chen, Peter Schroeder, and Jacqueline Rhodes deserve particular thanks. Others who have read and commented on some or all of the manuscript at various stages include Christine Bolus-Reichart, Martin Harris, and Sean McDowell. The readers at University of Illinois Press provided me with that most valuable of gifts, encouragement, at a crucial stage of the process. Indeed, their comments on the initial draft of the book helped to remind me of the value of the work (something easy to lose sight of when one is several years into a project). In thanking all these persons, I should also offer the standard caveat: all remaining flaws in this book are my own responsibility. Undoubtedly, there would have been many more of them without the expertise of others.

Special thanks go out to my family for many years of love and encouragement. I would particularly like to acknowledge my father, Albert E. Carlson, who regrettably passed away shortly before I completed my doctorate. Though frequently puzzled by some of my educational choices ("You are majoring in English?" "You want to go to Sri Lanka?"), my father always trusted me to find my own path and supported each of the choices I made along the way. For this and many other reasons, I dedicate this book to his memory. Finally, my wife, Alison Wiles, deserves particular mention, for she continues to be my greatest source of support and inspiration. This book is for her as well.

A portion of chapter 5 first appeared in *American Indian Quarterly,* volume 25, number 4 (Fall 2001). © 2002 University of Nebraska Press. I am grateful for permission to republish that material here.

SOVEREIGN SELVES

Introduction

For scholars interested in the conjunction between law and literature, one of the most significant early examples of what we would now call "ideological analysis" appears in Alexis de Tocqueville's 1835 classic *Democracy in America*. In chapter 16 of the first volume, Tocqueville suggests that the cultural fabric of early America had been shaped in significant ways by the dissemination of legal language. Commenting on the role that legal professionals played in preventing majoritarian tyranny in the young republic, he notes that in the United States "the language of the law thus becomes, in some measure, a vulgar tongue," while "the spirit of the law, which is produced in the schools and the courts of justice, gradually penetrates beyond their walls into the bosom of society" (290). In considering the possibility of an *ideological* connection between law and national identity, Tocqueville was well ahead of his time. Indeed, his theses anticipate the contemporary field of law and literature scholarship, particularly that strain focusing on the relationship between legal discourse (a term encompassing both the language and institutions of law) and identity formation. *Sovereign Selves* may be best understood as a part of that critical tradition. It represents the first stage of a broad inquiry into the relationship between legal models of self and the autobiographical acts of a variety of subjects writing during the period from the Revolution to the beginning of the twentieth century. At this stage, I focus particularly on autobiographies by early Native American writers, whose experience can be usefully understood under the broad rubric of colonialism.[1] In doing so, I aim to contribute to three major critical conversations: (1) debates over the generic definition of autobiography; (2) attempts to define a critical methodology for law and literature scholarship; and (3) concerns about the viability of "authenticity" as a critical term in the study of Native American literatures.

Adequately framing my entry into the first of these conversations requires a brief overview of some of the major trends in autobiography scholarship since the 1960s. Before the middle decades of the twentieth century, the study of autobiography had been more or less limited to treatments of texts as historical documents (often seen as limited by their subjective perspective) or to inquiries into the origins and history of the autobiographical form.[2] Since Roy Pascal's *Design and Truth in Autobiography* (1960), though, many scholars have taken issue with what we might call the "referential fallacy" (the idea that autobiography offers a transparent, objective window onto historical events) and the related notion that authorial veracity is *the* central critical issue in reading autobiographical writing. Pascal's innovation was to argue that the subject of autobiography is not historical fact, but *experience,* the organization of fact through consciousness to create meaning (17–19). His work thus opened the door for the literary criticism of autobiography, built on a greater appreciation of the relationship between autobiography and other forms of imaginative writing (like fiction). Of course, in doing so Pascal introduced a host of new theoretical problems. For if autobiography's defining characteristic is the presence of an ordering consciousness recording its experience of the world, how are we to make generic distinctions between, say, an autobiographical novel, a memoir, a diary, a confessional record, or a poem? Attempts to make such distinctions, meeting with only limited success, have dominated a significant strand of autobiography theory ever since.

The fundamental problem with efforts to create a taxonomy of autobiography has been the difficulty of applying traditional (normative, or rule-based) theories of genre to autobiographical writing. For years, critics have struggled with the fact that in its apparent variety, autobiography seems unlike almost any other literary "form." One can say that the sestina, for instance, is a poetic structure self-consciously used in Western versification, originating in the thirteenth century, and possessing certain formal characteristics. In this sense, the sestina is easily designated as a literary "object" with a definite history. In such a case, one can readily conceive of genre, in its normative sense, without much trouble. It is difficult to make such confident pronouncements about autobiography, however. The briefest survey of the relevant critical literature reveals thoughtful arguments that the autobiographical tradition begins with texts as different as Egyptian tomb hieroglyphics,

Augustine's *Confessions,* Petrarch's *Secretum,* Rousseau's *Confessions,* and Benjamin Franklin's *Autobiography.* Even critics trying to offer definitions that emphasize process (focusing on the autobiographical turn of mind) have often fallen back into some version of what we might call the "normative fallacy." In his early and important book *Metaphors of Self* (1972), for example, James Olney theorizes autobiography in terms of the "vital impulse to order that has always caused man to create" (1). Almost immediately, though, he grafts a broadly normative definition of autobiography (*as a noun*) onto his theory of the autobiographical impulse (*as a verb*). Olney argues that the essence of "order" in autobiography is the adoption of a unique, coherent, and individual point of view. Thus, the act of self-becoming must involve the creation of a unified identity around a complex of metaphors. The problem with such a fusion, linking a normative generic definition with the functional idea that autobiography is a response to experience, is that the former designates a specific "thing" (a literary object with certain characteristics, like unity and cohesiveness) while the latter designates an impulse (whose result might well vary cross-culturally and historically). These two kinds of definitions are not congruent.

The limitations of approaches to autobiography like that in *Metaphors of Self* suggest the need for theoretical distinctions between specific norms, or "models" of identity, and the broader processes of self-definition. The consequences of failing to do so extend well beyond academic debates regarding the contents of the literary canon. Without a distinction between self as an object and self-definition as an action, claims that autobiography is defined by characteristics X, Y, and Z commit both critic and reader to some difficult corollary positions. Having posited a series of characteristic elements, many traditional generic approaches go on to use these elements as a litmus test for defining not just the canon of autobiography, but also the canon of significant selfhood. In effect, then, in spite of a critic's best intentions, such scholarship can amount to a *de facto* argument that there are only certain models of identity that are authentic, legitimate, interesting, or valuable. Persons who fail to represent themselves according to these models either fail to show up at all on the critical radar screen (becoming non-persons) or find themselves relegated to a lesser status. No contemporary literary critic would consciously use the language of primitivism or "savagism" so much in vogue during the eighteenth and nineteenth centuries. Still, one cannot help but recognize the subordinate position an Australian aborigine occupies in a world where the development of self-expression is tied, in the words of one prominent scholar, to the emergence of "individuality" and the "full form of historical mindedness" embodied by men like Rousseau, Franklin, and Goethe.[3]

The central critical problem I am tracing here involves the failure of many scholars to start from the premise that there are various kinds of writing we might call autobiographical, all of which represent the attempts of discrete persons to understand the nature of self and identity. The study of autobiography implicates any critic, whether he or she wishes it, into a broader discussion of the nature of human identity and selfhood. Every statement we make about autobiographical writing, however innocent, has implications for the way we perceive ourselves, others, and human history. In this respect, we can see that the act of reading and writing about autobiography carries with it a unique set of ethical demands. To produce a transhistorical definition of autobiography *understood only as a specific form* is, in a sense, to produce a transhistorical definition of selfhood as a form. Such a notion may have been commonplace during the eighteenth century, but even without claiming great expertise in anthropology, philosophy, or comparative religion, readers of our era should feel uneasy about such universalism. Increasingly, scholars from a variety of fields maintain that selfhood is not a "thing," but a category or signifier, variously conceived by individuals and cultures throughout human history.[4] This point suggests an ethical imperative to reformulate the terms of literary analysis and to ask a different set of questions in analyzing autobiographical texts. In the study that follows, then, my critical orientation will be toward what we might call the *autobiographical impulse* (a mode of consciousness and linguistic action that involves generating a concept of personal identity within a specific cultural context) rather than on a specific definition of *autobiography* as a generic thing. (The autobiographical impulse is, of course, a mode with its own history, but the study of that history involves considering not what *the* autobiographical ur-text *is* in some absolute sense, but what various kinds of texts *do* in different times and places.) Such an orientation places the present work within the realm of the philosophy of language, suggesting a dynamic, "performative" understanding of genre, as opposed to a rigidly formalistic and normative one.

As developed in the work of thinkers like J. L. Austin and John Searle, the term "performative" designates the capacity of language not simply to reflect reality, but to actually constitute a form of action (shaping reality). Performative language, as Austin would say, "makes things happen."[5] Understood as a kind of performance, autobiography becomes the *act* of self-making through the use of language. Such an understanding of autobiographical writing links my work with the scholarship of Philippe

Lejeune and Elizabeth Bruss.[6] In his essay "Autobiography and Literary History," Lejeune (drawing on reader-response critics like Wolfgang Iser and Hans Robert Jauss) argues that genre is a historically specific code between authors and readers that enables works to be produced and circulated. Genre is not something inherent in the text itself, in other words; it is the product of a communicative circuit that influences the creation and reception of texts. Lejeune's insight draws attention to the idea that what we generally refer to today as autobiography emerged in conjunction with a particular historical paradigm regarding what constitutes a "self," a "life," and a life story.

As generic objects, the modern autobiographies of Rousseau or Franklin, for example, are particular manifestations of the broadly human autobiographical impulse, filtered through a cultural matrix (tied to modern individualism, in this case). Bruss's work foregrounds the idea that this matrix is a sociolinguistic one. In *Autobiographical Acts: The Changing Situation of a Literary Genre,* she argues that genre is an "institutional" reality, tied to the recognition by both author and audience of rules and norms regarding identity. This is, of course, just another way of suggesting that we view genre as the product of a communicative process, not necessarily as a description of fixed properties inherent in texts themselves. At the same time, though, Bruss draws our attention to the embeddedness of autobiographical writing within its particular social and historical context. Autobiographical forms emerge and acquire legitimacy within specific systems of intersubjective communication that can, of course, change over time (6–7). Following such an understanding, a number of the key principles of this study emerge: (1) the autobiographical impulse does not point us toward a single "referent" (*the* Self) that can be defined transhistorically; (2) autobiographical expression is not focused on a self or a life which exists outside or prior to it, but rather constitutes ("performs") that self in the act of narration; this is what Bruss, drawing on the philosophy of language, has referred to as the "autobiographical act"; (3) the nature and form of an autobiographical act is tied to the cultural context in which it occurs; (4) understanding that context requires close attentiveness to the discursive situation of the autobiographer (i.e., his or her relationship to the culture's ways of knowing the self and the institutions that legitimize and authorize those ways of knowing).[7]

The analyses of Native American autobiographies that form the heart of this book are attempts to understand how *specific* instances of autobiographical self-performance take place within *equally specific* linguistic and cultural contexts. This is a key point, for the understanding of autobiography I propose has a significant impact on the way I read the Native

6   *Introduction*

American texts I have chosen. (It also helps to explain my resistance to the discourse of authenticity pervading some Native Americanist scholarship, an issue I will take up shortly). Bruss's argument that autobiographies, as particular kinds of language acts, are made possible by certain "constitutive rules" and institutions seems to me to be another way of saying that autobiographical selves emerge within the context of some kind of normative universe, or *nomos*, the nature of which will have a profound impact on the way the autobiographical impulse plays out. The one element that is missing from Bruss's theoretical account of autobiographical performance and its context, though, is a clear discussion of the institutional structures that help define and disseminate the "symbolic systems" undergirding autobiographies.[8] This book marks my attempt to bring at least one example of those structures into sharper focus by looking at autobiographies produced within the particularly pressurized communicative context of internal colonialism in the United States.

In this study, I argue for the centrality of legal discourse in defining the sociolinguistic context of early Native American writers' autobiographical acts. Between the Revolutionary War and the early twentieth century, these autobiographers produced their acts of self-definition in the shadow of a hegemonic legal system designed explicitly to reshape their sense of identity. During this period, legal models of identity profoundly influenced not only the political and cultural landscape confronting Native American writers, but also the broader literary tradition of autobiography from which they might draw inspiration (and in which their non-Indian readers expected them to situate themselves). Generally speaking, from the late eighteenth through the early twentieth centuries, the sense of what was both possible and acceptable in American lifewriting became increasingly circumscribed by the normative characteristics of what we might call the "liberal autobiography," a form that itself takes shape largely within the context of the legal discourse of emergent capitalism.[9] Such constraints had enormous implications for the concurrent emergence of a tradition of American Indian lifewriting. As a result, Native American autobiographies provide a fascinating (if extreme) starting point for an inquiry into the deep and broad connections between legal discourse and autobiographical action in the United States.

As this discussion of the legal context of Native American autobiographical acts should suggest, however, besides making a theoretical contribution to the study of autobiography as a "genre," I also hope that this book will be germane to the increasingly vibrant field of law and literature scholarship. Again, understanding the nature of this connection requires a brief overview of recent scholarly trends. When one surveys the work done in law and literature over the last twenty years or so, three main areas of inquiry emerge. The first grew out of a recognition that practitioners of law and students of literature share a common interest in the nature of interpretation and the possibility of interpretive certainty. In this context, a number of critics have begun to consider whether the hermeneutic theories and practices of literary criticism can offer anything of value to legal scholars and professionals. Others have questioned the validity and ethics of such approaches in situations (like the courtroom) where the stakes of "correct" interpretation are often extremely high.[10] While there is much interesting work being done by the "hermeneutic wing" of the law and literature movement, this study engages with the other two main subfields in the discipline. These subfields involve both attempts to articulate the historical and ideological connection between legal and literary narratives and also to understand the ways both legal and literary texts function, in James Boyd White's term, as "constitutive rhetorics" where "character and community . . . are defined and made real in performances of language" (xi). These "ideological" and "rhetorical" approaches to law and literature scholarship each speak to different facets of the way legal discourse disseminates models of self. "Ideological" inquiry tends to focus on the law's content (both manifest and latent/structural) and its reproduction in literature. The "rhetorically" oriented work stresses the linguistic situation and intersubjective construction of identity by speakers working through and with the language and institutions of law. In different ways, both of these areas are crucially implicated in the contemporary debates about the subtle relationship between the language we use and the identities we assume. As such, they have a great deal to offer scholars interested in autobiographical writing.

In light of what seems to be the clear potential for convergence between two important fields of scholarship, it is surprising that almost no critical work has been done on the relationship between law and autobiography in nineteenth-century America. In spite of the proliferation in recent years of law and literature scholarship dealing especially with that historical period, and in spite of the exemplary work that has been done on the relationship between religious discourse and autobiography, critics have generally overlooked the potential connections between legal discourse and autobiographical expression. Perhaps this critical neglect derives from a lingering sense among some Americanists that autobiography cannot be treated as "literature," that its claim to factuality renders it a problematic object of study. This would be a curious objection, though, especially in light of the work done on autobiography by literary critics during the past thirty years. In my view, the marriage of a performative theory of autobiography and the ideological/rhetorical wings of law and literature scholarship is both natural and overdue. Regrettably, though, there are few models to help in developing such a critical synthesis. Even the most promising attempts to address the connections between law and literature inadequately theorize the relationship between legal models of self and literary representations of subjectivity.

Probably the best-known book-length study of nineteenth-century American legal ideology and its relationship to literature is Brook Thomas's *Cross Examinations of Law and Literature* (1987). Thomas draws on the work of two prominent legal scholars, Robert Cover and Morton Horwitz, in an attempt to bring welcome attention to the power of legal narrative to influence the literary representation of various models of identity. From Cover's essay "Nomos and Narrative," he takes the idea that the power and legitimacy of legal institutions derive from their close relationship to the cultural narratives that produce meaning and make human behavior comprehensible: as Cover puts it, "law and narrative are inseparably related" (96). Horwitz's extremely influential work *The Transformation of American Law: 1780–1860* offers Thomas a pair of related insights. Complementing Cover's sense of the importance of legal narrative, Horwitz asserts that the best place to look for evidence regarding the nature and development of the legal system is in appellate law and its legal "stories." Addressing the ideological dimensions of those legal narratives, he goes on to argue that antebellum law facilitated a shift (a "transformation") from economic and social conservatism and principles of equity to an emphasis on economic growth and production, individualism, and freedom of contract, a shift that enabled the accumulation of vast amounts of wealth in the hands of a privileged upper class. Drawing on these two scholars (and later on Mark Tushnet's work on slave law), Thomas goes on to discuss the transformation of American property law as it is represented in Cooper's *The Pioneers*, the changing image of the judiciary suggested in Hawthorne's *The House of Seven Gables*, and the ideological conflicts surrounding slavery reflected in Stowe's *Uncle Tom's Cabin*, Melville's "Benito Cereno," and other texts. In each case, he looks at how the transformations made manifest in various legal narratives relate to the content of these works of literature.

Despite the impressive scholarship on which Thomas draws in setting up his project, *Cross-Examination of Law and Literature* has some shortcomings. Those shortcomings, though, are extremely instructive ones, for they help draw attention to another contribution I hope to make with this study. In my view, the most significant weakness in

Thomas's work is its failure to adequately explore the nature of the relationship between the legal and literary narratives he discusses. With a few exceptions (such as where biographical connections, like Melville's relationship with his father-in-law Lemuel Shaw, appear), his book primarily *suggests* parallels between legal ideology and literary narratives, without explaining *how* that ideology is disseminated in the culture. In many respects, Thomas falls back on a form of "reflection" theory that characterized the approach of so-called "vulgar Marxist" criticism. His work thus reveals the need for a more rigorous analysis of how legal language functions through and within institutions (and of how and why its models of identity have been brought to bear on American subjects and literature). One of the contributions of this book is to address this need by looking closely at how encounters with legal institutions have shaped the communicative context of autobiographical self-definition. Focusing on autobiographical writings produced by manifestly "colonized" persons (whose relationships to institutional power are more easily isolated and analyzed), we get a clearer sense both of the dynamics of autobiographical action and of the nature of the connections between legal and literary language. Law and literature scholars interested in literary forms other than autobiography will hopefully find value in the present work for this reason.

Foregrounding the *colonial* context of the interaction between Native American law and autobiography draws attention to the final (and perhaps most complicated) critical context for this book. It is my hope that the readings of Indian autobiographies here will be appreciated as a constructive foray into the ongoing debate within the field of Native American Studies regarding the issue of "authenticity" in American Indian writing. Of course, readers of Native American autobiography share with students of *all* varieties of autobiographical writing several of the fundamental critical problems addressed earlier. Foremost among these is that most basic, generic question: what distinguishes a "Native American" or "American Indian" autobiography from other kinds of texts? Yet there are particular challenges in answering such a question, owing to the context—New World colonialism—within which autobiographical works by Indians have been produced. (Parallel debates have been going on for decades in African American literary criticism.) For many scholars, the most straightforward solution to the problem of genre has been simply to posit that Native American autobiography is centrally concerned with an individual's articulation of his or her "Indian" identity. Critics who have tried to apply such a definition, though, have immediately run into serious theoretical (and political) complications. The history of colonial contact between Native Americans and Euro-American settlers has largely taken shape as a conflict over the nature and meaning of "Indianness." Especially in the case of Native American authors writing before the middle decades of the twentieth century, then, the impulse toward self-definition and the mechanisms of colonial control have inevitably come into conflict, a fact that complicates our ability to read and understand these autobiographical acts. Recognizing this tension, some critics have gone so far as to question the ability of the colonized "other" to be heard at all within the representational order of the dominant culture.[11] Clearly, colonialism has placed normative genre definitions (which enter into Native American Studies through the discourse of "authenticity") at the heart of Indian autobiography criticism.

It is undeniable that the legacy of colonial domination raises important methodological questions for readers and critics of American Indian autobiography, questions that have helped determine my choice of materials for this book. The first problem involves ambiguities surrounding authorship and the control of textual production.[12] Frequently, we find that so-called Indian autobiographies were written either entirely by, or in unequal collaboration with, non-Indian editors. James Seaver's *A Narrative of the Life of Mrs. Mary Jemison* (1824), J. B. Patterson's *The Narrative of the Life of Black Hawk* (1833), and John D. Neihardt's *Black Elk Speaks* (1932), to name just a few of the most well-known examples, all share in common the mediation of a non-Indian collaborator or amanuensis. Increasingly, critics have sought to recognize and analyze this mediation. Arnold Krupat, who has written extensively on this issue, goes so far as to propose a distinction between "Native American autobiography" (the composite form produced under the auspices of a non-Indian ghostwriter or editor) and "autobiography by Native Americans" (the "independent" and unmediated form).[13] While I find Krupat's terms to be rhetorically awkward, his broader point about the need to understand the context in which textual representations of Indian identity are produced remains an important one.[14] Indeed, a persistent weakness in some scholarship on Indian autobiography has been a willingness to overlook or underemphasize the presence of a mediator while trying to make meaning from these works.[15]

Once readers of Native American autobiography have managed to clarify the situation of textual production, though, they must then move on to other interpretive problems. Because of the dominance of normative models of identity in understanding the processes of decolonization, critics reading texts produced collaboratively have often found themselves engaged in the thorny task of trying to separate the voices (and identities) within texts. As a result, metaphors of divided selves, persons "caught between worlds," dominate much of the critical literature. Yet as Miwok novelist and scholar Greg Sarris wisely cautions in his essay "American Indian Lives and Others' Selves," there is always a great danger of essentialism in this kind of critical thinking. Often, whatever strikes the critic as unfamiliar ("other") in the text becomes "Indian," a monolith defined in ahistorical opposition to a no less monolithic "Euro-American" perspective. Critical "sifting" also dominates much criticism of the writings of Indians perceived as having (at least partly) "assimilated" into Euro-American culture. Anishinaabe writer and essayist Gerald Vizenor has gone so far as to question the authenticity of *any* written texts purporting to represent what he characterizes as a fundamentally oral sense of self-consciousness. From such a radical perspective, all written autobiography becomes an inauthentic account of Native identity.[16] As we can see, this results in a continually decreasing number of texts that can be included within the canon of Indian autobiography. By extension, this involves radically circumscribing our sense of the possible range of Indian identities.

On the other end of the spectrum, there have been some critics, like Gretchen Bataille and Kathleen Mullen Sands, who have been perhaps too eager to read Indian autobiographies as "an insightful, complete, and varied means of entrance into the private and public worlds of the American Indian" (viii). Such an approach probably finds its roots in the collection of numerous Indian autobiographies under the impetus of "objective" anthropological science during the early decades of the twentieth century. It is also clearly tied to a real desire to read autobiography as a literature of "survival," a place where precontact culture can be preserved and passed on to subsequent generations. One problem with this approach, however, is that it marks a potentially troubling retreat in our theoretical understanding of the nature of autobiographical writing, taking us back to the time, before Roy Pascal's work, when autobiographies were read and appreciated primarily for their historical value and "truthfulness." Understandably, such a way of reading appeals to many Native Americanists, who (by and large) feel a strong imperative to bring to light a body of textual documentation of historical injustice and to champion Indian sovereignty. It may also be true that some texts do provide a reasonably "accurate" window into a culture. Yet if we let such assumptions dominate our expectations of Indian autobiography, we risk finding ourselves engaged yet again in a kind of normative criticism. If the texts that we value most are the ones that give us access to the "real" world of the Indian, what room is there for writers like William

Apess, whose sense of Indianness is as deeply informed by Methodism and the common law as by tribal memory and oral tradition?

It is vital for us to recognize that while questions of truth and authenticity in Native American autobiography emerge quite naturally from the highly charged ideological debates within Native American Studies (and from the complex political situation of Indian peoples in the United States), such questions can prevent us from seeing elements in the literature that deserve further notice. A willingness to think more broadly about how individual autobiographers "perform" their Indianness within particular institutional contexts can open up the conversation in useful ways. Recent work by Robert Allen Warrior provides a useful challenge (from within the Native American scholarly community) to the discourse of authenticity, one that relates to the work I try to do in this book. In his book *Tribal Secrets,* Warrior sets out to derive a critical language for the study of Indian texts that emerges "primarily from Indian sources." Particularly interesting in Warrior's argument, though, is his point that such a project (which is part of the struggle to establish what Devon Mihesuah and others refer to as "decolonizing methodologies") must inevitably challenge both "idealistic" and "essentialist" definitions of Indianness.[17] Warrior argues that "both American Indian and Native Americanist discourses continue to be preoccupied with parochial questions of identity and authenticity" rather than engaging in "the myriad critical issues crucial to an Indian future" (xix). For Warrior, a productively engaged discourse of Native Americanist criticism should be as interested in the Charles Eastman "who attended Mark Twain's seventieth birthday party or who read a paper at the First Universal Races Congress with W. E. B. Du Bois" as in the Eastman who "grew up in a traditional Sioux home" (xx). Warrior's point here is that the focus on "authenticity" fixes Indian identity in the past, denies the possibility that "Indian" self-definition can change (or vary) in productive ways within a colonial context, and prevents Native peoples from engaging in necessary self-criticism. Appreciating the intellectual diversity within the tradition of Native American thinking becomes difficult when the critical focus remains on denying certain writers a place at the table.

Throughout this book, I attempt to broaden our sense of the ways the Native American writers have conceived of their Indianness in the wake of colonialism. In doing so I focus on a pair of related issues: (1) the relationship between individual autobiographers' rhetorical and political strategies and the models of identity available to them as writers working in a colonial context and writing back to power; and (2) the implications of this relationship for our understanding of the development of a canon of Native American autobiography. In order to explore these issues with a manageable number of critical complications, I have chosen to focus on autobiographical texts written by Native Americans without (or with a limited degree of) direct involvement by a non-Indian editor. To help draw further attention to the *process* of autobiographical self-definition, I center my argument around two Indian writers who produced a *series* of autobiographical texts—William Apess and Charles Eastman. As the preceding discussion suggests, in studying Native American autobiographies I want to pay close attention to the dynamic of cultural contact within which such texts have been produced. Such an examination has led me to look broadly at the history of the colonial legal discourse of Indianness and at the overall careers of two writers who interest me tremendously.

Chapter 1 theorizes the rhetorical dynamics of colonial contact (using a linguistic framework drawn from speech-act theory) before mapping the basic contours of the legal discourse of Indianness during what I am calling the "early national period" of Indian policy (dating roughly from the Revolutionary War to the end of the removal period during the 1840s). This discussion, which establishes the centrality of the treaty as a paradigm for understanding the dynamic of engagement, leads directly into the following chapter's more detailed treatment of the rise of a divergent rhetoric of Indianness among the Seneca during the nineteenth century. This discussion of the Seneca in chapter 2, culminating with an extended treatment of the writings of Ely S. Parker, is intended to provide a broad sense of context for the later discussions of Apess and Eastman. It also highlights the difficulties confronting Indian writers of this time period who sought to engage with colonial legal discourse. Chapters 3 and 4 deal with the autobiographical writings of William Apess, one of the earliest American Indian autobiographers to gain a popular audience. Chapter 3 situates Apess's first autobiographical forays within the context of early Indian conversion narratives and the religious institutions that grounded them. In doing so, I discuss some of the constraints placed on Native American spiritual autobiographers during this historical period as a way of explaining Apess's gradual shift toward legal discourse in his search for a rhetoric of self-definition and political activism. Chapter 4 discusses Apess's use of this new rhetoric, which I am calling "Indian liberalism," in much more detail. Many of the issues raised in these early chapters will be picked up again in chapters 5 and 6, which focus on Charles Eastman's allotment-era autobiographies. Chapter 5 maps the changing legal discourse of the allotment period, setting up a reading of Eastman's initial autobiographical act, *Indian Boyhood.* Chapter

6 traces Eastman's gradual redefinition of self in his later writings as he moved away from the paternalistic rhetoric of the allotment policy to a more complex definition of Indian "character" and a new form of "rights talk." The concluding section outlines some areas for future study in the twentieth century and highlights the pioneering nature of Apess and Eastman, situating them within what I hope to be a more complexly understood Native American intellectual tradition.

In the end, this book argues that criticism of Native American auto-biography should start with a broad sense of the way colonial discourse functioned in the nineteenth century, then proceed to close readings of individual texts. Such an approach to the study of autobiography will lead me, from time to time, to position my own readings against those of other critics whose criticism has struck me as tending toward the "normative" mode. I have tried to express those disagreements in a way that acknowledges the great debts I feel toward those who have written extensively on these issues before me. At the same time, though, the more I reflect on the dynamics of colonial contact, the more I tend to view the authenticity debate as a critical dead-end (as Warrior suggests), against which I feel the need to speak strongly. It seems to me that for critics to rely on a standard of cultural "purity" (even a veiled one) in the wake of colonial contact is both illogical and frequently detrimental to the political interests of Native American peoples. My performative and rhetorical approach to the study of autobiographical acts (and colonial contact) seeks to stake out an alternative position, less radical perhaps than some recent visions of "decolonizing methodologies" (such as Linda Tuhiwai Smith's), but useful nevertheless for our historical understanding of Native American responses to colonialism. I challenge the notion that we should concentrate our energies on dividing texts into "white" or "Indian" parts. I question the assumption that the tradition of Native American autobiography must be understood in terms of restrictive definitions of Indianness. Instead, I hope to show how individual auto-biographical acts can reveal a *process* of self-definition whose engine was engagement with legal models of Indianness in a highly charged communicative context. These acts produced something more complex than capitulation to colonial power; they produced a vibrant tradition of Native American literary and political discourse that should be better appreciated today.

1 *The Discourse of Indian Law*

Since the pioneering work of Edward Said, scholars have recognized that imperialist discourses define their subjects in ways that render them both radically different from, and subordinate to, the dominant group or population. Put slightly differently, we might say that the ideology of colonialism first enables, and then reifies, a way of knowing the "alien" place, its culture, and those who inhabit it. Thus, as Said has noted in *Culture and Imperialism,* colonialism is "supported and perhaps even impelled by impressive ideological formations that include notions that certain territories and people *require* and beseech domination, as well as forms of knowledge affiliated with domination" (9). To analyze the culture of colonialism, then, is to attend both to such "notions" and to the mechanisms of power that apply them to the lives of ordinary people. It is to understand how colonialist ideology precedes, and subsequently buttresses, the development of imperial institutions that disseminate its ways of knowing. Marxist theorist Louis Althusser would designate this conjunction as the union of "ideological" and "repressive" state apparatuses; following Foucault, throughout this book I will refer to such a combination of knowledge and power as a "discourse." Whatever terminology we use, we are still left with a stark picture of the colonial experience. Confronted with complex discursive systems, colonized peoples have inevitably found their own acts of self-definition framed in various ways. The central theoretical problem for postcolonial studies (whether from a literary, sociological, or anthropological perspective) has always been understanding the nature (and degree) of this experience.

As one might expect, the primary challenge in thinking and writing about Native American autobiography as a form of postcolonial literature is to develop a critical model that adequately addresses the intersection between language, colonial institutions, and self-definition in the "New World." The work of Mary Louise Pratt provides a useful starting point for such an endeavor. In her important book *Imperial Eyes* (and in an earlier essay titled "Arts of the Contact Zone"), Pratt develops the term "contact zone" as a way of discussing the dynamics of colonial encounters in the Americas. As she defines it, the contact zone is a "social [space] where disparate cultures meet, clash, and grapple with each other, often in highly asymmetrical relations of domination and subordination—like colonialism, slavery or their aftermaths" (Pratt, *Imperial* 4). While she refers explicitly to "social spaces" here, Pratt is particularly interested in the more abstract "space" of writing. The strength of her definition, then, lies in its attentiveness to the social conditions and power dynamics surrounding and reflected in colonial texts. As her language reveals, Pratt's interest centers around both the violence of imperialist discourse and the ways in which colonized "others" meet and contest that violence in writing. The metaphor of texts as embodiments of geographical "contact zones" can be a particularly suggestive analytical tool for assessing the complex interplay of rhetorical modes found in colonial writing (as in a collaborative autobiography such as James Seaver's *A Narrative of the Life of Mrs. Mary Jemison*, for example). Not surprisingly, then, Pratt's work has been taken up by a number of critics interested in studying these issues.

Yet despite its strengths, Pratt's notion of the contact zone raises certain complications for the student of Native American literature (in the United States especially). In *Imperial Eyes* (a book focused on travel writing), Pratt acknowledges having borrowed the term "contact" from linguistics, where it refers to the development of hybrid, pidgin languages to facilitate communication between speakers of different native tongues. However, the addition of the spatial term "zone" to create a central critical metaphor renders suspect certain aspects of Pratt's application of a linguistic model. The problems become apparent when we consider the corollary concepts she introduces to explain more fully the dynamics of the contact zone. First, Pratt speaks of "trans-culturation," a process where subordinated groups "select and invent from materials *transmitted to them* by a dominant culture" [emphasis added] (*Imperial* 6). Equally relevant for students of autobiographical writing, she also uses the term "autoethnography" to designate kinds of writing "in which colonized subjects undertake to represent themselves in ways that *engage with* the colonizer's own terms" (7). Pratt's use of the ideas of selection, invention, and engagement highlights her concern (which I share) with thinking about ways that the writing of colonized peoples can be resistant, often indirectly, to colonizing discourses and their models of identity. At the same time, though, her dualistic image of *transmission* draws attention to some of the limitations of spatial thinking about linguistic exchange, limitations that have profound implications for the constitution of a "canon" of American Indian writing.

Putting all of Pratt's terms together, we seem to have a picture of an imperialist culture projecting its ideology across a cultural "frontier" and the subordinate, colonized culture digesting that ideology and transmitting it back in a manner that involves subtle resistance. Despite the sense of interchange, though, the image of a boundary line between transmitter and receiver seems to remain relatively intact. In the introduction to *Imperial Eyes,* Pratt herself notes that the "contact zone . . . is often synonymous with 'colonial frontier'" (6). In using such a spatial metaphor, we risk unconsciously internalizing a model that maintains that the "other" is always "over there," beyond our cultural borders. The problems with such assumptions in the field of Native American Studies are relatively clear. Any attempt to apply a predominantly geographical conception of cultural contact to the experience of Native Americans in the United States would involve willfully ignoring the peculiar position Indian peoples have occupied historically (both inside and outside the nation's geographical borders). Chief Justice John Marshall's phrase "domestic dependent nations" (coined in the seminal 1831 case *Cherokee Nation v. Georgia*) highlights the way the U.S. legal system has addressed such peculiarity. In such a context, the idea of "transmission" across a cultural boundary line is perhaps not the best way to conceive of the dynamics of the relationship between the Pequots and the citizens of Connecticut in the 1800s, to take one example. To think of cultural boundaries as synonymous with geographical borders, then, would seem to risk continuing to "displace" Native peoples and perpetuating the myth of the "vanishing Indian." Even though Pratt (who is focused on texts, not maps) avoids such an error, those who draw upon her metaphorical formulation may not.

Besides potentially blurring the historical realities of U.S.–Native American relations, thinking about colonial contact in spatial terms can also lead us into the rigidly dualistic thinking about identity that plagues some postcolonial literary criticism, thinking that focuses on a writer's position either "inside" or "outside" of a dominant culture and on how texts embody such positions. We should note in this regard how Pratt's metaphors lead her directly into the problematic issue of "authenticity." Discussing "autoethnographic writing," she argues that such texts are not "what are usually thought of as 'authentic' or autochthonous forms of self-representation . . . Rather, autoethnography involves partial collaboration with and appropriation of the idioms of the conqueror" (7). This formulation, particularly the notion of "partial" engagement, seems to turn on the problematic assumption that even after contact, the dominant and subordinate cultures will remain theoretically "pure" and distinct. Pratt's model seems to suggest that we would be able to map the geography of a text and to distinguish the "Indian" parts of a Native American autobiography from its "non-Indian" or "Western" parts. The "true" voice of the colonized would become something uncontaminated by any hint of the colonizer or his or her "idioms." This, of course, is frequently the way such texts have been read. A troubling corollary of this position, however, has been the assumption that "authenticity" is often synonymous with silence—that the "real" voice is found between the lines, if at all. Such a position has been argued with particular force by those, like Gerald Vizenor, who maintain that Native American culture is *essentially* an oral one, and that any foray into writing can entail a self-alienating sacrifice. (Vizenor's complex response to this dilemma has been to assume the role of a literary trickster and to write in a perpetually ironic mode that frustrates readers' and critics' attempts to pin down either his own subject-position as an author or the identities of his various fictional characters and personae.) Alternately, one often finds an attempt to construct an idealized model of precontact identity against which writers are measured. Doubtless there is some merit in both approaches, and each one does help us see part of the picture of the colonial experience. Yet neither of them is entirely satisfactory. In both cases, the theoretical problem derives from recourse to the root metaphor of travel between cultures as the basis for a theory of contact and/or decolonization. This formulation prevents us from seeing a more complex form of blending going on—both rhetorically and, perhaps, experientially.

It may be that a more productive way of conceptualizing the "contact zone" as an interpretive tool would be to abandon the binary thinking that often dominates our conceptualization of culture. In his 1997 essay "Resketching Anglo-Amerindian Identity Politics," Scott Michaelsen does just that, addressing the inadequacies of dualistic, spatial models of cultural contact with disarming simplicity. "Contact changes everything," Michaelsen notes (226). In making such a claim, he takes issue with the notion that "cultures can be crossed—that people can live biculturally—but that fundamental cultural positions remain unchanged" (246). It is easy to see how the latter position feeds readily into theses about authenticity and ethnic purity (theses that have worked both for and against Native Americans in the contemporary political and legal climate of the United States, and that tend to fuel increasingly rancorous debates within the Native American Studies community). The problem, as Michaelsen suggests, lies with a tendency to conceptualize culture exclusively in terms of place, rather than as a phenomenon of language. If, on the other hand, we try to think of culture as a symbolic system (as Pratt initially suggests, following the thinking of Clifford Geertz), contact becomes a more complex form of *communication*, a continuous circuit rather than a series of unidirectional transmissions.[1] Such a move opens up new ways of reading a genre like Native American autobiography and may enable us to challenge some of contemporary postcolonial theory's most troubling orthodoxies.

Drawing more broadly on linguistics as a model, it becomes difficult to dismiss an individual utterance as inauthentic because it engages with the utterance of an interlocutor. Engaging with new ideas or linguistic structures in the course of a conversation (demonstrating code competence) is not, axiomatically, a process of total subjection or alienation; it is not precisely analogous to being uprooted in a geographical sense. It is possible, surely, to imagine a speaker reinterpreting pieces of code that were not part of his or her original linguistic repertoire in a way that both reflects a changed sense of linguistic possibility and a changed sense of self. Following this model, communicative engagement in autobiographical writings could be understood as a dialogic (or, better yet, multivocal) reformulation of identity. We must be cautious about such claims, of course, for it is clearly possible to manipulate language without being radically transformed by it. It is on this point that postcolonial criticism must part ways with Foucault. Many Indian speakers/writers play with codes without ever wholly embracing them. But we should also consider the possibility that an *ongoing* process of engagement with identity-defining discourses might produce lasting effects on a writer's rhetoric, politics, and worldview. Only by getting beyond the critical framework of authenticity, though, can we meaningfully begin to conceptualize such a process and broaden our consideration of the ways that colonial contact has led (at least some) Native American autobiographers to create new definitions of self.

It seems to me, then, that Pratt's terms provide a useful starting point for an inquiry into the ways that a number of early Native American autobiographers defined their "Indian" identity in the wake of colonialism. Nevertheless, Pratt leaves us with the need to work toward a more precise critical understanding of the dynamic of colonial contact as it relates to these texts. Fortunately, the appeal to a linguistic foundation in her definition of "contact" points us in a helpful direction, toward the strain of autobiography criticism developed by critics such as Elizabeth Bruss. Bruss's critical model (as was discussed in the introduction) suggests that autobiography should be understood generally as a kind of performative utterance, a speech act whose primary function is the constitution of identity through writing. To conceive of autobiographical writing in this way, as a kind of perlocutionary speech act, is to foreground its social/communicative aspects and its "structure," in the sense that Roland Barthes uses the term.[2] The ordinary language philosophy on which Bruss draws stresses that there is really no private speech or writing.[3] What we say has meaning (and *does* something—J. L. Austin's definition of a perlocutionary utterance) in accordance with culturally specific codes and in relation to some interlocutor or interlocutors.[4] As a form of linguistic action, then, all autobiography is a *communicative act of self-definition* and thus by extension involves a complex process of engagement. Autobiographers draw on available models of self (codes) to become known and knowable (both to themselves and to their audience). In this sense, the study of autobiography, generally speaking, concerns itself with identifying these historically and socially embedded models and understanding how and why writers come to use them "competently" in the autobiographical act of self-constitution.

Of course, something important must distinguish our understanding of the linguistic context of Native American autobiographies from that of many other forms of autobiographical utterance. Owing to the historical realities of colonialism, the former texts represent communicative acts that are particularly contested and proscribed. Put slightly differently, we might say that the conditions of autobiographical performances by Native Americans were more precisely defined than those of their Anglo-American counterparts, in a manner somewhat (but not entirely) analogous to the African American slave narrative. "Competent" code usage is bound up in a larger set of power relations and ideological pressures. What I hope to foreground in this chapter is the way that (during the historical period addressed in this book) the linguistic rules of engagement for Native American autobiographers were profoundly shaped by colonial legal discourse. Because it was backed by potent military, political, and educational institutions, Indian law in nineteenth-century America was particularly insistent in its imposition of a specific model of self and in its delineation of the relationship between writer and audience. The central challenge in studying Native American writing during this period, then, involves understanding how this body of law shaped the communicative circuit between the colonizer and colonized. Once we have set up such a context, mapping the process of rhetorical engagement in Native American autobiography (the central concern of the other chapters of the book) becomes more straightforward.

In the opening of his monumental (and still essential) *Handbook of Federal Indian Law* (first published in 1942), Felix S. Cohen observes that "law dominates Indian life in a way not duplicated in other segments of American society."[5] He might have added that as the discursive centerpiece of colonial power, law "dominates" Indian life in a way not duplicated by any other discourse. Cohen's sense of the centrality of law in the experience of American Indians can be confirmed, empirically if not scientifically, by something as simple as a quick glance at the Native American Studies section of any major bookstore. Such a survey reveals a host of titles (both contemporary and historical) dealing with issues like sovereignty, water rights, religious liberty, repatriation of remains, treaties, and other manifestly legal concerns. Similarly, if we skim titles of Indian autobiographies (especially nineteenth-century texts) we find that legal issues, terms, and concepts are prominently represented. Two obvious examples would include William Apess's *Indian Nullification* (1835) and Sarah Winnemucca Hopkins's *Life among the Piutes: Their Wrongs and Claims* (1883). The reason for the centrality of law in many of these texts is not, of course, that legal discourse provides the *only* source of models of transcultural Indian identity in a colonial context. Indeed, to chart a full history of colonial models of Indianness, we would need to look at literary texts, religious texts, travel writing, anthropological writing, legal writing, and a range of other sources.[6] Such an endeavor is well beyond the scope of this book, though, and would also place our focus more on the history of ideas than on the rhetorical strategies of Indian writers themselves. If we trust those writers to guide us in identifying the most imposing strain of colonialist discourse, our focus narrows to a consideration of the legal sphere that Cohen has identified.

Merely citing bibliographical evidence of Indians' concern with legal issues does not, however, fully establish the centrality of Indian law for this study or provide an adequate basis for theorizing the dynamic of contact. Doing so requires a consideration of what I see as an important distinction between those models of Indianness that are "imposing" (which we can designate as "discursive," in the strict Foucauldian sense) and others that are not. The particular qualities and characteristics ascribed generally to law within the Western tradition, and the fact that legal language is wholly and directly integrated into a coercive, normative, institutional system, provide the primary explanations for this power. As Arnold Krupat has noted, "laws are the specific outcome of successful rhetoric, public speaking oriented toward persuasion. Once that outcome has been written into law, however, these texts are no longer persuasive but coercive, and may be enforced with the full power of the state" (*Ethnocriticism* 130). It is the second half of Krupat's formulation (his invocation of state power as central to the shift from persuasion to coercion) that marks the crucial distinction between legal language and other forms of language. Legal historian Lon L. Fuller has defined law as "the enterprise of subjecting human conduct to the governance of rules" (106). Such a formulation helps us to distinguish law from, say, anthropology, for it rightly stresses the primacy of legal *action* over the static identification of law only with the body of rules itself. Law is much more than a book of statutes or a collection of philosophical texts. A full understanding of how law functions, as a form of discourse, considers how institutions translate legal language into modes of governance, shaping social interaction according to the ideological assumptions contained within that language.[7] By definition, then, the discourse of Indian law is an active force, rooted in linguistic constructions of Indian identity, but functioning through a range of institutions and practices to regulate Native identity and social interaction both within and across political boundaries.[8]

An important corollary point grows out of this functional definition of law. Clearly not every colonialist construction of Indian identity originates in a legal system. If such models are integrated into the normative institutions of law, however, they *become* discursive codes capable of imposing themselves more effectively upon Indian subjects. This is an important point to grasp as we seek to understand both the complex relationship between church and state during the first three centuries of American colonialism and the importance of the conversion narrative form in the emergence of Indian autobiography. The early history of colonial contact between English settlers and Native Americans suggests that the impact of Christian models of identity on the latter was closely related to the incorporation of those models into coercive legal systems by the former. Consider, for example, the "successful" missionary work taking place in colonial Massachusetts during the seventeenth century under the stewardship of John Eliot. Clear evidence that the evangelical mandate to convert was essentially a part of the "mode of governance" appears in the fact that the seal of the Massachusetts General Court represented an Indian pleading "come over and help us." Not surprisingly, the influence of the Puritans' Calvinist model of self on Eliot's "Praying Indians" was also directly related to the General Court's placement of those Indians on plantations under the jurisdiction of English guardians and magistrates. The importance of this integration of religious models into a legal system becomes clear when recalling the failure of Eliot's evangelism to make much of an impression on the indigenous population without the backing of the force of the state.[9] As Francis Jennings notes in *The Invasion of America,* those Indians taken up for civilization and religious instruction "were first compelled to subject themselves to the governance of Massachusetts" and subsequently "placed under the authority of a military officer who appointed Indian commissioners to enforce among their people the laws made by the English" (251–52).[10] When incorporated within the political system, then, the religious language of conversion became a part of colonial legal discourse, exerting considerable power over Indian subjects. Native American engagement with this language should be understood within its legal context, which helps to explain both the appeal of, and the gradual shift away from, the conversion narrative form by early autobiographers such as William Apess.

With these clarifications, I trust that readers will be prepared to entertain my hypothesis that engagement with colonial *legal* discourse is central to the development of early Indian autobiography. What is required next is a closer analysis of the content of that discourse. Several related areas—legal doctrine, forms, and institutions—are relevant here. An analysis of legal doctrine enables us to outline the model of "Indian" identity encoded within the tradition of U.S. Indian law. The consideration of forms and institutions clarifies the manner in which that model was brought to bear on Indian subjects. At the same time, it helps us to begin to understand the process by which Native Americans began to generate their own oppositional rhetoric in the shadow of colonialism.

To comprehend the colonial legal model of Indianness, we must begin by looking back to the roots of modern Western law. Indeed, both the complexity and structural anomalies of U.S. Indian law have largely been the result of the diverse sources that have fed into it.[11] Indian law derives partly from the international law tradition, and as such, some of its strongest roots reach back to Europe during the late Middle Ages (the period when Roman law was beginning to be rearticulated to form the basis for a modern international legal system). Several key concepts of U.S. Indian law also derive from English sources. The common law tradition, infused during the eighteenth century with many of the principles of liberal contractarian thought, provides another prominent root. Both of these sources were subsequently shaped anew by the particularities of American history. All these components, therefore, should concern us as we seek to understand the ways in which Indian law has sought to construct the Indian self.

Well before the formal codification of Indian law in the United States, or even the nominal discovery of the "New World," the medieval cant of crusading provided the first fully articulated legal models of non-Christian identity and suggested mechanisms for regulating colonial contact. In his essay "The Medieval Discourse of Crusade," Robert A. Williams Jr. traces the manner in which Church leaders and jurists developed a systematic legal explanation of colonization during the historical period of the Crusades, justifying the confiscation of "pagan" lands by conquest in accordance with certain natural law principles (a blend of Christian theology and Roman law).[12] The theory of the Universal Church (which asserted papal primacy over the spiritual well-being of the entire world) was reinforced by Augustinian just war (*bellum justum*) theory to produce over time a full-fledged Crusading ideology. One of its key components involved defining the relative subject positions of the Christian European and the non-Christian "others" found elsewhere. A seminal text like Pope Innocent IV's thirteenth-century legal commentary *Quod super his* delineated a transnational Christian self (tied to a notion of the Universal Church) and a complementary pagan or infidel self (one who rejected Christianity and the natural law principles it was seen to buttress). The ideology of Crusade articulated by Innocent IV consequently asserted a natural law right to property for civilized Christians, but denied the same right of *dominium* to infidels (who were seen as failing to live up to certain normative assumptions about "natural" human behavior). The failure of infidels to adhere to Christian Europe's norms of subjectivity was seen as justification for secular intervention by Christian princes, acting under a papal mandate to protect the affairs of all subjects of the Church, whether actual or potential. Overall, then, the era of the Crusades served to establish law as the central mechanism of colonial power, codifying in the process a particular model of the colonizeable (non-Christian) other. Indeed, this body of law established a principle that would be manifest in U.S. Indian law throughout the nineteenth century—the equation of "civilized" identity with the Christian state.[13]

Beginning in the late fifteenth century, when the long period of exploration and colonization of the Americas began, the papal mandate for "interference" in the lives of non-Christian peoples influenced the development of a more complex body of colonial law for the New World. Pope Alexander VI's famous Bull of Donation to Spain in 1493 was the most ambitious attempt to apply the papal right of *dominium* in a colonial context. Yet because of the realities of European politics, canon law could not, finally, provide an adequate basis for European colonialism in the New World. Papal authority provided only the impetus for the subsequent development of a secular Indian law in English colonies. Many European powers (most notably England, France, and the Netherlands) rejected the papal sovereignty component of Crusading discourse informing Alexander's Bull as well as the subsequent partition of the New World between Spain and Portugal in the Treaty of Tordesillas (1494). However, the basic distinction that the Crusaders had drawn between Christian (and civilized) Europe and pagan others persisted, offering a model of how a more broadly acceptable legal basis for colonialism might be established. The legacy of the law of Crusade for colonialism in the English colonies, then, came in the form of two key customary doctrines of European international law. The first, the doctrine of two spheres, argued that the European system of international relations did not apply in the Western hemisphere. This allowed for the creation of a discrete body of Indian law that did not need to recognize the Indian as possessing the same sovereign rights as the European. The second principle, necessary to limit the lawlessness of colonial competition initiated by the first, was the doctrine of discovery (Falkowski 14). It allowed for a more complete picture of the Indian self to be drawn in law.

The doctrine of discovery posited that European powers initially possessed only a "right of occupancy" over uncivilized lands they had claimed, but argued that such a right became the more stable "right of possession" when such lands were settled and the indigenous peoples "removed."[14] Such removal could be achieved either through purchase (the route preferred by the English) or by conquest (the more typical approach of the Spanish). Not surprisingly, debates raged from the sixteenth through the eighteenth centuries regarding the legal rights of indigenous peoples to resist removal and dispossession and the "just war" limits to conquest. Writing in the eighteenth century, Emmerich de Vattel, the most prominent proponent of a broad application of the law of discovery, extended the concept so far as to claim that lands peopled by "wandering tribes" should not even be seen as "occupied" (Vattel 92).[15] With such a claim, Vattel provided probably the most aggressive legal justification for colonization and the rejection of the rights of indigenous peoples. On the other side of the question, the sixteenth-century Jesuit scholar Francisco Vitoria provided the most developed and well-reasoned refutation of the law of discovery as it was commonly applied to Native Americans. In a pair of treatises ("On the American Indians" [1537–38] and "On the Law of War" [1539]) he developed the natural law theory of Indian sovereignty (which broadened later into the sovereign equality of states doctrine in international law). Vitoria rejected both the notion of the supremacy of European princes in the temporal affairs of the peoples of the Americas and the "just war" apology for military conquest. Yet even he accepted a basic hierarchical distinction between civilized and uncivilized cultures; the Indian was sovereign, but he was not equal to the Christian European. Thus, although Vitoria rejected the idea that Indians could be coerced into giving up their lands and rights, he nevertheless articulated a kind of "trust" relationship between Indians and Europeans, the goal being to help the Indian develop self-government and other trappings of Christian society. This notion of a trust relationship (later formally integrated into concrete legal structures) came to serve as the root of a long-standing tradition of paternalism in Indian law in the North American colonies.[16] At the same time, the idea of a "trust responsibility" has been central to the development of treaty relationships with Native tribes and to the subsequent interpretation of treaty law by the courts. Both issues have been important ones, not just in the history of Indian "politics" but also in the development of Indian autobiographical writing.

The English colonial system along the Atlantic coast was, of course, deeply influenced by these debates and by the widespread recognition of violent excesses in New Spain.[17] Admittedly, the early decades of English colonialism in North America saw territorial acquisition by violent means. The genocidal Pequot War of 1636–37 in New England and the subjugation of the Powhatan in Virginia between 1622 and 1646 provide probably the strongest examples of colonialism by conquest in the English territories. In the long run, though, competition with the French and Spanish, the considerable strength of inland nations like the Iroquois and the Creek, and unease in London about duplicating the pattern of the Spanish conquistadors and the encomienda system led to the attempt to create a system of Indian law more rooted in the treaty side of the law of discovery. By the middle of the seventeenth century, the English sought to centralize their land acquisition policies and began to rely exclusively on treaties, rather than naked coercion, to secure new territories. There were numerous abuses and inequalities in the treaty system, of course (one of the most infamous early examples being the Walking Purchase from the Delaware), but these abuses were often facilitated by collaboration with other Indian nations.[18] Consequently, the law of discovery came to be applied primarily as a means to assert exclusive English right (with regards to other European powers) to purchase Indian lands. By the mid-eighteenth century, the British system had been further consolidated to the point where two Indian superintendents (one for the north and one for the south) had control of Indian policy and territorial acquisition. These superintendents (Sir William Johnson in the north, Edmond Atkin and John Stuart in the south) served, in effect, as ambassadors to the Indian nations in their spheres.[19] Johnson, in particular, was instrumental in preserving the "covenant chain" between the British, Iroquois, and other nations, all in service of English colonial interests. Significantly, in dealing with the Indians in this "chain" and committing themselves to the treaty as the legal basis of colonialism, the English acknowledged a considerable degree of Indian sovereignty (an acknowledgment that remains central to the federal judiciary's interpretation of the United States's trust responsibility to Native peoples). At the same time they sought to increase Indian dependency through trade and missionary work, preserving a general model of cultural and political paternalism, a model with which Indian writers were forced to engage throughout the eighteenth and nineteenth centuries.

There was a tension, of course, between official British imperial policy toward the Indian tribes and the thinking of many of the colonists, who exerted constant pressure to expand westward and who also tended to manifest a more aggressively paternalistic attitude.[20] These tensions formed part of the general collection of grievances that drove the colonies and the Crown apart after the collapse of French power in North America. Not surprisingly, then, with the end of British rule came a change in the tenor of Indian policy and law. Subsequently, during the revolutionary and early national periods, we find in U.S. Indian law an ambiguous blend of the international law principles of discovery and legal paternalism, complicated by a range of political factors (persistent conflict with Great Britain, the relative weakness of the colonies immediately following independence, and conflict between the interests of the federal government, the states, and private citizens). Indian participation in the Revolutionary War provided a convenient justification for displacement based on the law of conquest, for those inclined to such an interpretation. Even those uncomfortable with the idea of forcibly removing Indian peoples from lands in the east often maintained that the government had a right to do so, though "humanity" dictated that such a right not be exercised.

In a letter written to James Duane on September 7, 1783, George Washington provides a fairly representative example of the thinking (and rhetoric) that characterized American policy through the 1780s and early 1790s: "That as they [the Indians] maugre all the advice and admonition which could be given them at the commencement; and during the prosecution of the War could not be restrained from acts of Hostility, but were determined to join their arms to those of G Britain and to share their fortune; so, consequently, with a less generous People than Americans they would be made to share the same fate; and be compelled to retire along with them beyond the Lakes. But as we prefer Peace to a state of Warfare, as we consider them a deluded People, as we persuade ourselves that they are convinced, from experience, of their error in taking up the Hatchet against us, and that their true Interest and safety must now depend on *our* friendship" (qtd. in Prucha, *Documents* 1). Like many of his contemporaries, Washington argues that the Indians (tellingly, he makes no distinction among various nations) be seen as enemies defeated in a just war, who therefore have no "right" to expect leniency from the victorious Americans. At the same time he notes that a sign of American "generosity" is a preference for peace rather than continued war, and pity for these poor "deluded" people. This "generosity," of course, was less a consequence of pure benevolence than of military realities (the potentially dangerous threat still posed by some of the eastern tribes) and political factors (the danger for Americans fighting under a banner of universal rights in being seen by sympathetic European powers as oppressors of the Native population).[21] If Americans would not exercise their rights as conquerors, though, Washington nonetheless stresses the cultivation of a new, even more vigorously paternalistic relationship with the Indians than that which characterized English colonialism. In practical terms, this meant a return to a treaty system for regulating colonial contact, a system that was significantly more imbalanced against the Indian nations following the end of European colonial rivalries in North America.[22] One of the legacies of the return to the treaty system was a renewed commitment to establishing boundaries between the Indians and civilized whites, largely for the "protection" of the former. In his letter to Duane, Washington intimates that Indians not currently beyond these boundaries would have to be moved eventually, presumably by means of land purchase. The principle of purchasing Indian land by treaty (a legacy of the law of discovery) was not limited to removal of Indians beyond the Fort Stanwix line, though. Treaty making also provided the basis for subsequent expansion under the broad principles of the law of discovery.

All of Washington's comments to Duane emerge in the context of broader assumptions about the inevitable decline and passing of the Indian, assumptions that involve a series of pointed claims regarding Indian identity. Toward the end of his letter, Washington notes: "I am clear in my opinion, that policy and oeconomy point very strongly to the expediency of being upon good terms with the Indians, and the propriety of purchasing their Lands in preference to attempting to drive them by force of arms out of their Country; which as we have seen is like driving the Wild Beasts of the Forest which will return as soon as the pursuit is at an end and fall perhaps on those that are left there; when the gradual extension of our Settlements will as certainly cause the Savage as the Wolf to retire; both being beasts of prey tho' they differ in shape" (qtd. in Prucha, *Documents* 2). Although Washington's expression of faith in the "vanishing Indian" idea here seems more extreme and fatalistic than the views of some of his contemporaries (Jefferson, for instance, who was a steadfast supporter of the ideal of assimilation), his remarks (and the policies they represent) are generally indicative of a central thread in the legal discourse of Indianness during the early national period. Regardless of whether emphasis fell on the law of conquest or the commitment to treaty relations, early U.S. Indian policy and law located the Native self in a precivilized state and failed to recognize in the Indian the same sovereign identity and rights possessed by American citizens.

The idea that the Indian represents a kind of self anterior to European civil society (a notion implicit in the international law of discovery, whether in its more militant or paternalistic strains) was buttressed and made more explicit by other facets of the legal order in early national America, most notably the common law tradition and the broader ideology of contractarianism. The thinking of John Locke serves as a touchstone for understanding both these related areas. Social contract theory, which stands as one of the roots of our constitutional system, had its own ways of making the Indian knowable. All the prominent contractarian theories formulated through the eighteenth century (those of Hobbes, Shaftesbury, Locke, and Rousseau) conceptualized the political and legal structures of modern European civil society through a form of speculative historiography that looked back to a prior, uncivilized age—the state of nature. In the English colonies and later United States, though, Locke's particular formulation of the social contract and the subjects who compose it proved the most dominant in shaping the colonial mind and its conception of the Indian self.[23] Beyond its influence on constitutional debates in the American colonies, Lockean theory was connected to the American legal system even more broadly by way of William Blackstone and his four-volume *Commentaries on the Laws of England* (1765–69) (and later by James Kent's four-volume *Commentaries on American Law* [1826–1830]). For many years (until the appearance of Kent's writings) the most influential legal texts in the United States, Blackstone's works, especially the second volume of the *Commentaries* ("Of the Rights of

Things"—dealing with property law), achieved a remarkable synthesis of Lockean theory and the English common law tradition. Thus, both in its constitutionalism and common law past, early American legal consciousness can largely be characterized as Lockean. The Lockean tenor of early American jurisprudence ensured the persistence of powerful ways of knowing the Native American.[24]

Much of the import of Locke's system for Native American peoples becomes apparent when we recall his comment in the *Second Treatise of Civil Government* (1690) regarding the state of nature: "In the beginning, all the world was America" (301). The centerpiece of Locke's political philosophy, as articulated in the *Second Treatise*, was the following assumption: although "property" (which for a seventeenth-century English intellectual referred primarily to land) was shared in common by men in the state of nature, the right—the imperative, in fact—to make possession of such property exclusive was also a part of the natural order. The Lockean man, a type designated by C. B. MacPherson as the "possessive individual," is autonomous, "owning" the full measure of his person and labor. Such self-possession stands at the root of his ability not only to assert private ownership of the fruits of nature, but also to come together with other individuals to constitute a civil society, government, and legal order that might protect such property rights. With its sense of value added through individual labor and the related notion of undeveloped land as "waste," Lockean theory renders the more communally oriented economic and social order characteristic of most precontact Native American communities as the obverse of civilization. Indian possession of a wilderness to which they are seen as having "added" nothing thus becomes temporary and alienable. Though it is debatable whether Locke himself would have condoned violent displacement, the legal and moral justification for dispossession characteristic of "discovery" could clearly be grounded further in the norms of contractarian subjectivity. Both rendered the Indian knowable, but only as a kind of prehistorical vestige of the state of nature.

In addition to buttressing the legal justifications for colonial expansion and the displacement of the Indian, Lockean contractarianism also informed another key component of Indian law in colonial and antebellum America—the attempt to develop mechanisms of assimilation. By positing individualism and a desire for private property as both antecedent to civil society and "natural," Locke's social contract suggested the viability and validity of certain state mechanisms to civilize the children of nature. The Indian's failure to adopt the natural and rational course (the path to civilization followed by white Europeans) provided further justification (on top of the international law principles we have already discussed) for the paternalistic control needed to remold his identity. In this context, Lockean psychology and epistemology (developed in the 1690 *Essay on Human Understanding*) proved as influential as contractarianism, furthering the image of the Indian as an impressionable cultural "child" and suggesting policies and institutional mechanisms by which he might be "matured." These mechanisms were conceived at the time as primarily educational.

Though there were debates during the early national period about whether religious education or more secular, vocational training should serve as the foundation for "bringing up" the nation's Indian children, governmental policies to further the general project of training Indian subjects advanced along several fronts in the early 1800s. Missionary agencies were established among numerous Indian nations and received direct political and financial support from the federal government. Day schools (both religious and secular) were founded to begin shaping Indians' identities at childhood, when they were seen as being most malleable. Finally, at the urging of Indian Superintendent Thomas L. McKenney, Congress in 1819 created a $10,000 civilization fund, which was used for such varied purposes as the purchase of farm equipment and seed and the support of farmers sent to live among Indian communities. The language of the 1819 Civilization Fund Act provides a good summary of the overall purposes and assumptions behind the assimilationist component of Indian law:

> For the purpose of providing against the further decline and final extinction of the Indian tribes, adjoining the frontier settlements of the United States, and for introducing among them the habits and arts of civilization, the President of the United States shall be, and he is hereby authorized, in every case where he shall judge improvement in the habits and condition of such Indians practicable, and that the means of instruction can be introduced with their own good consent, to employ persons of good moral character, to instruct them in the mode of agriculture suited to their situation; and for teaching their children in reading, writing, and arithmetic, and performing other duties as may be enjoined, according to such instructions and rules as the President may give and prescribe for the regulation of their conduct, in the discharge of their duties. (qtd. in Prucha, *Documents* 33)

Representative of the broad ideological spectrum called "Jeffersonian Philanthropy" by historian Bernard Sheehan, this statute codified all the key legal assumptions about Indian identity I have been discussing.

Taken as a whole, then, these various threads (international law, common law, and contractarianism) formed the basis of the body of antebellum Indian law and its model of Indian identity. With such complex roots, it goes without saying that the discourse of Indian law was not always clear in its pronouncements about Native identity. A good example of the complicated ways in which these notions of Indianness sometimes manifested themselves in colonialist discourse appears in a key nineteenth-century text produced by one of the most prominent figures in Native American legal history: Chief Justice John Marshall. In his decision in *Johnson and Graham's Lessee v. William McIntosh* (1823), Marshall's main concern was to address the complex nature of Indian land title. At the same time, though, the opinion shows that a key part of the content (the referential dimension) of Indian law centered around the construction or reproduction of the tangled models of Indianness I have traced here.

The legal issue in *Johnson and Graham's Lessee v. William McIntosh* involved a question of title to a parcel of land in Illinois that had been bought by one party directly from a group of Illinois Indians and granted to another by the federal government. In his decision, Marshall points out that the U.S. government had legally succeeded the British as the ruling authority in its territory and posits a basic continuity of key legal principles (both international law and common law) vis-à-vis the Indian population. "They [the United States] maintain," he writes, "that discovery gave an exclusive right to extinguish the Indian title of occupancy, either by purchase or conquest; and gave also a right to such degree of sovereignty, as the circumstances of the people would allow them to exercise" (qtd. in Prucha, *Documents* 35).[25] As the decision proceeds, though, Marshall makes several additional points that are worth quoting at length. He writes:

> We will not enter into the controversy, whether agriculturalists, merchants, and manufacturers, have a right, on abstract principles, to expel hunters from the territory they possess, or to contract their limits. Conquest gives a title which the Courts of the conqueror cannot deny ... The title by conquest is acquired and maintained by force. The conqueror prescribes its limits. Humanity, however, acting on public opinion, has established, as a general rule, that the conquered shall not be wantonly oppressed, and that their condition shall remain as eligible as is compatible with the objects of the conquest. Most usually, they are incorporated with the victorious nation, and become subjects or citizens of the government with which they are connected ... But the tribes of Indians inhabiting this country were fierce savages, whose occupation was war, and whose subsistence was drawn chiefly from the forest. To leave them in possession of their country was to leave the country a

wilderness; to govern them as a distinct people, was impossible, because they were as brave and high spirited as they were fierce, and were ready to repel by arms every attempt on their independence. What was the inevitable consequence of this state of things? Frequent and bloody wars, in which the whites were not always the aggressor, unavoidably ensued. European policy, numbers, and skill, prevailed. As the white population advanced, that of the Indian necessarily receded. The game fled into the thicker and more unbroken forests, and the Indians followed. The soil, to which the crown originally claimed title, being no longer occupied by its ancient inhabitants, was parceled out according to the will of the sovereign power, and taken possession of by persons who claimed immediately from the crown, or mediately, through its grantees and deputies . . . However extravagant the pretension of converting the discovery of an inhabited country into conquest may appear; if the principle has been asserted in the first instance, and afterward sustained, if a country has been acquired and held under it; if the property of the great mass of the community originates in it, it becomes the law of the land. So, too, with respect to the concomitant principle, that the Indian inhabitants are to be considered merely as occupants, to be protected, indeed, while in peace, in possession of their lands, but to be deemed incapable of transferring the absolute title to others. (36–37)

In this decision (large portions of which would be repeated verbatim in Kent's discussion of Indian property rights in volume three of his *Commentaries*), Marshall initially seems to skirt the issue of whether contractarian principles *automatically* justify the displacement of precivilized peoples (i.e., whether the rights of those who "use" the land trump the rights of those who hunt on it).[26] At the same time, by suggesting the impossibility of leaving the Indians in possession of their lands (because doing so would be to leave it a wilderness), he seems to argue for a natural, inevitable progression from the state of nature (where the Indian is located) into civil society. There are some significant contradictions in Marshall's decision, of course. In asserting a continuity of law between British colonial domination of Indians and U.S. control, for instance, he mistakenly asserts that conquest had *always* been the basis of English claims. At the same time, he claims that the Indian "right of possession has never been questioned" and that the federal government has the "exclusive power of acquiring that right" (by treaty). Marshall's decision also contains elements of both paternalism (the idea that Indians must be protected) and the suggestion of assimilationism, both of which are balanced, nevertheless, by suggestions that the Indian's primitive and warlike nature render him difficult to manage or change.

The kind of density and complexity that we see writ large here in a key decision by the nation's highest court is characteristic of U.S. Indian law as a colonial discourse, especially in the nineteenth century. Indeed, the attempt to produce a coherent Indian policy against a backdrop of often inconsistent legal doctrines produced a great deal of creative jurisprudence (Marshall's "domestic dependent nations" formulation, for instance). As we study the relationship between law and Native American autobiography, therefore, we must pay close attention to the specific historical context of the texts in question, being cautious about grand generalizations. Nevertheless, regardless of occasional confusion regarding the specific legal foundation for colonial power or the particularities of colonial policy, the texts we have been examining present us with a rough outline of the basic model of Indianness pervading early national legal language. The Indian was made knowable as a particular kind of precivilized other and child of nature.

Of course, the mere fact that Indian law presents a roughly coherent model of Indianness does not by itself unlock its relationship to Native American autobiography. When we consider such a model as part of a *discursive system*, though, we can begin to form a more complete picture of the process of engagement. The "referential" component of Indian law (i.e., its model of Indian identity) remained generally consistent throughout the nineteenth century. What accounts for the influence of this model on the development of Indian autobiography are the forms and institutions at the heart of American colonialism. I have already alluded to the importance of institutions such as schools for the dissemination of legal ideology. (I will have more to say about such institutions in subsequent chapters.) To close this chapter, however, I want to focus attention on the most important legal *form* in the early history of U.S. Indian law—the treaty.[27] Because of a range of historical factors, the Indian treaty helped define the rhetorical structure of engagement during the nineteenth century. Reflecting on the nature of treaty making as a language act, then, can help us see more *specifically* how the legal model of Indianness shaped the work of a range of Indian writers. It will also allow me to complete this retheorization of the contact zone as a site of discursive engagement.

In spite of Marshall's claim to the contrary in *Johnson and Graham's Lessee v. William McIntosh*, the treaty did serve as the primary legal mechanism regulating colonial contact in the English colonies and the United States until 1871, when Congress prohibited the negotiation of further agreements.[28] Furthermore, the "trust" model of U.S-Indian relations implicit in treaty law has proven highly influential in other areas of Indian jurisprudence. Indeed, for more than three hundred years, treaties (both as texts and events) have provided one of the best maps of the "primal scene" of contact between Native Americans and Euro-Americans, as well as a tool for understanding the history of those relationships. For all these reasons, then, treaties should take center stage in our study of the dynamic of colonial engagement and of the autobiographical texts produced in the context of such engagement.

Admittedly, during the seventeenth and eighteenth centuries, the nature of treaty making underwent significant changes. As Dorothy Jones points out in *License for Empire,* by the mid-eighteenth century the British had committed themselves for a variety of political reasons to a comprehensive, multilateral treaty system. The effectiveness of that system was grounded both in the Iroquois's dominance of other nations and their seeming acceptance of a European conception of empire "with its assumptions of the right to dispose of the land of imperial dependents" (71). Yet by the mid-1780s the Iroquois had lost much of their influence and consequently the ability to secure favorable terms in bargaining with the colonizers. From that point onward, Indian nations (not just those in the east) were rarely able to negotiate on relatively even footing with the U.S. (One of the rare instances was during the 1860s, when the effects of the Civil War and the strong initial resistance of Plains tribes to white encroachment led to the signing of the Treaty of Fort Laramie, which was broken within ten years.) Treaty making as a central component of U.S. Indian law thus became much more clearly a mechanism of domination during the late eighteenth and nineteenth centuries than it had been under British rule. Nevertheless, the treaty remained (and still remains) a prominent model for cross-cultural contact *both for Native Americans and European Americans.* If we remain aware of shifts in the nature of treaty making, then, the idea of the "treaty" provides a useful way to understand the dynamic of colonial contact (and its impact on early Native American autobiography).

Historically, the commitment of Indian peoples to the treaty model of colonial engagement has grown out of a broader, indigenous tradition of diplomatic exchange. Probably the clearest examples of this phenomenon (owing to the large amount of useful primary source material) are to be found among the Iroquois. As Robert A. Williams Jr. demonstrates in *Linking Arms Together,* treaty making provided a centerpiece of Indian life in the eastern woodlands well before the domination of Native peoples by colonial powers. A blend of ceremonialism, storytelling, and ritualized gift giving, early Indian treaties (often negotiated between nations with widely disparate cultural practices and languages) represented a remarkably flexible model of diplomatic engagement. As Williams (drawing on the language of legal scholar Robert Cover) puts it, "the parties to a treaty had to agree to create and sustain a *nomos*, a normative universe of shared meanings" (47). This approach to treaty making was, generally speaking, an extension of indigenous assumptions about kinship, rooted in the idea that one must extend and solidify a network of relationships with those around oneself.[29] Before the advent of colonial bureaucracies and other mechanisms of domination, then, Native peoples had developed an approach to diplomacy centered on the development of a shared language and a commitment to reciprocal exchange. We might say, therefore, that indigenous tradition had long prepared the Indians of the eastern woodlands to "engage with the terms of the other" (an approximation of Pratt's definition of autoethnography). Clearly nations like the Iroquois were not accustomed to the *unequal* exchanges characteristic of diplomatic relations with the United States. Yet they were still remarkably well-prepared to adapt to the new realities of colonialism by engaging with the *nomos* being imposed upon them.

To fully comprehend this colonialist *nomos*, we must combine our understanding of the legal model of Indianness with a recognition of how the U.S. legal system conceived of treaty making. In thinking generally about the treaty as a *colonial* legal form, the first key point to recognize is that treaty law represents a commitment both to the idea of contractual relations between a colonial power and Native Americans and to a trusteeship concept of colonization (both of which entail, in limited ways, some conception of Indian sovereignty).[30] Treaties thus provide Indians with some degree of "standing" in the legal system of the colonizer. These aspects of treaty law are encoded at the formal level of treaty language itself, and they structure the dynamic of colonial contact by interpellating participants into specific subject positions (as parties to a contract). By foregrounding particular models of intersubjective relations, then, treaties disseminated new modes of self-definition; these modes would be instrumental in the development of written Indian literature, especially autobiography, during the eighteenth and nineteenth centuries. As Dorothy Jones has pointed out, through treaties Indians gained a "toehold in the American legal system which eventually gave them a wholly unique position in American society" (157). Such a "toehold," though, required engagement with the legal models of identity encoded within those same treaties. It required Indians to accept the treaty, on some level, as a performative language act defining them in the terms of the colonizers.

Interestingly enough, the Indian treaty is perhaps the easiest of all legal forms to recognize as a "performative" utterance. In fulfilling its various roles, *any* treaty is a highly structured communicative act designed to have a very real impact upon its participants; it is, in other words, a good example of "law in action." Yet the (now archaic) meaning of the term "treaty" during the colonial and early national period reinforces even further this sense of "performativity." Formerly, speaking of an Indian "treaty" referred not only to the written agreement itself, but also to the *act of negotiation and the actual meeting where it was reached* (Prucha, *American Indian Treaties* 24). As an "act," the Indian treaty clearly functioned in multifaceted ways—both as a contract between theoretically independent parties and as a direct manifestation of colonial power. As a legal contract, a treaty also rests upon a notion of sovereignty (just as a modern private contract rests upon the assumption that the participants possess sovereign rights in their own person). Thus, treaty making works (initially at least) to develop and reify the concept of Indian sovereignty and the related notion of the "tribe" as a corporate political unit. In this sense, Indian treaties construct (and, over time, reproduce) the parties and sovereign communities that they bind together. At the same time, of course, very real power disparities generally characterized the colonial treaty-making endeavor, disparities that became increasingly pronounced in the "negotiations" taking place after the Revolutionary War. As the power of Native American communities relative to English-speaking ones declined, treaty-making exchanges became more unequal, and the rules of communication increasingly determined by the colonizing powers. In this sense, the act of treaty making also served to produce the kinds of hierarchical relations characteristic of colonialism. In theory, though, even this system of subordination has included a mandate that the federal government fulfill a range of obligations to Indian peoples and protect specific tribal rights. Not without reason, then, has Francis Prucha referred to this legal form as a political "anomaly."

If it is an anomaly, though, the Indian treaty has nevertheless proven to be a remarkable powerful model of legal relations and linguistic contact. Granted, the meaning of such agreements has often been the subject of debate, and the willingness of the U.S. government to live up to its treaty commitments has varied considerably over time. Still, the persistence of the form should draw our attention to the existence of an indigenous model of "legal engagement," one that helps explain why early Indian autobiographers were so capable of writing "autoethnographically" within the framework of American law. Such acts of engagement were not always easy, of course, but the readings to follow in subsequent chapters will show that the process was consistently taking place. Native American writers in the nineteenth and early twentieth centuries could not ignore that insistent discourse of Indian law. Instead, they endeavored to articulate a new language of self-definition that could provide the basis for a viable rhetoric of political resistance. In the chapters that follow, I will examine that rhetoric in several different historical and cultural contexts. Before turning to the complex autobiographical mediations of William Apess and Charles Eastman (in chapters 3 through 6), I will explore the legal dynamics of engagement among the Seneca. For in the writings of Maris Bryant Pierce, Nathaniel Thayer Strong, and Ely S. Parker, we can get a clearer sense of the difficulties Native peoples faced in trying to make the discourse of law, in some sense, work for (and not against) them.

2 Seneca Politics and the Rhetoric of Engagement

Throughout the middle decades of the nineteenth century, the Seneca nation engaged in a long struggle to preserve their reservation lands from encroachment and to prevent their removal to the west. This struggle proved to be instrumental in the development of Seneca literature in English, beginning in the 1840s with figures such as Maris B. Pierce, Nathaniel T. Strong, and Peter Wilson. The beginning of the process of engagement represented in these writers' works, though, can be found at the end of the Revolutionary War—with a treaty. On October 22, 1784, after several days of negotiation, the United States and the Six Nations of the Iroquois League signed the Treaty of Fort Stanwix, formally ending the hostilities of the American Revolution. As the settlement of a military conflict won by the American army, this agreement provides an extreme example of the power-saturated kind of communicative circuit often found in U.S.–Indian relations. Because of the disparities in economic, military, and political power between the Americans and the Iroquois, the relative positions of the various negotiators were manifestly unequal. Consequently, the terms of this settlement were unilaterally imposed on the Six Nations by the United States.

The written content of the Fort Stanwix agreement provides a clear sense of how the colonizing power (the United States) meant for the treaty to function, as a legal act. The final version of the agreement reads as follows:

The United States of America give peace to the Senecas, Mohawks, Onondagas and Cayugas, and receive them into their protection upon the following conditions:

ARTICLE 1: Six hostages shall be immediately delivered to the commissioners by the said nations, to remain in possession of the United States, till the prisoners, white and black, which were taken by the said Senecas, Mohawks, Onondagas and Cayugas, or by any of them, in the late war, from among the people of the United States, shall be delivered up.

ARTICLE 2: The Oneidas and Tuscarora nations shall be secured in the possession of the lands on which they are settled.

ARTICLE 3: A line shall be drawn, beginning at the mouth of a creek about four miles east of Niagra, called Oyonwayea, or Johnston's Landing-Place, upon the lake named by the Indians Oswego, and by us Ontario; from thence southerly in a direction always four miles east of the carrying path, between Lake Erie and Ontario, to the mouth of Tehoseroron or Buffaloe Creek on Lake Erie; thence south to the north boundary of the state of Pennsylvania; thence west to the end of the said north boundary; thence south along the west boundary of such state to the River Ohio; the said line from the mouth of the Oyonwayea to the Ohio shall be the western boundary of the lands of the Six Nations, so that the Six Nations shall and do yield to the United States, all claims to the country west of said boundary, and then they shall be secured in the peaceful possession of the lands they inhabit east and north of the same, reserving only six miles square round the fort of Oswego, to the United States for the support of the same.

ARTICLE 4: The Commissioners of the United States, in consideration of the present circumstances of the Six Nations, and in the execution of the humane and liberal views of the United States upon the signing of the above articles, will order goods to be delivered to the said six nations for their use and comfort. (qtd. in Prucha, *Documents* 5)

As a manifestation of colonial power (and indeed, of military conquest), the text clearly defines the parties in a hierarchical relationship. The first (dominant) participant in this communicative act is the United States government, speaking through its representatives. At Fort Stanwix, Oliver Wolcott, Gen. Richard Butler, and Arthur Lee acted as commissioners plenipotentiary (i.e., invested with full governmental powers) from the United States. They negotiated in the name of the government, and thus, when they had the final treaty read aloud to the Indians present, they in effect spoke with the voice of that government. The other (subordinate) participants were the members of the Six Nations and a few members of the Shawnee tribe. We can see immediately how the predicative language in the treaty functions to place them in a subordinate position. The United States (speaking through the commissioners) "give peace" to the Indians and "receive them into their protection," thereby establishing a paternalistic (trust) relationship with the tribes. Here, the very *act* of predication (which, just like reference, is a form of linguistic action, defining actors and objects) assigns hierarchical subject positions to the parties involved.[1] The language of the treaty works to naturalize these positions as it goes, and thus a particular normative universe (*nomos*) begins to take shape.

Beyond the choice of verb form, the effacement of human agency through the use of the passive voice in Articles I–III also advances the ideological assumptions behind the treaty. The Indians are told that "hostages shall be immediately delivered by the said nations," that they "shall be secured in the possession of the lands on which they are settled," and that "a line shall be drawn" defining the boundaries between white and Native American lands. Particularly in the case of these last two provisions, the mysterious agency that will carry out these actions remains vague. It would seem that the utterance itself (as a transcendental voice of the natural order of law) functions less to perform the "securing" and "drawing" in question than to simply point it out; the passive voice masks the threat of coercion behind this discourse, transforming it from a kind of command into a form of "knowledge." Only when we come to Article IV does human agency return as the subject of predicative action. In that article we are told that the commissioners of the United States "will order goods to be delivered" to the tribes. It is interesting that in this, the only point in the treaty where the American government actively undertakes any obligation of its own (i.e., the only place where this utterance "acts" on them), it no longer seems to be a transcendent order which speaks. The text tells us that it is "in execution of the humane and liberal views of the United States" that the goods in question will be delivered. Whereas the language of the treaty suggests that the transcendent, natural order of law secures property and sets boundaries *around* the Indians, American benevolence here is construed as a free act of goodwill, almost an afterthought. It stands somehow in the margins of the normative legal universe taking shape in this text and reinforces the idea of a paternalistic relationship between the parties.

The referential action of the treaty also merits attention. The text invokes a number of "institutional facts" (to use John Searle's term), all of which relate to the models of Indianness and civilization deployed in early national Indian law. The legal notion of national borders implicit in the treaty emerges as the most obvious. The notions of property lines or estates of land held in fee simple are not "facts" that members of the Six Nations would necessarily have considered natural, yet the text treats them as such.[2] Second, the notion of "protection" in the preamble derives from the paternalistic trustee model so widely influential in colonial law. In yet another manifestation of the hierarchical nature of this discourse, Article 1 refers to an exchange of Indian "hostages" for white and black "prisoners" taken during the Revolutionary War. Through a set of institutional facts, based on the law of war, the Indians are designated here as a "foreign" people defeated in war. They are also designated as a dishonorable people, who must be coerced into compliance by having some of their number become "hostages" (why not, we should ask, call them also "prisoners of war"?). In conjunction with its predicative acts, then, the referential dimension of treaty reifies a particular way of "knowing" (representing) the American Indians. The overall picture shows the United States (whose institutions are natural and ratified by a transcendent law) having defeated in just war a barbarous foreign people. As a result of this defeat, the natural order (one where property is guaranteed and the lines between savage and civilized are clearly drawn) can be restored, as soon as the Indians assume their natural position as subordinated dependents of a paternalistic white society, which deigns to deal with them in the form of a treaty rather than by simply punishing them by force of arms. The United States agrees out of moral goodness to provide generous boons to these children of the forests.

There is little doubt that the Treaty of Fort Stanwix was a "meaningful" performative legal utterance; it is an intentional invocation of codes by a speaker with the goal of producing an action on the part of its auditors, who recognized both the codes and the intention. The commissioners convey a representation of the natural order of things to the Six Nations, and from their perspective the latter are obliged to understand and accept that order. In making such a gesture, they also commit the United States to the terms established by this discourse (to this system of knowledge/power), communicating quite clearly to the Six Nations that this kind of law will structure the relationship between them. Undoubtedly, the representatives of the Six Nations saw the Fort Stanwix treaty as a coercive linguistic act whose legitimacy was based solely on force. From their perspective, the action called for by this performative utterance was not merely understanding, but acquiescence to an imperious command. Records indicate that after the commissioners had presented the conditions of the treaty, one of the most important Seneca leaders, Cornplanter, responded in the following way: "You have this day declared your minds to us fully, and without disguise. We thank you for it; this is acting like men, for thus men speak. We will take what you have said into our most serious consideration, and when we have prepared ourselves to answer to what you have proposed, you shall hear our voice" (qtd. in Prucha, *American Indian Treaties* 47). The resignation in this short speech (especially when we see it in contrast with some of the proud declamations earlier in the "negotiations") attests to the way this treaty was understood. The Six Nations, cowed by the threat of force and recognizing the futility of resistance, gave in to the commissioners' demands. They did what the treaty bade them, turning over five chiefs as hostages and accepting American territorial claims. Though clearly not understood by the Six Nations to be natural or valid, those claims could not simply be ignored. The Indians realized that the nature of "engagement" in treaty exchanges had changed from the days when the Iroquois League had been a major power broker between the English and French. This was to be no Treaty of Lancaster, the much more complex diplomatic exchange of 1744 made famous in Benjamin Franklin's printed edition. The Seneca were now in the shadow of a new kind of legal discourse.

Merely analyzing the ideological assumptions of the Fort Stanwix agreement only tells part of the story of colonial contact, however. We have yet to see how, recalling Mary Louise Pratt's phrasing, "colonized subjects undertake to represent themselves in ways that *engage with* the colonizer's own terms." We have also not seen how that engagement might subsequently shape the horizons of Indian literary expression and autobiographical acts of self-definition. By itself, of course, acquiescence to blatant coercive force and imperious command does not constitute a form of "engagement" with colonial models of identity. We can probably feel confident in the assumption that the Seneca, who up to that time had enjoyed a position of independence and sovereign power in the British colonial order, would not have immediately felt a strong commitment to the model of identity put forward by the Treaty of Fort Stanwix. But the *process* of engagement is a historical one, taking shape over time and through a sustained encounter with legal models, forms, and institutions. Focusing solely on the ways that this one treaty seeks to define Indian identity does not fully explain the dynamic of contact. But it does help us locate the beginning of Seneca engagement with the discourse of U.S. Indian law and with the assumptions put forward at Fort Stanwix.

Two of the characteristics that distinguish a legal act like the treaty from other kinds of communicative acts are longevity and putative solidity. As noted earlier, in making the Treaty of Fort Stanwix, the commissioners committed the United States to a particular kind of long-term relationship with the tribes of the Six Nations. Notwithstanding their vulnerable political situation, the Seneca gained from this agreement (and others like it) an understanding of how they would need to address themselves to the colonizing power in the future if they were to have any chance for the redress of their wrongs (Dorothy Jones's idea of a "toehold"). In other words, the treaty established the parameters for subsequent communication and provided the possibility at least of finding a way to "write back" to the colonizing power in a way that it might understand and recognize. From 1784 onward, the Seneca leadership demonstrated an impressive grasp of their complicated position in the American legal system, and they changed their modes of self-expression as a result. In 1790, for example, Cornplanter delivered a speech to President Washington demonstrating the kind of sophisticated strategy of rhetorical engagement the Seneca used to cope with encroaching Americans.[3] Speaking of his people's concerns that their remaining lands would be lost, Cornplanter addresses Washington in the language of paternalism, calling him "Father" and "great councillor" to the Seneca in a way that fuses their newly subservient position with the form of kinship relations that had characterized relations under the English treaty system. Shrewdly, he also opens his speech with a description of the fear that followed Washington's name during the Revolution, when the "town destroyer's" army ravaged the Seneca nation (a specific reference to the Sullivan Campaign of 1777). This comment is designed to reinforce the postwar commitment of the federal government to protect its defeated children. Cornplanter subsequently uses treaty language (which designates a promise both as a form of contract and as a trust responsibility) to try to transform the Indians' subservient colonial position into a stronger legal position, noting, "When you gave us peace, we called you Father, *because you then promised to secure to us the possession of our lands.* Do this, and so long as the land shall remain, that beloved name shall live in the heart of every Seneca" [my emphasis] (qtd. in Coleman 63).[4] Moving on from his claim regarding Washington's contractual obligations to the Seneca, Cornplanter proceeds (much in line with the Declaration of Independence) to list the grievances of his people. He presents his argument in legalistic language ("Father, hear our case"). In doing so, he demonstrates a full awareness of the jurisdictional conflicts (between state and federal authorities) that plagued antebellum Indian law, commenting on the fact that "first one and then another comes and claims by authority of the very people who *he* told us had promised to secure this land to us for ever" (64). Finally, Cornplanter cleverly couches his plea that the Great Father fulfill his trustee responsibilities with an invocation of a key component of the colonial discourse of Indianness (mentioning the legal imperative of "civilization"): "Father, the game

which the Great Spirit sent into our country for us to live on, is fast going from among us. We had thought that it was his intention that we
should till the ground with the plough, as the white population, and we
have talked to one another about it. But before we come to any conclusion about this, we must know whether you intend to leave our children
any land to till . . . We have heard that you were wise, and we now wait
your answer to what we have said, that we may see if you are just" (65).
What is most interesting in a speech like this is the way an attempt to
use the *nomos* of treaty law as a shield against colonial power begins to
draw on the models of Indian identity pervading the discourse of Indian
law. Speaking only six years after Fort Stanwix, Cornplanter may well
have been dissembling in his comments about the Seneca's understanding the imperative to become "civilized" freeholders and in his willing
acceptance of the protection of the Great Father. Indeed, his adherence
to the contractual language of the treaty suggests the persistence of a
sense of corporate identity and a subtle form of resistance to the individualization implicit in the ideology of assimilation and civilization. At
the same time, though, Cornplanter had clearly and rapidly learned the
new language of colonial contact and was prepared to use it with great
facility.[5] Within a generation, the continual use of that language by a
new group of Seneca mediators would lead to their deeper engagement
with colonial models of identity, and, not surprisingly, to intratribal conflict. At the same time, it would profoundly influence the emergence of
Seneca literature in English. The struggle over removal proved to be the
catalyst.

———————

Throughout the early decades of the nineteenth century, U.S. Indian law
continued to dominate the lives of the Seneca in ways that extended well
beyond the persistence of old contractual agreements. In this respect, the
Treaty of Fort Stanwix marked only the beginning of their struggle with
a more aggressive strain of colonial discourse. Two years after the Fort
Stanwix agreement was signed, the states of Massachusetts and New
York resolved a legal dispute of their own that would have significant
consequences for the Seneca in the coming decades. Both Massachusetts
and New York had sought to claim large areas of the nation's territory
within the boundaries of New York state. In their 1786 settlement, Massachusetts ceded to New York jurisdiction over the lands in question,
while New York granted Massachusetts "pre-emptive rights" to purchase
the lands from the Seneca should they decide to sell. This pre-emptive
right (a form of exclusive purchasing power derived from the right of

discovery) was sold three times in subsequent years before finally ending up in the hands of a private interest, the Ogden Land Company, in
1810. Throughout this period, but especially once the Ogden Land Company became involved, considerable pressure was placed on the Seneca
to induce them to sell their lands.[6] Recognizing the precariousness of
their situation, the nation continued its process of engagement with the
colonial legal order, even if different leaders held divergent visions of the
proper approach and goals of such engagement.

Cornplanter's speech to Washington represents the general tenor
of the dominant form of Seneca diplomacy after the Revolutionary War
and the collapse of Iroquois power. Recognizing their ambiguous status
within the American legal system, many Seneca embraced their treaty
relationship with the federal government as the best chance for survival.
Agreements subsequent to Fort Stanwix (like the 1794 Treaty of Peace
and Friendship and the Treaty of Big Tree in 1797) guaranteed the nation
possession of their reservations unless they chose to sell. In 1802, as pressure from private land speculators increased, the Seneca appealed to the
U.S. government to fulfill its paternalistic trusteeship role as protector
of Native interests. In the process, they obtained another guarantee of
their land rights in a treaty signed at Buffalo Creek. Tensions between the
federal government's treaty relations with the Seneca and the emergent
removal policy (tensions that would be resolved unfavorably in the case
of the Cherokee) ensured that the Indian position was never a secure one;
the continual renegotiation of agreements during this period attests to
this fundamental instability. Nevertheless, the government's commitment to treaty making (which treated the Indian nation as a corporate
or collective entity) worked against the drive toward assimilation of the
Indian as a possessive "individual." In spite of, or perhaps because of,
these contradictions, the centerpiece of their relationship with white
America continued to be Indian leaders' increasing engagement (through
the treaty form) with Anglo-American legal discourse.

Notwithstanding their obvious reluctance to emigrate, the Seneca
continued to receive considerable pressure to sell their lands from representatives of the Ogden Land Company and the state of New York well
into the late 1830s. In 1823 and 1826, Ogden agents (often masquer-
ading as private purchasers) managed to obtain large tracts along the
Genesee River and near the Buffalo Creek Reservation in western New
York. Through the 1823 agreement, the Ogden Land Company gained
possession of most of former captive (and later adopted Seneca) Mary
Jemison's Gardeau Reservation, a sizeable tract occupied by about fifty
of Jemison's Indian relatives. Indicative of the complex legal maneuver-

ing taking place around the Seneca after the Revolution, the ability of the "White Woman" of the Genesee (as the author of her "autobiography," James Seaver, refers to her) to sell these lands rested primarily on a state bill passed in 1817 granting her New York citizenship and full title to the reserve (which had earlier been granted to her by the Seneca themselves in the 1797 Treaty of Big Tree). The 1817 statute allowed Jemison's subsequent cession "treaty" to the Ogden Land Company to be viewed as a private contract (a position accepted by Secretary of War Calhoun in a letter to the Six Nations' subagent, Jasper Parrish, in 1824), effectively removing the federal government's trust responsibility from consideration.[7] Jemison's own account of land transactions in the 1824 *A Narrative of the Life of Mrs. Mary Jemison* highlights the way that this type of sleight of hand placed her at an extreme disadvantage. Discussing her sale of the Gardeau lands, she provides readers with a familiar drama of fraudulent land exchange between literate whites and illiterate Indians: "Then they read the deed which my friends had prepared before he came from home, describing a piece of land by certain bounds that were a specified number of chains and links from each other. Not understanding the length of a chain or link, I described the bounds of the piece of land I intended Jemison [George Jemison, a supposed 'relative'] should have, which they said was just the same that the deed contained and no more" (145). Of course, the deed actually specified ten times more land than Jemison had intended to sell, much to her subsequent surprise. As a private contract, though, and not a true Indian "treaty," this agreement was not subject to federal oversight. The "trust" relationship encoded in the legal discourse of treaty had been effectively sidestepped. The lands were lost.

The fact that Jemison had been defrauded of her Gardeau lands by a combination of state and private interests was not overlooked by the other Seneca communities. In the wake of the *federally authorized* 1826 treaty ceding all remaining Genesee Valley lands, the Seneca began to challenge the local development interests by appealing to the national government. The influential Seneca leader Red Jacket (who had originally opposed Jemison's 1797 land grant) led the opposition to the 1826 agreement, which was never ratified by the U.S. Senate (the 1828 vote was 20-20). The Seneca protest led President Adams to appoint a commissioner to investigate the agreement, and the investigation highlighted numerous improprieties on the part of the Ogden Land Company. Red Jacket's victory was only a partial one, however. The 1826 treaty was never resubmitted to the Senate, but it was allowed to stand without ratification. It was not until the late 1960s and early 1970s that the

Seneca would receive compensation for the lost territory (compensation they would not have received, admittedly, had the treaty been ratified in 1828). In the end, then, the loss of the Genesee country provided a bitter learning experience for the Seneca. Clearly, their only hope for legal redress and protection from the encroaching power of state government and private interests lay in federal law, but appeals to Washington seemingly needed to be supported by broader appeals to public opinion. This, in turn, required the emergence not only of a new rhetoric but also of writers capable of engaging, in printed English, with American audiences and legal systems. By the late 1830s such writers were beginning to appear.

The removal crisis in Seneca country peaked in 1838, when a treaty of questionable legitimacy was signed whereby the nation sold off its remaining lands and agreed to move to Kansas. Similar to the infamous Treaty of New Echota with the Cherokee, only a minority of the Seneca signed the 1838 agreement, with many of the signers reportedly being bribed or intimidated. Conflict ensued between tribal factions, as did a legal struggle over the legitimacy of the treaty and the federal government's obligations toward the Seneca. In 1842 a compromise treaty was negotiated and some, but not all, of the lands were saved from purchase. Nevertheless, the issues surrounding the removal crisis continued to be debated throughout the 1840s. Such debates contributed to what critic Daniel F. Littlefield has called the "genesis of Seneca literature in English," rooted in the emergence of the kind of proto-elite from which a tradition of Indian autobiography would develop elsewhere across the country throughout the nineteenth century.[8] The members of this younger generation, who came of age during the debates surrounding the treaty of 1838 and its aftermath, all show signs of the deepening influence of Indian law on Seneca rhetoric. At the same time, their political writings provide the background for the development of a new language of self-definition.

A series of pamphlets on the Seneca removal crisis published by the Society of Friends provides ample evidence of the pervasiveness of legal forms and institutions in the daily life of all the Seneca (not merely its literary spokespersons) by the mid-nineteenth century. A significant portion of the 1840 Quaker pamphlet (titled "The Case of the Seneca Indians in the State of New York, Illustrated by Facts") consists of sworn affidavits by individual members of the Seneca nation. In the affidavits, a written legal form that became quite familiar to them, members of the nation attest to fraud and other illegalities in the treaty negotiations. The Quakers also reproduced several memorials drafted and sent both to members of

Congress and President Van Buren by small groups of Seneca. The writers of these memorials adopted the appropriate legal language as they sought to articulate the Seneca position. In a document sent to Senator Samuel Prentiss, for example, the twelve Seneca signatories from Buffalo Creek sought to "make a full statement of our grievances," arguing that "[i]n the sight of God who looks down upon us, *it cannot be wrong* for us to lay claim to our own rights, and we implore the protection of the Senate in so doing" (Coleman 120).[9] The Prentiss memorial exemplifies the subtle influence of legal discourse on Indian subjects who engage with it. The "rights" asserted in the text appear to be the Indians' rights, as wards, to the protection of the federal government. The signatories find themselves in the increasingly familiar position of embracing the paternalistic regime of treaty law as the best means of preserving their own cultural identity. At the same time, the memorial shows a subtle movement away from an exclusive sense of corporate identity as a result of such continuous engagement with the legal system.[10] The authors indicate a willingness to compromise with the faction that wished to emigrate and to make an "equitable division" of reservation lands between parties that would enable "those who wish to take their share of the public property and dispose of it as they please" to do so (118). Such a disposition represents a significant shift toward "civilized," individualistic modes of social organization, a shift also reflected in the language of those at the forefront of attempts to mediate the crisis.

The Quakers published records of 1842 treaty negotiations between the Seneca, a representative of the Ogden Land Company, the states of Massachusetts and New York, and federal commissioners, records that provide interesting evidence of the ways that the dynamic of legal engagement was reshaping the diplomatic speech of tribal leaders. The 1842 council represented an attempt to find a compromise solution to the conflict and to somehow rewrite the 1838 treaty. Speakers on all sides followed many of the customs of traditional Iroquoian diplomacy; for example, they addressed each other as "brothers" and opened with ceremonial invocations. And yet a pragmatic recognition of changed circumstances dominates the proceedings. Contact, and the legal disappointments of the past, had clearly changed something. Initially the text shows the Quaker representatives encouraging their Seneca friends to resist illegal removal, but also to accept the need to adopt a "civilized" life. As the council continues, this proves to be precisely the rhetorical strategy used by the Indian speakers in their attempt to engage with the powerful institutions confronting them. Israel Jemison, acting as primary spokesperson for the Seneca, opens the discussion by observing that "we are fully convinced, that if our nation would adopt your habits and mode of life, they would be made prosperous and happy" (15). But this statement is followed up immediately with the serious business of discussing the new treaty. Jemison engages in a communicative act that first accepts the model of subjectivity advocated by his Quaker supporters and then moves on to a pragmatic attempt to build on that foundation and hold on to as much of the Seneca's traditional lands as possible. As the conversation continues, interestingly enough, it is only the Quaker speakers who discourse in the metaphorical language of earlier forest diplomacy (speaking effusively of how their hearts are "bleeding" for their Indian friends, for example). The Seneca participants in the treaty, in contrast, are blunt and businesslike, seemingly an acknowledgment of the changed realities of mid-nineteenth-century America. The questions various Seneca chiefs ask about the new, compromise treaty (after hearing it read aloud and interpreted) are clear-eyed and pragmatic—suggesting canny negotiators trying to keep their options open and to get the best possible deal for themselves within the hegemonic legal framework of the colonizing power. "If the Indians, at some future day, conclude to sell the Cattaraugus and Allegheny reservations, will they be obliged to sell them at the price presented in the former treaty?" asks one speaker (25). "If the chiefs should ratify this Treaty and soon after conclude to go West, can they go?" asked another (24). The rhetorical foundation for the give and take of negotiation reflects an increasing commitment to engage with the discourse of U.S. Indian law. We have come some distance from the rhetoric of Cornplanter's turn-of-the-century diplomacy, but the progression is nevertheless clear and traceable.

If the Quaker-produced materials show us both the degree to which law impacted the daily lives of the rank-and-file Seneca and the ways legal engagement was shifting tribal members' approaches to treaty negotiations, the writings of the nation's literary spokespersons provide even deeper insight into the role of legal discourse in shaping an emerging rhetoric of Indian identity—the kind of rhetoric that would eventually become important for Seneca autobiography. One of the best examples of this is Maris Bryant Pierce's 1838 "Address on the Present Condition and Prospects of the Aboriginal Inhabitants of North America, with Special Reference to the Seneca Nation," a work that stands as one of the most forceful arguments against removal.[11] In justifying himself to his white readership, Pierce (who was educated at Dartmouth and had close ties to the Quakers) seems to accept the idea of a hierarchical distinction between Indian life and civilized life, as well as the basic environmentalist assumptions behind the civilization policy: "Hitherto our cause has been advocated almost exclusively, though ably and humanely, by the friends of human right and human weal, belonging by *nature* to a different, and by *circumstances* and *education*, to a superior race of men." (56) Further evidence of Pierce's engagement with legal models of identity is that a key part of his argument against removal turns on the assertion that the Indian can and should be elevated through such education (a position strongly maintained by the Quakers, especially with regard to the "domestic instruction" of Seneca women). He stresses that the Seneca possess the "capacity of apprehending and appreciating any of the principles which form the basis of Christian civilization" (57). Later in the "Address," Pierce argues for the equitable application of treaty law, actually invoking the law of discovery as justification (since the Indian's "original and undisputed possession of this country" dictate that land transfers take place through treaty). In doing so, he does not question the prescriptive right of the Ogden Land Company to purchase Indian lands or the desirability of elevating the Indians "to the rank which civilization and Christianity bestow" (59). Rather, Pierce *only* disputes the legality of the 1838 treaty (the signatures to which he sees as having been illicitly obtained), while stressing that the reason so few Seneca were willing to sign it was that their present location and circumstances remain the most conducive to advancement. When he closes by pointing out that selling land at two dollars an acre constitutes bad business (wondering "Is the offer liberal?"), Pierce demonstrates precisely the kind of economic sense his readers would expect of a "civilized" possessive individual (63). In this sense, the implicit "claims" about his own identity as an educated Seneca that emerge in his polemic buttress his larger argument about the need for Indians to be transformed in accordance with legal models. The text connotes even more than it says about the impact of Indian law on Pierce's own changing sense of his rhetorical position and role as an Indian leader.

Similar to the Seneca memorialists, Pierce's move to embrace treaty law (which addresses the "Indian" as a collective entity, or "nation") as a means to securing the right and ability to become civilized (an "individual" model of identity) reveals the complexity of his new rhetoric of self. Another Seneca voice on the other side of the debate, that of Nathaniel Thayer Strong, manifests the influence of law to an even greater degree. An interpreter and assistant to James Stryker, subagent to the New York Indians at Buffalo, Strong had actively worked behind the scene with agents of the Ogden Land Company to secure the initial signatures to the 1838 treaty and subsequently to see it ratified. To the latter end, in 1841 he penned an "Appeal to the Christian Community on the Conditions

and Prospects of the New York Indians," where he stresses the legitimacy
of the treaty sale and rejects the Quakers' involvement as both "incompatible with the law of Christian charity" and full of "misrepresenta-
tions" (4). In the pamphlet, Strong makes the case for the legitimacy and
desirability of the land sale, invoking the Seneca's "secure and inviolable
. . . rights under the treaty," the "constitutional" actions of the Senate
and president, and the true spirit of Christian benevolence. In his view,
all three dictate delivering his people from "bondage, degradation, and
misery" and removing them to the "asylum provided . . . by your government" (3–4). As Strong presents it, the Ogden Land Company's purchase
represents neither a subversion of the trust responsibilities of the federal
government nor a threat to the long-term welfare of the Seneca.

Strong's involvement in the efforts by the Ogden agents to bribe
Seneca chiefs into signing the treaty has struck some critics as evidence
of his unreliability as a source (Littlefield 93). A careful reading of his
text, though, suggests that he may not have been simply acting as a
mouthpiece for the Ogden Land Company. His direct treatment of the
bribery issue in the "Appeal" serves as one piece of evidence of the degree to which his engagement with the discourse of Indian law (and his
employment by the War Department) led him to a sophisticated act of
rhetorical redefinition. As Strong correctly notes in the text, the practice
of distributing "presents" during treaty negotiations was a long-standing
one, dating back in Seneca memory to the covenant chain between the
Iroquois League and the British. However, under the rule of the United
States a subtle shift had taken place; the practice of offering explicit financial compensation to individual chiefs as part of the final agreement
became common. The cynical intent of change in policy was, in Andrew
Jackson's words, to "corrupt a few [Indian] leaders . . . and induce them
to adopt the plans embraced by the government" (qtd. in Prucha, *American Indian Treaties* 154). At the same time, though, the act of bribing
individual chiefs supported the overall policy of "civilizing" the tribes
by breaking down corporate models of identity. As an Indian participant
in the system, Strong puts the policy in an interesting light:

> Let me ask what is the meaning of the term *bribery* as applied to Indi-
> ans? If a right to personal gratuities be the privilege of chiefs according
> to the general and well understood usage of Indian communities, then
> the acceptance of them, being consistent with official fidelity, involves
> no violation of duty, and the payment of them is not bribery. According
> to the unbroken custom which has prevailed among the Seneca since
> the first sale of their extensive possessions in this state, the chiefs have
> demanded and received personal allowances . . . At this day, and espe-

cially among tribes whose constant intercourse with white men has taught them that money is the surest means of purchasing both luxuries and comforts—when the increased value of their lands enhances their official importance and busy white advisors are ready to stimulate their cupidity, it is not strange that the chiefs should be disposed to make the most of their official perquisites. (20)

The remarkable straightforwardness with which he addresses the issue of financial payments to the chiefs reveals Strong's desire to show that "personal allowances" to the chiefs were in no way inconsistent with Indian custom. What once were called "presents," he argues, are now inaccurately designated bribes. Clearly, such a claim overlooks the real differences between goods distributed to a community through the mediation of the chiefs (the earlier practice) and what are in effect personal "wages" paid by the government to savvy and self-interested leaders. However, the very fact that he *claims* that no difference existed between the two practices may in fact testify to the impact of legal engagement on Strong's own definition of Indian identity. His willingness to participate overtly in the bribery system and his manner of defending it may attest not to cynicism but rather to a subtly changed sense of what it means to be "Indian," or at least how to talk about being Indian. Strong presents *individual* self-interest as totally consistent with his conception of Indian identity and culture. Rather than defending himself from charges of being a "corrupt" chief, he presents himself as a rational, individual Seneca.

Beyond his remarkably unselfconscious advocacy of the "bribery" system, many of Strong's arguments in favor of the removal treaty suggest other ways in which he was actively engaged with the discourse of Indian law, and not simply acting as a pawn of the Ogden Land Company. Generally speaking, he comes across as remarkably open-eyed with regard to the evils of the colonial system. Unlike even an opponent of removal like Pierce, Strong challenges the basic legitimacy of the law of discovery and the roots of colonial domination: "The aborigines of this continent, from their first intercourse with the nations of Europe, have been the victims of that most unjust principle of colonization upon which the government of each nation first discovering any particular portion of this vast country, assumed over it unqualified dominion, both as to its soil and its inhabitants" (27). Despite the "injustice" of European claims, Strong acknowledges the weight of history and legal precedent in shaping the present, commenting that "the rights of Great Britain and her colonies, which have passed by the revolution to the states, have since been asserted and exercised by them" (28). For this reason, he notes,

Indians "hold our lands by a title comparatively worthless, and as to personal rights are placed under restrictions equally severe and humiliating." Confronted with this harsh reality, Strong's support of removal appears to grow out of a pragmatic conviction that the best path for the future, and the only way for the Indian to attain full equality with the civilized American, is to emigrate to a place where title to land can be firmly established. To take such a position is to accept the legal model of possessive individualism as the only viable basis for Indian self-definition in the future. Strong's argument (which *is* oppositional) takes place within the terms established by Anglo-American legal discourse. "The rights of property," he tells us, "are the very basis of the political institutions of Great Britain." For this reason, "we find that the capacity [of the English] to acquire and hold individual property, and the power to transfer it, at pleasure, and transfer it by will, were essential elements of civilization" (31). The Seneca find themselves in a contrasting situation where they are "without the capacity to take or hold lands (otherwise than by mere occupation) or to dispose of them—shut out from all civil and political rights—a distinct and degraded and despised class of society." Ironically, only removal to the west, Strong insists, will enable the Indians to establish themselves as equal participants in civilized life through solid land title.

By framing the debate over the removal treaty in such a way, Strong makes clear his basic acceptance of the dominant models of identity deployed in Indian law. This is because, in his view, the Indian struggle for "civil and political rights" would increasingly take place within the normative register of Anglo-American law and classical liberalism. Though his suggestion (late in the text) that the negro slave is better off than the Indian may strike a modern reader as hyperbolic, such a rhetorical move is reminiscent of the revolutionary discourse of the American Whigs. Here, as throughout the "Appeal," Strong comes across as remarkably well-versed in the dominant ideological assumptions of early national America. Some of the passages cited above could easily have been taken from John Marshall's legal opinions, or from Blackstone. Yet Strong does not seem merely to be parroting the discourse of colonial domination. The text does not idealize the colonial past, and Strong seems to see himself as a defender of the Indian way of life. The manner in which he adopts legal thinking in his criticism of the legal oppression of the Seneca renders his text a useful example of what can happen in the process of engagement. Strong's "Appeal" provides further illumination of the way that, over time, Indian law was coming to dominate the communicative dynamic of colonial contact in the nineteenth century, in ways that were profoundly shaping the *language* of self-definition, especially among the "literary" elite. The terms of the debate in which Pierce and Strong were engaged, from what appear on the surface to be such radically different positions, place them both in the shadow of the same legal models of Indian identity. And yet we can also see new forms of protest and accommodation, as well as new ways of conceptualizing "Indian" identity, emerging from this context. It is little wonder, then, that the explicitly autobiographical writing emerging from Seneca country in the wake of removal would also speak in a recognizably legal dialect.

The pronounced impact of legal engagement on Maris Pierce's and Nathaniel Strong's sense of Indian identity foreshadows much of what we find in the writings (especially the short autobiography) of Ely S. Parker, perhaps the most famous and influential Seneca intellectual of the nineteenth century. Like Pierce and Strong, Parker came of age during the conflict over the removal treaty. He studied law during the 1840s and served as secretary to the Tonawando Seneca during the crisis. In the process, he met and began a collaboration with the pioneering American anthropologist Lewis Henry Morgan (acting as Morgan's principal informant in writing the *League of the Iroquois* [1851], a text itself highly influenced by legal thinking).[12] Parker subsequently became involved in changes in the governmental structure of the Seneca reservations that overthrew the traditional tribal government in favor of a ballot-driven system. He also worked for the election of public officials and for the passage of laws by the state of New York that extended some of the state's criminal jurisdiction over tribal lands, allowed the nation to sue in state court, and funded schools. Unable to find employment as a lawyer (New York prohibited Indians from practicing law), he later supported himself for a time as a civil engineer. During the Civil War, Parker came to national prominence as an adjutant general and member of Ulysses S. Grant's staff. After the war, Grant appointed him to be commissioner of Indian affairs, the first Indian to serve in that post. Parker's tenure as commissioner (from 1869 to 1871), perhaps more than any other biographical detail, attests to the extent of his engagement with the evolving discourse of Indian law and to his immersion in its institutions. As with Pierce and Strong, such engagement seems to have profoundly shaped his sense of Indian identity and rhetoric.[13]

As with many nineteenth-century Indian writers, Parker's formative encounters with the *nomos* of Indian law took place in white-run schools. Parker's unpublished manuscripts contain several compositions written while he was a student at the Baptist Mission School of Tonawanda and at the Yates and Cayuga Academies during the late 1830s and

1840s. These writings reveal a young man struggling both to learn a new *cultural* language and to find a middle ground between assimilationism and traditionalism. A pair of 1845 essays on "The Age of Improvement" and "The Beneficence of the Great Spirit" (composed on different sides of the same piece of paper) highlight Parker's complex rhetorical and social position.[14] In the first of these, he notes that "the present is particularly characterized as an age of improvement" and goes on to speak approvingly of the steam engine (and its "subjugation of various powers of water and fire for the benefit of man") and telegraph (which has converted the "electrical car" of "Old Jupiter" into a "mail carrier") (PP). Such praise of modernity is tempered, however, by a concern for the impact of technology on the "inner world." Sounding a bit Emersonian, Parker laments the tendency of men to place "too much dependence upon the powers of others" and their lack of original thought (PP). It is difficult not to read Parker's anxiety over "dependence" as a reflection of his position as a reservation Indian in the mid-1800s; indeed, his remarks both on progress and self-reliance foreshadow his later advocacy of the allotment policy (which he saw as a means of forcing Indian self-reliance) as commissioner of Indian affairs. When we turn the page over and look at Parker's second composition, though, we also find evidence of his ambivalence toward the present age. Written in a form suggestive of traditional Seneca ritual prayer, "The Beneficence of the Great Spirit" consists of effusive thanks to the "Great Spirit" for nature in its many forms, as well as particular thanks to the thunder, addressed as "Great Grandfather." The emphasis here is rather different from the "subjugation" of nature through technology that is lauded on the other side of the paper. The materiality of this "two-sided" composition stands as an obvious metaphor for Parker's own inner struggle to find a language of self-expression within the discourse of colonialism. As a young man, at least, he seems both committed to a process of engagement and anxious about its alienating effects.

Parker explores these paradoxes directly in another school composition, dated November 13, 1845. This piece, called "On Happiness; the Savage versus the Civilized Life," is addressed (almost as if intended as a speech) directly to his classmates and teachers. The occasion seems to have involved a visitor to the school who overheard Parker take the position in a school debate that the "savage" is happier than the "civilized man." Parker notes that this gentleman then posed the following question: "Why, if the savage life is more conducive to happiness than the civilized, has Mr. Parker abandoned that life, and now is studying to acquire that knowledge of the arts and sciences which prevails among civilized people . . . ?" Parker's response is initially defensive and angry, for he notes that he is "accountable to no human" for his "beliefs or opinions" (PP). Yet clearly, on some level, he indeed felt "accountable," for he goes on to address the accusatory question with a fairly extensive autobiographical apologia. "I am one of the remnants of that race of beings generally denominated savages," Parker begins. He then reviews the position he took in the debate, noting, "I have seen that the happiness of the savage consists in the gratification of his desires. Their appetites are few and not being [word illegible] are easily supplied" (PP). Having offered that assertion, he goes on to provide a list of primitive "virtues" (bravery, friendship, universal benevolence, hospitality, and strict honesty). As for his decision to leave this happy life, Parker explains that "it was rumored in my ears that the civilized life was able to produce more happiness than the savage," a claim that he notes having thus far been unable to substantiate. He then closes his apologia with a highly nuanced statement: "If we do not find it, if happiness shall still be our aim, we shall resume the blanket (the bended bow and the arrow, the [word illegible] and feathers), the tomahawk and knife, and resume savage life in all its wildness, and then you may justly say 'do what you will the Indian will be an Indian still'" (PP). What sort of statement is this? Parker seems to hold out hope that happiness will be found, but that hope is couched in language that is both threatening (suggesting that Indians *will* take up the tomahawk and knife again), resigned (questioning whether happiness can still be a viable goal), and fatalistic (suggesting that the failure of cultural contact will only prove to whites that the Indian—the "remnant" of the race to which he belongs—cannot be changed or saved). In the end, rather than offering a sustained defense of the position he had apparently taken in the aforementioned debate, Parker offers poignant testimony of his own constrained position. Many of the options he mentions in his conclusion are clearly not viable. Can the Seneca, hemmed in on all sides by the growing settlements of a populous state, really take up the tomahawk or resume "savage" life in a meaningful way? Is Parker willing to simply give up and accept the narrative of the vanishing Indian? Or is he implying that the only real option is to redefine himself, to accept the need for engagement with the institutions of "civilization," even though this means surrendering the search for a happiness equivalent to that of "savage" life? Is this his understanding of the colonial relationships put in force by nineteenth-century treaty relations?

Many of Parker's other school compositions, and the path of his own career (in the military and in the Indian service), suggest that he grudgingly accepted the final two propositions listed above. Comments made in pieces like "The Intellectual Character of the Indian" (dated March 21, 1843) are more representative of his school writings than the essay "On Happiness," and they foreshadow his eventual support for the allotment policy and his gradually shifting articulation of Indianness. As early as this 1843 piece, Parker was arguing that Indians accepted the need for improvement through individualism, being aware that "without industry they must die" (PP). He goes further—noting (in a manner similar to later writers like Charles Eastman) that Indian people are uniquely adaptable. Their minds are free, Parker writes, and "there is no race on the earth that has so many interesting features of intellectual character as the untutored Indian" (PP). In an autobiographical turn, Parker then alludes to the value of the kind of schooling he was then receiving, reflecting on the benefits the "untutored" mind received from exposure to the arts and sciences. He thanks his classmates for their support and speaks of returning to the forest bearing their feelings of love and support. In doing so, Parker accepts the responsibility of becoming a "representative" Indian, one who can demonstrate the viability of assimilation as a survival strategy. The alternative it seems, is that which he had described earlier in the essay—the prospect that the "remnants" of the race must "go into the far west, to valleys undisturbed by the injustice and oppression of the white man, but [which] in my apprehension will be to the Indians the valley of the shadow of death" (PP).

By the time he assumed the post of Indian commissioner, Parker's reflections on these grim alternatives seem to have led him to become increasingly committed to the idea of the Indian *individual* as a future model of identity (a position similar in some respects to Nathaniel Strong's). In spite of his earlier defense of the Seneca's treaty rights during the removal crisis, *as commissioner* Parker came to reject the validity of continued treaty negotiations with Indian nations. In his annual report to Congress in 1869, he notes that negotiating treaties had led Indians to become "falsely impressed with the notion of national independence" and thus interfered with the government's attempts to elevate them into civilized life. Parker remarks that according to the "stern letter of the law," Indians "are held to be wards of the government, and the only title the law concedes them to the land they occupy or claim is a mere possessory one" (qtd. in Prucha, *Documents* 134). He goes on to suggest that "as civilization advances and their possessions of land are required for settlement, such legislation should be granted to them as a wise, liberal, and just government ought to extend to subjects holding their dependent relation" (135). Taken together, these statements imply a rejection of the corporate model of Indian identity, coupled with the

continued acceptance of the paternalistic notion of the Indian-as-child
needing to be raised into the legal form of civilized adulthood. Such an
ideological conjunction would subsequently serve as the basis for the
federal allotment policy (the impact of which on the autobiographical
acts of Charles Eastman provides the subject for chapters 5 and 6).

Parker's remarks in his congressional report (and his advocacy of allotment) exemplify his ongoing struggle to engage with the discourse of
Indian law. What might have begun at one point in his life as a defensive
process of accommodation seems to have become, in time, a deep, though
ambivalent, internalization of colonial ideology. One of Parker's numerous letters to his friend Harriet Maxwell Converse (written sometime
in 1881) appears to shed some light on what the process of engagement
meant for his sense of self:

> I beg you not to tell me that because the beautiful snow has fallen and
> covered the lovely bosom of Mother Earth, and because the North Wind
> howls and screams in every crack and crevice of man's shelter, I should
> be reveling in legendary and forest lore. No. Dreamland, fairyland, and
> storyland are all good and charming for those who have the time and
> talent that way. For me there is but one world to deal with at present,
> viz., the world of stern reality, and all other fancies are pushed aside for
> life's actual strifes.
>
> Do you know, or can you believe, that sometimes the idea obtrudes
> itself into my obtuse and lethargic brain, whether it has been well that I
> have sought civilization with its bothersome commitments, and wheth-
> er it would not have been better, even now, being convinced of my
> weakness and failure to continue in the gladiatorial contests of modern
> life, to return to the darkest and most secret wilds (if any such can be
> found) of our country, and there to vegetate and expire silently, hap-
> pily and forgotten, as do the birds of the air and the beasts of the field.
> The thought is a happy one, but perhaps impracticable. (qtd. in Parker,
> "Writings" 523)

Parker's comments here are fascinating on a number of levels. He
sets up a clear contrast between the "stern realities" of "civilization,"
which he feels compelled to confront, and a primitivist dreamworld that
can only be identified in this context with "Indian" life. The appeal his
Indian past holds for him registers as a nihilistic pull, a desire to vanish,
suggesting the influence of contractarian thinking (with its emphasis on
the progression from the state of nature to the state of civilization) on his
self-consciousness. As Parker's practical side argues for the need to confront his present "modern life," he foregrounds how his immersion in the
Indian/civilization dichotomy at the heart of Indian law problematizes
his attempt to develop a retrospective "experience" of Indian selfhood

(the kind of process that stands at the heart of the autobiographical act). Emerging from the broader context of his long-term engagement with that discourse, Parker's letter suggests a generally melancholic internalization of colonial models of identity.

Not surprisingly, the struggle we find in his letter to Harriet Maxwell Converse also shapes and complicates Parker's one sustained attempt at formal autobiographical expression. Though we have no date for its composition, "General Parker's Autobiography" was first published in 1905 by his great-nephew, the anthropologist and Indian activist Arthur C. Parker. In his introductory remarks, Arthur Parker notes that the text was apparently intended as a public address, though he cannot say whether or where it was ever actually delivered. He justifies its publication both because of its "personal and historical characters" and the fact that it is "perhaps the only autobiography of a Seneca Indian preserved in literature."[15] (Parker obviously did not consider the as-told-to narrative of Mary Jemison to be an example of authentic Seneca lifewriting.) At the same time, the book may also have interested him as a manifestation of a phenomenon he would cite years later in a discussion of the degree to which Indians had become "civilized" in America. Toward the end of his 1927 work *The Indian How Book*, Parker quite simply notes that "Indians take to law" (332).

Ely Parker's autobiography begins with some remarks that link him in subtle ways to a number of assumptions implicit in the modern, civilized model of possessive individualism. The opening rhetorical gesture notes the audience's desire to know him as an individual: "I must then perforce open your eyes as to who and what I am. I do this because when we read books we want to know as much about the authors of them as it is possible to know. Or when we look upon a new machine, instrument or invention of any kind, we want to know all about the inventor" (qtd. in Parker, "Writings" 527). The relationship Parker establishes between himself and his own autobiography (and by extension, the life he imagines in it) becomes analogous to an author's or inventor's personal, proprietary interest in his creation (an interest that is figured in the modern world, through copyright and patent law, as an issue of property). Having thus intimated an individualist notion of self-possession, Parker goes on to pose the quintessential autobiographical question—"Who is General Parker?" At that point, he begins what his Anglo-American readers might expect—a chronological narrative of his life, starting with his Seneca roots. Interestingly, as he does so, Parker begins to use the third person: "That the general is an Indian you can see for yourself. Some fifty years or so ago, he was born . . ." (528). This process suggests a degree of distance and dissociation from his precivilized Indian roots. (This use of the third person for such purposes will come up again, in much more detail, in the treatment of Charles Eastman in chapter 5.) The hint of dissociation and self-alienation cuts two ways, of course; Parker's reference to himself as "the general" suggests an incomplete identification with that role as well. The opening lines of the autobiography, then, manifest a deep sense of ambivalence surrounding Parker's sense of individual identity, ambivalence rooted in his colonial experience.

In the opening paragraph, Parker shows that he understands the act of writing autobiographically as an act of radical individuation. For a Seneca who had lived his life immersed in Indian law, the implication of this understanding would seem to be that autobiography is the tale of how to become not-Indian. In this sense, Parker's story converges with the history of Indian law and policy. As he tries to work through the obvious complications arising from such a fusion, Parker reveals the degree to which the colonial experience and contact with Indian law had come to dominate his sense of the significance of his life. He fills his autobiography with a series of digressive comments on the failures of various attempts by the American government to civilize the Indian. In fact, throughout the text Parker seems to appreciate the meaning of his own experiences primarily in relation to such legal history. He recalls having been educated under the "manual labor system" at a mission school, but comments that he is "not a believer, notwithstanding all the benefits that I may have personally received, in the missionary system as it has generally been practiced up to the present time" (528). Contrary to the missionary approach to "civilization" first through religious conversion, Parker advances the position he took as Indian commissioner, arguing that Indians first must be "localized and made to abandon their roving habits." In this context, his own life and "successful" assimilation stand as an aberration, contradicting his own legal ideology. His own story is not adding up.

Because Parker's personal experience does not validate his stance on colonial policy, it largely drops out of the text, making "General Parker's Autobiography" a rather peculiar example of the genre. In a profound sense, the story Parker seems to *want* to tell is that of the legal model of the Indian fostered by colonial legal discourse; the fact that his personal experience apparently complicates the picture leads to its effacement from the text. When he discusses his early education and involvement in the Seneca removal crisis, Parker does re-enter his life story, but only briefly. The bulk of that section of the text turns into a discussion of the removal policy itself. Interestingly, Parker now represents removal as a policy flawed in its execution, though not its conception: "The argument was plausible. The Indians were to be concentrated upon lands which were to be patented to them and to be made inalienable to them and their children forever. The government was to build houses for them, provide them with stock and agricultural implements for farming purposes. School houses and churches were to be built and teachers and missionaries sent among them. The government in short was to civilize them and when civilized they were to be organized into a territory with all the paraphernalia of a territorial government, with the privilege of seating a Delegate in Congress" (531). Overall, Parker seems comfortable with all the basic assumptions about Indian identity behind the removal policy. The problem, he suggests, lay in private individuals, like those of the Ogden Land Company. "Behind all this plausibility," he notes, "this plea of humanity and Christian feeling for the Indian, stood an army of speculators ready to lay greedy hands upon the lands that were to be vacated" (532). Parker's commitment to the ideology of the removal policy, if not its execution, becomes clear as he moves immediately to rail against the absurdity of negotiating treaties with Indian tribes (as he had in his earlier report to Congress). Further evidence of his engagement with law appears when he notes that in the War of 1812 and in the Civil War, Indians fought with all Americans "for the Supremacy of the Constitution and the establishment of liberty and equal rights for all men" (534). With this invocation of the Civil War, Parker re-enters his autobiography, but again only briefly. He quickly digresses into an anecdote about Lee's surrender to Grant at Appomattox.

As the preceding examples show, throughout his autobiographical text Parker almost perversely avoids self-reference, opting instead to discuss various aspects of Indian law. Such an avoidance seems to be a manifestation of the self-negating rhetoric visible not just in his 1881 letter to Harriet Maxwell Converse, but also in a later piece of correspondence, dated January 11, 1887:[16]

> In your note you remark "*I know you.*" From the bottom of my heart, I wish you did. There are so many sides to my nature that I sometimes scarcely know myself on my introspection inspections. I sometimes fancy myself as a chameleon, ever changing color in thought with every changing circumstance. If you do know me you have a far deeper insight into this mysterious human nature than I possess over my own earthly kingdom.
>
> Now [illegible] I will cease to wrangle, I will restore my tomahawk to my belt, my scalping knife to its sheath and unstring my bow. These primitive weapons are no match for your [illegible] pen. Like Scotts

coon, I say "Don't shoot." I will come down and resume the manners
and customs of civilized mankind and the rest of the world, and look
only at the surface of things, which is all I generally submit to the outside world. What you read above are only the meteoric flashes of my
romantic, ethereal brain and are harmless.

Your Insenitable [*sic*] Cousin,
Donehogawa the Wolf

Here Parker confesses both his autobiographical uncertainty and his
rhetorical self-consciousness. He does not know how to describe who he
is, especially when he "inspects" himself like a general or a bureaucrat.
At the same time, he reveals the difficulty in finding the right language
to represent this inner turmoil. The tone of this letter is complex and
deeply conflicted—at times, fatalistic (wishing for self-knowledge that
he deems impossible), at times darkly ironic (identifying his own melancholy with the stereotypical sullen, hatchet-wielding Indian), at times
pathetic ("Don't shoot"), and at times brutally honest (confessing that
all he can show the world is an ever-changing surface). Read alongside
his autobiography, the letter suggests that Parker's particularly deep engagement with the discourse of Indian law throughout his life rendered
the language of Indianness a continual problem for him. Unable to treat
his past self in positive terms, his life story (in the autobiography) de-
volves into the story of Indian law—a story he is not able to rework
into a satisfactory autobiographical act. Parker's claim toward the end
of the autobiography that "now you perhaps know as much about General Parker as he knows of himself" is a particularly poignant sign of the
melancholy "wrangling" referred to above (535). His apparent inability to
articulate a sense of personal identity (which he clearly sees is expected
of him as an autobiographer) and his subsequent attempt to situate his
own experience exclusively within the narrative of assimilation mapped
out by Indian law says much about the powerful impact of colonialism
on his ability to craft a life story. At the end of the (tellingly, unfinished)
autobiographical manuscript, all Parker can do is trail off, complaining
about his lack of a pension for his military service and commenting on
the dire situation facing the western Indians if they continue to struggle
against their "irresistible fate."

As I suggested at the opening of chapter 1, in reading Native American autobiography we can benefit by being attentive to the particular
contexts in which individual writers lived and wrote, and by remaining
wary of broad, normative generalizations. The first Seneca autobiographer, Ely Parker provides a particularly stark example of the ways colo-

nial legal discourse could overwhelm the autobiographical purpose of a writer and complicate his or her articulation of Indian identity. Parker indeed lived in a world of "stern realities," and *in his case* engagement with the discourse of Indianness seems to have led him to an imaginative and rhetorical collapse. His abortive act of self-definition thus provides eloquent testimony regarding the difficulties Native American writers faced in developing a new rhetoric of Indianness during the nineteenth century. In this respect, Parker's writings (and those of his Seneca predecessors) establish a context for our evaluation of the achievement of other Indian writers, who were able to redefine themselves more successfully and publish complete autobiographical manuscripts. Parker was an exceptional individual, whose political accomplishments were also considerable. To see the degree to which even he struggled to find a satisfactory rhetoric of self-definition should highlight for us the challenges of discursive engagement during this time period.

The discussion of Seneca history offered in this chapter has been intended to further suggest *why and how* the language of law exerted such a profound influence on the autobiographical acts of nineteenth-century Native Americans. Along the way, I have tried to demonstrate how critical readings of nineteenth-century Indian autobiography will be enhanced by a historical inquiry into (1) the specific models of Indianness disseminated through legal forms and institutions and (2) the way *particular* Indian subjects engaged with those models over time, as a result of their own distinctive life experiences. That not every writer responded to that model in the same way should not lead us to narrow our own view of the literary tradition—to leave out some writers as "inauthentic." Indeed, a full recognition and appreciation of the diverse responses to the hegemony of Indian law seems essential, both in scholarly and political terms. As students of colonial contact, we need to understand the *semiotic* battle over the term "Indian" (a battle that indeed has ongoing "legal" ramifications). Viewed in such a context (as an *individual* struggling to define his Indianness while engaging with powerful discursive formations), Ely Parker becomes a complicated and compelling figure in a larger tradition, not just a failed autobiographer.

The focus of this chapter has been broadly historical, tracing a community's process of legal engagement from the Revolutionary War to the late nineteenth century. From this point onward, however, I intend to narrow the view. In the balance of this book, I will discuss in detail the works of a pair of major Indian autobiographers, reading their specific textual strategies of engagement against the background of their historical periods and the writings of their contemporaries. William Apess (who wrote during the removal era) and Charles Eastman (who came of age during the allotment era) both struggled through a similar autoethnographic *process* as Ely Parker and his Seneca contemporaries. Apess's and Eastman's autobiographical acts, however, represent more coherent culminations of that process. In the end, though, what interests me most as a reader is that none of these "Indian" writers define their Indianness in exactly the same way. It is my hope that having developed an understanding of their Seneca contemporaries will enable us to better see how and why Apess and Eastman produced such different autobiographical acts during their own respective careers. One common thread that holds all these writers together, though, is that they were all involved in an ongoing engagement with Indian law and its powerful institutions of self.

3 *William Apess and the Constraints of Conversion*

> And in the war, which we made against them, God's
> hand from heaven was so manifested that a very few
> of our men in a short time pursued them through the
> wilderness, slew, and took prisoners about 1,400 of
> them, even all they could find, to the great terror and
> amazement of all Indians to this day; so that the name
> of the Pequots (as of Amalech) is blotted out from under
> heaven, there being not one that is, or (at least) dare call
> himself a Pequot.
>
> —John Mason's 1643 Puritan account of the Pequot War
> (quoted in Laurence M. Hauptman, "The Pequot War
> and Its Legacies," 1990)

According to law, the first American Indian to produce an extensive body of autobiographical writing during the nineteenth century should not have existed at all. Yet between 1829 and 1836, the name "William Apess, a Pequot" appeared roughly half a dozen times on the title pages of publications. These events signaled to those who were paying attention the rise of an unexpected and important new voice in antebellum America. Indeed, during this period of American literary history, only in Frederick Douglass's act of "subscribing himself" at the end of his 1845 *Narrative* can we find an equally provocative signature. In his short but remarkably productive literary career, Apess emerged from the shadow of legally sanctioned genocide to become the first major Native American autobiographer. Only Samson Occom, a missionary-educated Mohegan, is known to have written an autobiography in English before him. Occom's "A Short Narrative of My Life" (1768) runs to only a few thousand words, though, in contrast to Apess's three substantial autobiographical works, *A Son of the Forest* (1829, 1831), "The Experience of the Missionary" (1833), and *Indian Nullification* (1835), which total nearly two hundred pages.[1] Owing both to this quantitative difference and to his much more overt commitment to social protest, it is Apess who has come to occupy the more central position for critics interested in the literary tradition of Native American autobiography.[2] Modern readers may take what comfort they will in the grim irony that his canonization stands in direct defiance of "the inevitable extinction that had long been decreed for the Pequots" (O'Connell, *On Our Own Ground* xvii).

In an important sense, the arc of Apess's autobiographical career begins almost two hundred years before he was born, for his is a story rooted in the early history of colonial contact. At the outset of English colonial expansion, the Pequot nation inhabited an area along the southern coast of New England, in present-day Rhode Island and Connecticut. Coupled with the strategic location of Pequot lands, trade rivalries and territorial conflicts between European powers and among the various English settlements initially garnered Apess's ancestors considerable power and influence. By the early 1630s, in fact, the nation was one of the most potent players in colonial affairs in the region. However, during the bloody Pequot War of 1636–37, the English moved to break their power, ruthlessly and without compromise. Both in the prosecution of the war and in its aftermath, the colonials showed their resolve to obliterate the Indian nation completely from memory. In the course of the conflict, English militia forces massacred a large portion of the Pequot population, first in one of their principal villages near the Mystic River, and later in a swamp near New Haven. Subsequently, the Treaty of Hartford that ended the conflict stipulated that the name "Pequot" never be used again, and that Pequot place names likewise be replaced. The survivors of the war were divided up among friendlier tribes (the Narragansetts, the Mohegans, and the eastern Niantecs) or sold into slavery in Bermuda. The success of the English in thus erasing the Pequots from the pages of history can be seen in the fact that in antebellum America the most prominent references to them appear in Timothy Dwight's poem "Greenfield Hill" (in a section recounting their extermination) and in Herman Melville's use of their name in *Moby Dick* to christen his doomed whaler.[3]

Yet despite such grim history, the existence of a series of texts written by "William Apess, a Pequot" proves that 1637 did not mark the end of this Indian nation. From the end of the Pequot War until the time of Apess's birth, the remnants of his people in New England lived on, albeit

in a continual struggle with the institutions and legal apparatuses of colonial domination. The initial division of survivors among other nations
lasted only a short time. By the 1650s two separate groups of Pequots
had achieved their independence from the control of the Mohegans and
Narragansetts. This achievement served merely to deliver them from one
form of subjugation to another, however, for the General Court of Connecticut stepped in to assert its authority directly. The legislature established four Indian towns, supervised by two Indian "governors" chosen
by the English. The eastern Pequots were driven from their lands across
the Paucatuck River into two of these towns, located near Stonington,
and in 1685 the colony purchased two hundred eighty acres in that area
for a reservation (where the present-day Paucatuck Pequots still reside).
Meanwhile, the western, or Mashantucket, Pequots commenced a more
prolonged period of conflict with the colony. Connecticut sought for a
time to settle them on a two-thousand-acre reservation near the town of
Ledyard, but the Mashantucket leader Cassacinamon refused to cooperate
with the English. After his death, the general court appointed another
tribal governor and two new colonial "advisors," who facilitated the
move. Throughout the eighteenth century the Mashantuckets continued
to engage in struggle after struggle with the colonial government, before
the legislature, and in the courts. These conflicts focused both on land
claims and their frequent dissatisfaction with white "overseers," salaried
trustees (paid with tribal money) who controlled all tribal income (from
land leases, sale of firewood, and interest from their bank account) and
who also were responsible for making any petitions to the government
on their behalf. The Mashantuckets resisted such paternalistic control
and legal domination as best they could. Nevertheless, by 1800 many
had been forced to move off reservation lands (about half of which had
been leased to white farmers under the auspices of the overseers) and
were indentured to white households and farms. In fact, by 1854 the
Connecticut state legislature had totally abrogated the tribe's right to
control their own land, passing an act that allowed the state to sell territory without their consent.[4]

Into such a context, initially of attempted erasure and subsequently
of aggressive legal control, William Apess was born in 1798. Regrettably,
many of the details of his biography remain sketchy, and no scholar has
yet been able to provide an adequate description of his life independent
of his autobiographical writings.[5] Based on what we do know of Apess
and the history of his people, however, it is clear that he was born into an
environment of diaspora and colonial domination. In both of his explicitly
autobiographical texts, "The Experience of the Missionary" and *A Son*

of the Forest, Apess tells us that his grandfather was a white man who married a Pequot woman and subsequently was adopted by the tribe. His grandparents did not live on one of the reservations, settling instead in the woods outside Colrain, Massachusetts, near the Connecticut River. Apess was born there, but he moved soon after to Colchester, Connecticut, with his family. In Connecticut, he found himself in a condition of deep poverty and legal disenfranchisement. Because of the dispersion of his people, he also seems to have lacked a well-developed "tribal" support network that could help him develop a clear sense of Indian identity. Instead, Apess was raised and came to self-consciousness under the shadow of the colonial system, indentured to white foster families and attending white schools for much of his youth. The legal domination of his "extinct" people by the states of Massachusetts and Connecticut thus stands as the most significant shaping force in his early experience.

As this brief background should suggest, the fact that Apess produced any autobiographical writings stands as a remarkable achievement. There has been considerable critical debate, though, over how best to interpret that achievement.[6] Some scholars have read his autobiographies as monuments to Indian resistance and subversiveness. Others find in them examples of the loss of an "authentic" Indian voice within a colonial context. Such radically divergent interpretations of the earliest major Native American autobiographer recall the series of larger questions raised in the introduction: What does it mean to call Apess an "Indian" autobiographer? What model of self emerges in his autobiographical acts, and from where does that model come? And finally, having answered those questions, how can we place his texts within a tradition of autobiographical writings by Native Americans? As I see it, much of the critical confusion surrounding Apess's writings emerges from a failure to appreciate fully the relationship between his autobiographical acts and the models of self made available through the powerful discursive formations surrounding him. The commitment of some scholars to normative, *a priori* definitions of Indianness (and to the spatial model of cultural contact discussed earlier) has often forced them into limited pronouncements about Apess's authenticity. Consequently, such readings address only a limited part of the picture. In contrast, I hope to foreground the *process* by which Apess, working out of a particular historical context and experience of colonial contact, constructed a new rhetoric of Indian selfhood in his autobiographical writings. For him, as for many early Native American writers, this process involved a progressive engagement with legal models of identity. Evaluating and interpreting Apess's work as a manifestation of the communicative dynamic of colonial contact,

I hope to provide a more nuanced way of thinking about the teleology of his acts of self-definition. In the process, I will further advance the framework suggested in the last chapter for rethinking the broader tradition of Native American autobiography.

In this chapter and the next, I will re-evaluate the full range of Apess's writings, reading them together as evidence of his engagement with colonial institutions and the legal models they disseminate. As with much previous scholarship on his work, a central part of my initial discussion revolves around Apess's concern with manifestly religious issues and his conversion to Christianity. However, I will try to illustrate how a narrow focus on his evangelical language has led readers to overlook important elements in the shape of Apess's autobiographical career. Critics have regularly failed to account adequately for the place of the religious discourse of conversion within the broader spectrum of nineteenth-century colonialism and Indian law. Consequently, they have missed some of the differences between Apess's two principal autobiographies, "The Experience of the Missionary," and *A Son of the Forest*. A lack of close attentiveness to legal context has also contributed to other misunderstandings of the way these texts function as autobiographical acts of engagement. Again, following the binary thinking that often plagues postcolonial criticism, readers have frequently seen Apess either as a man brainwashed by colonialism and its discourses or radically subversive of them. In my view, neither of these extreme views is accurate. When read as a sequence, Apess's autobiographical texts record his evolving articulation of Indian identity and reveal something different from either precontact authenticity or postcontact interpellation. Growing out of a progressive engagement with Indian law, his autobiographical career tells the story of the emergence of a new form of Indian rights talk. I would argue that this also represents the development of a postcontact model of Indian identity that enabled Apess's opposition to colonialism from within the ideological framework of the liberal state and its legal order. It is a model, I would suggest, best referred to as Indian liberalism.

Paradoxically, of course, in finally achieving this kind of oppositional voice, Apess does seem to have abandoned the attempt to articulate an Indian identity wholly independent of the discursive structures of colonial law. In this respect, though, he only draws our attention back to the maxim (discussed in the introduction) that "contact changes everything." Admittedly, Apess may offer an extreme example of such change, owing to the extreme circumstances of his life. But if he clothes himself in a form of legal subjectivity that is tied to the modern liberal state, Apess does so in a way that is neither meekly submissive to the colonial order nor wholly independent of it. Without question, Apess's autobiographical career highlights anxieties many Native Americans continue to feel in their struggle to define themselves in the wake of colonialism. His example raises persistent questions about whether real resistance can be best achieved by preserving (or recovering) "traditional" Indianness or by adapting to change in sometimes radical ways. Devoting our energy to deciding whether Apess's texts are really "Indian" prevents us from engaging in the more fruitful consideration of how he uses autobiography to reinterpret Indianness as part of a struggle for survival. In the end, Apess's experiences led him to formulate a model of Indian selfhood that is not readily categorizable through traditional terminology. Doing justice to that sense of self remains our challenge as modern readers of his work. As a record of his engagement with colonial legal institutions, his autobiographies allow us to develop new ways of thinking about the postcolonial condition. I would submit that understanding Apess's engagement with the law is the best way of doing so.

The tremendous challenges Apess faced in defining his Indianness, because of his colonial experience, manifest themselves throughout his first autobiographical text, "The Experience of the Missionary."[7] Indeed, Apess's use of the conversion narrative form to guide his initial foray into autobiography suggests the depths of his reliance on colonial models of identity in the process of self-definition; even the variations from convention in the text indicate not an evasion of such models, but rather the degree to which Apess was enmeshed in them. To understand how a work like "Experience" was produced, then, and the problems that render it a conflicted autobiographical act, we must first consider the connections between the missionary endeavor in antebellum New England, the broader structures of Indian law, and the Indian conversion narrative as a particularly overdetermined autobiographical form. When viewed in this larger historical context, we can see why Apess's attempt to construct a sense of Indian identity in this text proved unsatisfactory to him. At the same time, we can begin to understand how his attempt to work through this dissatisfaction provided the foundation for his subsequent autobiographical writings.

Apess's decision to write a conversion narrative links him with a number of other early Native American autobiographers. Samson Occom (Mohegan, 1723–1792), Peter Jones (Ojibwe, 1802–56), Peter Jacobs (Ojibwe, dates unknown), and George Copway (Ojibwe, 1818–68), all modeled their own personal narratives on this popular form of spiritual autobiography.[8] It also connects him to a range of other Indian "converts" who kept private journals and wrote copious numbers of letters to their English mentors offering proof of their ongoing spiritual struggles.[9] The power of this discourse of conversion in America (arguably it provided *the* dominant model of self in early American lifewriting) dates back to the Puritan hegemony in early New England. Its influence on such a wide range of Indian writers owes to more than just its longevity, though. One obvious contributing factor was that the majority of literate Indians before the late nineteenth century had been educated by missionaries, as opposed to secular authorities. Spiritual autobiography was thus very likely the first (and perhaps only) form of lifewriting to which they were introduced. Conversion narratives and so-called "dying Indian speeches" may even have played a role in the education of some Indian writers in these schools. John Eliot's *Indian Dialogues* (1671) provides an early example of the use of the "dramatic" accounts of conversion for such didactic purposes.[10] Texts like Experience Mayhew's *Indian Converts* (first printed in 1727) and Eliot's *Dying Speeches and Counsels of such Indians as Dyed in the Lord* (ca. 1685) exemplify the latter rhetorical mode.[11] Beyond the wide range of available models, though, probably the most important reason for the dominance of conversion rhetoric in early Indian writing was political. The tale of a "Native" becoming Christian seemed sure to exert the broadest possible appeal to the white audiences, and it was also the language *demanded* by the institutions Indian writers needed most to engage, both to make their own way in a changing world and to advance the cause of their brethren.

Because of these institutional factors, the choice to write a conversion narrative in the colonial context of eighteenth- and nineteenth-century New England created a number of complications for any Indian author.[12] Many of these difficulties are readily apparent at the generic level. As typically written in the New England colonies, the conversion form was rigorously normative and didactic, designed to document the autobiographer's progress through the various stages of religious experience leading to a sense of saving grace. Somewhat paradoxically, this emphasis on the experience of inner transformation means that the conversion narrative seldom emphasized the *political* significance of events. (If discussed, such happenings were typically personalized through the rhetoric of the jeremiad.) For writers in early Puritan New England, autobiographical experience was meant to provide occasions for self-reflection and self-criticism. (Quaker autobiographies, by John Woolman and Elizabeth Ashbridge for example, provide interesting, contrasting examples here, owing to their inclusion of overt political critique.) In this sense, the conversion narrative form, especially in its earliest manifestations, centered on a radical form of introspection, a critical inward turning that allowed limited opportunity for social criticism.[13] From its beginnings, the genre's primary social function was to facilitate a move from one circle of community (English colonial society) into a smaller circle within it (the community of the Christian elect); this was accomplished by providing public testimony of the results of rigorous self-policing, not by challenging the community's values and standards.[14] Being by definition much further outside the circle of the elect than his English counterparts, an Indian convert's narrative of religious experience emerges from an even more complex and potent set of external pressures and imperatives, tied to the dynamics of colonial contact. The model of self that continued to structure the conversion narrative, even after the breakdown of the early Puritan theocracy, provided limited resources with which such pressures might be managed.

A failure to appreciate fully the highly pressurized colonial context from which they are produced has shaped the critical reception of Apess's "The Experience of the Missionary" in problematic ways. Barry O'Connell, for example, inclines toward an interpretation of "Experience" as a kind of subversion of colonial norms. He argues that although most antebellum white readers would have seen "conversion" as a synonym for "assimilation," Apess uses the conversion narrative as "an affirmation of Indian pride and autonomy" (*On Our Own Ground* 118). In O'Connell's view, the text derives subversive power from the fact that it sets up a situation where "whites, not Indians, become those in need of conversion." In my view, though, his argument that "by expropriating the very language of white justification and turning it back upon them, Apess also engages in a linguistic conversion" remains suspect. Without a full acknowledgment and analysis of the work's context, the idea of a counterhegemonic "linguistic conversion" may amount only to a bit of metaphorical wishful thinking about the dynamics of colonial engagement. In making his claim for subversiveness in the text, O'Connell does not address the fact that for an early nineteenth-century Native American writer the religious language of conversion often continued to function within a broader colonial system. Indeed, his acknowledgment that Indian conversion and assimilation *were* synonymous for many antebellum Americans would seem to force us to qualify claims regarding Apess's ability simply to "expropriate" such colonial language.[15]

In reading a work like "The Experience of the Missionary," we should begin by acknowledging that conversion was a central component of Indian law and colonial policy during the early national period. As the first chapter's historical overview of the development of Indian law suggested, "religious" and "secular" models of Indianness came together quite explicitly in colonial legal discourse around the homology of the terms "civilized" and "Christian," a linkage that lingered well into the late nineteenth century. From the beginning of European colonization, the experience of Christianity for Indian converts was always linked to (and subordinate to) the experience of colonial domination and the broader discourse and institutions of Indian law.[16] In her book *Indian Education in the American Colonies*, historian Margaret Szasz has demonstrated convincingly that the philosophical underpinning of colonial schooling through the seventeenth and eighteenth centuries lay in the notion that civilization and Christianization were united endeavors; such thinking can be traced back (as we saw in chapter 1) to the legal discourse of Crusade, which established a link between the Christian state and civilization, and to the emergence of modern international law in the sixteenth and seventeenth centuries.[17] Running counter to a general shift in modern political thought, which has created a firm division between what we might call religious (i.e., canon law, or "divine" law) and secular legal discourses, Indian law continued to fuse those two spheres well into the nineteenth century. The prominent role of missionaries in the federal government's civilization schemes and the civilization fund established by Congress in the early national period provides some evidence of this. The centrality of missionary education in President Grant's "Peace Policy" during the late 1860s (taken up in more detail in chapter 5) provides even more. Most significantly, though, in the English colonies this linkage generally placed Christianization as subordinate to, and taking place after, civilization.[18] As James Axtell has noted, the English colonists believed that only bringing the Indians into "civility" would prepare them to admit "religion," and that such a process would ultimately solve the "Indian problem" by turning the Indians into Englishmen (266). "Civilization," of course, meant transforming the "savage" self by bringing the Indian into the civil and social order of the English. The means of effecting this transformation were institutional—the church, the school, apprenticeship, and the praying towns (267). Whether directly or indirectly supported by the state and the colonial legal system, then, the instruments of conversion remained implicated in legal models of Indian identity and assimilation.

This basic synchrony of church and state in the attempt to colonize the Indian population is not the only factor that we should consider in reading the early Indian conversion narratives. A significant element of the policy of Indian schooling involved training Indians themselves to go forth, proselytize, and convert their brethren, transforming them in accordance with property-centered models of possessive individualism. In the case of writers like Occom, Apess, Peter Jones, and others, this meant that the autobiographical act of penning a conversion narrative was linked in some way to their transformation into agents of civilization, functionaries within the colonial system itself. (Reflecting this, some critics have come to distinguish the "missionary narrative" as a specific subgenre of spiritual autobiography).[19] In his short autobiographical text, "Peter Jacobs's History of Himself" (1857), Jacobs (a Wesleyan-ordained Ojibwe) begins by stressing that before hearing the gospel he, like all of his tribe, was a "heathen" and thus "cruel and wicked" (qtd. in Peyer, *Elders* 101). He then recalls the saving influence of Peter Jones, who converted him, after which experience, tellingly, he "built . . . a large house and began keeping a store, and made a comfortable living by selling things." Noting his subsequent desire to become a missionary, Jacobs suggests that the meaning of his life from that point on involved his incessant work to convert his fellow Indians and to usher them out of their "heathen state" into modern commercial life. Although he maintains that much work remains to be done, Jacobs displays pride in his ability to "form seven classes" of Indians and to help them "to build eleven houses" (103). Overall, his example shows that for an Indian during the early national period to chronicle his "conversion" involved more than simply testifying to an inner transformation into an Englishman (or later, an "American"). Implicitly, it required deep identification with the colonial system and its normative legal models.[20]

That much of George Copway's *Life of Kah-ge-ga-gah-bowh* (1847) focuses on accounts of the author's arduous journeys as a missionary further supports this general point about the compromised nature of early Indian conversion narratives, while also suggesting how long into the nineteenth century the conjunction of conversion narratives and assimilationist institutions persisted. Copway, as numerous commentators have observed, self-consciously aligned himself with the institutions of colonial governance and used his autobiographical text as a platform to advance "civilization" schemes that would have benefited him directly. The title page of the 1850 edition of his autobiography explicitly identifies him as "projector of the Concentration of the North Western Indian Tribes, for the Better Promotion of their Physical Improvement," a colonial functionary, in other words (Ruoff 61). Copway goes on in his dedication to pray that "religion and science may lead us on to intelligence and virtue; that we may imitate the good white man, who, like the eagle, builds its nest on the top of some high rock . . ." (65). In such terms, he signals his commitment to the joint endeavor of civilization and conversion, a commitment manifested throughout his autobiographical text. Interestingly, biographical scholarship on Copway reveals him to have also had an equivocal public career in pursuit of these ends. He was often involved in questionable attempts to advance his own interests and to obtain paid positions from government and church officials in the U.S. and Canada. He was expelled from the Canadian Conference of the Methodist Church in 1846 for embezzlement, for example, just prior to publishing his autobiography. Subsequently, riding the wave of public interest generated by that work, he sought to advance a proposal for a Christian Indian territory in the northwest named "Kahgega," after himself. In the end, though, Copway fell out of favor with the prominent Americans (including Longfellow and Francis Parkman) whose friendship he had courted, and the story of the last twenty years of his life seems to have been one of mental instability and frequent attempts to obtain some form of government position. In his historical introduction to Copway's writings, Donald Smith notes that the missionary went so far as to volunteer in 1858 to assist the U.S. government in expelling the Seminole from Florida (46). This marked the equivocal endpoint of his *conversion* to the "civilized" view that "man is the one for whom the world is made" (qtd. in Smith 43).

While suggestive, these brief discussions of Jacobs's and Copway's narratives nevertheless provide us with only an overview of the tensions surrounding early Indian "spiritual autobiographies." Before turning to a consideration of Apess's "The Experience of the Missionary," we might seek a more complete sense of how the discourse of colonialism impacted the early Indian conversion narrative by looking in more detail at the work of Samson Occom. The first known Indian autobiographer in the English colonies, Occom was born in 1723 at Mohegan, near the town of New London, Connecticut. His mother, Sarah, had been converted by the Congregationalist missionary David Jewitt during the earlier years of the Great Awakening, and eventually Occom himself was sufficiently impressed by the evangelical fervor to convert and begin to educate himself. Partly because of his education, he was active in tribal leadership at an early age and assumed the rank of councillor (a liaison position between the tribe and colonial authorities) by age nineteen. At that time he also became directly involved in dealing with the colonial legal system, signing a memorial to the Connecticut General Assembly regarding a long-standing land dispute known as the "Mason Controversy."[21] The controversy dated back to events during the seventeenth century, including the revolt of the Mohegan lesser Sachem Uncas against

Pequot domination and the subsequent close alliance between the Mo-hegans and the British. Uncas had allegedly ceded lands belonging to the tribe to Connecticut settlers in 1640, and later deeded more land to John Mason in 1659. Mason subsequently deeded a large tract back to the Mohegans, with the provision that it subsequently be inalienable. After Uncas's death (around 1683) disputes arose between Connecticut, the Crown, and two different factions within the Mohegan nation itself, disputes that were not fully resolved until 1771.

Occom's involvement with the colonial legal order in the context of the Mason case (and his recognition of the need to deal effectively with that system) provided him with the motivation to further his education. In 1743, he began to study with the Reverend Eleazar Wheelock, the popular itinerant Congregationalist minister who went on to found the Moor's Indian Charity School in 1754 and later, with Occom's fund-raising help, Dartmouth College. Subsidized by the Boston Board of Commissioners of the New England Company (one of the three prominent missionary so-cieties active in the colonies), Occom studied with Wheelock until 1748, when poor eyesight forced him to stop. At that point, he commenced a long career as an Indian schoolmaster and minister. He spent twelve years among the Montauk Indians on Long Island and became active as a fund-raiser for Wheelock's ventures (a role that took him to England to preach before large crowds). Eventually, though, disillusionment with the missionary establishment and a falling out with Wheelock led Occom to strike out on his own. In 1785, along with his former pupil and son-in-law Joseph Johnson, he helped to found the independent Brotherton Christian Indian community in western New York, where he died in 1792.

Occom's decision to pen his autobiography in 1768 was influenced by his involvement in the Mason case, his missionary education, his personal relationship with Wheelock, and his general experience with the colonial system. Certain forces in the missionary community, un-happy both with Occom's inclination to speak out on the Mason issue and his increasingly high profile as a fund-raiser, commenced a campaign of defamation against him in the mid 1760s, going so far as to question his authenticity as a Mohegan. Part of Occom's intention in the "Short Narrative," then, was to respond to such challenges. Ironically, as it does so, the autobiography engages with much of the assimilationist rhetoric underpinning Indian law.[22] "A Short Narrative of My Life" opens with a statement that clearly points toward the institutional embeddedness of his Indian conversion narrative. "I was born a Heathen and brought up in Heathenism," Occom begins, before noting further that his parents, like all their fellow Mohican Indians in Connecticut, "Livd a wandering life" (qtd. in Peyer, *Elders* 12). It would not be unusual, of course, for a conversion narrative to open with an acknowledgment of sinfulness. Occom's text goes beyond such a confession, though, noting not simply that he was born a *heathen*, but into *heathenism*. The latter represents a broader cultural category, not just a reference to a personal state of depravity. In the text the term is explicitly linked to Indianness (being a "wandering" people), not just to Occom's particular selfhood. Later in the opening paragraph Occom comments on the lack of regard his people had for the Christian religion, excepting the blankets they received once a year from a New London minister: ". . . and all this Time there was not one among us, that made a Profession of Christianity—Neither did we cultivate our land, nor kept any creatures except Dogs, which we used in Hunting; and we dwelt in Wigwams. These are a Sort of Tents, Covered with Matts, made of Flags. And to this Time we were unacquainted with the English Tongue" (13). What might seem an odd string of statements in a "typical" conversion narrative makes perfect sense when we recall the fusion between the religious model of the converted self and the legal model of civilization in colonial discourse.[23] Occom seems to represent his people's "failure" to farm, to husband livestock, to settle down in "permanent" housing, or to learn English, as part and parcel of their failure to become reconciled to God. The influence of the normative models of Indian law on such claims is quite clear. Living as an Indian becomes equated, in toto, with heathenism, and heathenism is further defined as a lack of civilized forms, property, etc. It is the state of savagery (which is encoded in the heart of the law of discovery that provided the foundation for subsequent Indian law).

Opening as it does, Occom's spiritual autobiography shows the influence of a long tradition of colonialist discourse. As Francis Jennings points out in *The Invasion of America*, the legal and religious concepts of "savage" and "heathen" had been fused from the beginning of the colonial period. Cotton Mather's biography of John Eliot in *Magnalia Christi Americana*, provides only one of dozens of representative examples. Mather comments that "[t]he natives of the country now possessed by the New Englanders had been forlorn and wretched heathen ever since their first herding there; and though we know not when or how those Indians first became inhabitants of this mighty continent, yet we may guess that probably the devil decoyed those miserable salvages hither, in hopes that the gospel of the Lord Jesus Christ would never come here to destroy or disturb his absolute empire over them . . . No such estates are to be expected among them, as have been the baits which the pretended converters in other countries have snapped at . . . our shiftless

Indians were never owners of so much as a knife till we came among them" (qtd. in Lauter 435). The kind of rhetoric Mather employs here explicitly places God's empire, represented by the (fused) colonial order and Christian faith brought from England, in diametrical opposition to the savage society and heathenism of the Indian population. Deviltry, brutishness, the failure to grasp the legal concept of property, and a lack of land rights are all linked together in a neat justification of the colonial endeavor. Admittedly, the ferocity of Mather's strain of Puritan rhetoric diminished as the eighteenth century progressed, but the basic melding of Christ and civilization standing behind his text remained alive. If missionaries no longer feared the devils in the woods, and if ministers no longer justified wars of extermination with such "Barbarous Creatures" (as Increase Mather had in his 1676 *Brief History of the War with the Indians of New England*), the basic conviction remained that conversion and civilization were linked endeavors.

The source of Occom's engagement with such discourse and its definition of Indian identity was most likely his early immersion in, and lifelong struggle with, the missionary school system, which underwent a significant period of growth during his youth. The Great Awakening of the 1740s provided a strong push, renewing evangelical imperialism throughout New England, albeit with some new twists. The infusion of Enlightenment thought (especially that of Locke) into American Christianity (a figure like Jonathan Edwards being central here) led to important institutional advances in the colonial deployment of Christianity. Enlightenment beliefs in the universal human potential for advancement and the importance of education for such advancement supported a tighter fusion of missionary work and colonial assimilationist policy through the founding of boarding schools, often funded by the state. The years from the 1730s to the 1760s thus saw a flowering of experiments in Indian schooling and the rise of the manual boarding school system in which Occom would learn and later work. As a colonial institution, the manual schools played an important role in shaping the development of Indian autobiography as a form of conversion narrative by translating legal models of self into a specific assimilation program. Developed during the eighteenth century in several different areas (by the Moravians in Pennsylvania and the Ohio country, by John Brainard on the Delaware River, by John Sargent and Jonathan Edwards at Stockbridge, Massachusetts, and by Wheelock in Connecticut), the schools were the primary site where colonial models of identity were brought to bear on Native subjects, for the expressed purpose not only of "civilizing" them, but of making them agents of civilization. The manual school curriculum cen-

tered on a concept of total immersion, seeking to induce Indian students
to change their entire way of life.

In his foray into Indian schooling, Wheelock's "Grand Design" (his
phrase) for colonial education combined instruction in English grammar
and alphabet, the Westminster Assembly's Catechism, arithmetic, and
the pastorale classics of Greece and Rome.[24] Agriculture and wage labor
(learning some kind of trade) balanced out the few hours of classroom
time (Axtell 99). In conceptualizing his educational system in such a
manner, Wheelock was clear about the subordinate relationship of Christianization to the larger colonial endeavor of making possessive individu-
alists of the Indians. We can see further evidence of his (and the colonial
population's) sense of the primarily civil function of missionary work in
his skillful lobbying for economic assistance for his schools. Wheelock
argued to legislators that money spent on education would be a better
defense than that spent on expensive forts to pacify Indians (Szasz 220).
It seems that such arguments had some force, for over time he received
funding for his projects, not only from missionary societies and private
donors, but also from the colonial assemblies of Massachusetts and New
Hampshire. In a fundamental sense, then, both in ideology and structure,
Wheelock's mission school was a colonial institution, whose missionary
work was a central part of the legal discourse of Indianness.

Recognizing the fusion of the process of Christianization with that
of civilization in the mission schools both helps to clarify some of the
deeper and more profound divergences of Occom's "Short Narrative"
from the typical Puritan conversion narrative and to qualify further our
sense of its subversiveness of colonial models of identity. If a major part
of any conversion narrative involves the leaving behind of a past, sinful
self (to the limited degree that such a shedding is possible for fallen man),
because of the ways religious discourse was deployed within the colonial
order, Occom's "Short Narrative" chronicles a much more pronounced
process of fissuring. His "conversion" experience becomes a more radical kind of self-negation than would typically characterize the form.[25]
In this respect, by replicating the colonialist assumptions of his time,
the autobiography reinforces the reader's sense that the term "Christian
Indian" is itself a contradiction. (This is, of course, a grotesque irony, for
in his ministerial work, his organization of the Brotherton community,
and his correspondence, Occom reveals his commitment to developing
a more egalitarian vision of Christian community, one that sought to
transcend such contradictions).[26] To become Christian in the rhetorical
terms of colonialist discourse was to leave one's Indianness behind, to
internalize a polarity that marks Indianness as a negative cultural condi-

tion.[27] Occom's teacher, mentor, and sometimes adversary, Wheelock, provides clear evidence of this point. In a 1761 letter, which James Axtell claims "might well stand as the motto of Moor's Indian Charity School," he laments, "Few conceive aright of the Difficulty of Educating an Indian *and turning him into an Englishman* but those who undertake the Trial of it" [emphasis added] (qtd. in Axtell 206).

In light of these kinds of assumptions, we should also be cautious about overreading the potential subversiveness of Occom's autobiography, which turns early on to a discussion of his education and subsequent work as a missionary/teacher among the Montauk Indians. Admittedly, Occom complains about the lack of recognition and support he received from the missionary establishment after he had struck out on his own. He also takes some pains to point out the greater efficacy of his work among the Montauk when compared with his white predecessor. Still, it is difficult to see something deeply subversive about Occom's endeavor to stress his own success as what is, by definition, a colonial agent. That he was a more effective teacher than others, because of his sensitivity to his students' cultural location and historical experiences, comes across clearly in the text. However, such a move to self-justification and criticism of the missionary establishment may, in the end, be less of a departure from the "conversion" form than some critics have allowed. Indeed, what better way for a Christian Indian to attest to his own spiritual awakening and his negation of his Indianness than to point out his deep commitment (and ability) in educating and civilizing his brethren?

The most manifestly oppositional part of Occom's narrative comes toward the end, where he rails against the disparity between his wages and the pay of a white missionary who, he notes, had no family to support. In this respect, he does register a powerful protest regarding the social inequities (and racism) of the colonial situation in New England. Yet Occom's protest does not reflect a fundamental challenge to the assumptions of the colonial order. Instead, Occom adopts those assumptions, and they provide a basis for his own critical commentary. Echoing the opening of the narrative in an interesting way, he characterizes his "circumstances and manner of living" as a missionary in the following manner: "I Dwelt in a wigwam, a Small Hut with Small Poles and Covered with Matts made of Flags, and I was obliged to remove twice a Year, about two miles Distance, for reasons of scarcity of wood, for in one Neck of Land they [the Montauk Indians] Planted their Corn, and in another, they had their wood, and I was obliged to have my Corn carted and my hay also,—and I got my ground plowed every year" (16). The unnecessary repetition of the definition of a "wigwam" from the opening paragraph of the autobiography suggests a desire to make a point here through rhetorical emphasis. The repetition serves to draw attention to Occom's inability to rise fully above the state of his birth; I *still* dwell in a wigwam, he seems to intimate. In this passage, then, Occom draws attention to his endeavors to become civilized, to farm as well as to learn the gospel, before pointing out that poverty had forced him into taking numerous jobs and *wandering* (removing) from his home. The injustice he protests in the lines above is not really the attempt by whites to transform Indian selfhood and culture, then. Rather, he offers a form of class-based indictment of the failure of whites to allow that transformation fully to take place.

Drawing his "Narrative" to a close in this way, Occom recognizes that he is not following the expectations normally placed on a spiritual autobiographer—that he concentrate on his own sinfulness. Indeed, it is precisely at this point that he exposes the fundamental inadequacy of the conversion narrative form (with its rigorous inner-directedness) for the purpose of articulating a positive sense of Indian identity in his colonial context. Occom's narrative begins to break down as he observes, "I speak like a fool, but I am Constrained" (17).[28] Here we see his inchoate awareness that an autobiographical act by an Indian in his situation could not truly be adequate without a more outward-looking struggle with the eighteenth-century colonial order. At this historical moment, the conversion narrative form works to turn the Indian writer inward, against himself, because of the categorical fusion of Christianity and civilization within that order.[29] Yet even as he manifests this new awareness and moves to depart from the conversion form, Occom continues to demonstrate the remarkable *insistence* of the normative colonial models of Indianness. Despite pointing out the hypocrisy and prejudice of Christian New England (drawing a parallel between himself and an indentured "poor Indian boy" beaten because he is an Indian), he does not retreat from the basic equation of Indianness with heathenism, or the basic assumption that "civilization" and all that it entails is his desired end. The sin of white society seems to be not that it labels the savage as heathen, but that it fails to allow him to fully slough off his heathen self.

In this regard, Occom's closing remarks provide the final proof of his conflicted engagement with the colonial rhetoric of Indianness, even as he begins to voice his opposition to the colonial system. He writes: "So I am *ready* to Say, they have used me thus because I Can't influence the Indians so well as other missionaries; but I can *assure them* I have endeavored to teach them as well as I know how; but I *must Say*, 'I believe it is because I am a poor Indian.' I Can't help that God has made me so; I did not make myself so" (18). To the end, Occom defends his job performance as a civilizing influence on his Indian brethren. Beyond this, the use of the phrase "poor Indian" here connotes his sense of the failure of the missionary establishment to live up to its end of the bargain and incorporate him into civil society. The primary register of "poor Indian" is to point toward his lack of property—the centerpiece of liberal selfhood—and to his ongoing engagement with the colonial legal order. Occom's use of the phrase here is an almost direct echo of a 1766 letter where he laments the injustice of the Mason Controversy. In that letter, he writes: "I am afraid the poor Indians will never stand a good chance with the English in their land controversy, because they are very poor, they have no money. Money is allmighty [*sic*] now-a-days, and the Indians have no learning, to wit, no cunning; the English have it all" (qtd. in Peyer, "Samson Occom" 211). In light of these other remarks, as Dana D. Nelson has suggested, the force of the ending of the "Short Narrative" is to "powerfully [draw] our attention to how the colonizer . . . refused to share land, pay, and finally human dignity with the Indians" (Nelson 61). In other words, it highlights the missionaries' failure to allow the full flowering of possessive individualism among their wards. The roots of the critical consciousness emerging at the close of Occom's autobiography reach deep into the legal ideology of the Anglo-American state. To articulate his concerns in a different "voice," he would have to turn to other genres (such as hymns).

The prominent role of legal models of identity in Occom's "Short Narrative" suggests the importance of approaching William Apess's foray sixty years later into the conversion narrative form with similar attentiveness to its discursive context. Such care is especially warranted when we recall that Apess's exposure to the colonizing influence of religious education took place in the context of near cultural annihilation. Though he did not attend a missionary boarding school as Occom had, Apess experienced an even more direct, total, and early immersion in colonial legal structures and models of identity. An initially vigorous identification with that discourse probably influenced his decision to title his inaugural autobiography "The Experience of the *Missionary*" (my italics). Admittedly, such self-identification attests to a biographical fact—Apess did become a minister in the Methodist Church and actively preached to his brethren. At the same time, though, to delineate himself explicitly as a "missionary" is also to identify himself, as Occom had in his text, as one of the primary agents of colonial policy. Further evidence of such an identification appears when we recall that Apess published his narrative along with accounts of the conversions of some of his personal flock as

a book called *The Experiences of Five Christian Indians.* In addition to
his own conversion narrative (and the narrative of his wife Mary, written by herself), that text includes "The Experience of Hannah Caleb,"
"The Experience of Sally George," his aunt, and "The Experience of Anne
Wampy." The first two of these read as Native American hagiography,
testifying to the possibility of the "translation" of Indians formerly "convicted" of sin into the realm of God's grace. The third highlights Apess's
own role in bringing a wretched and sinful Indian woman to repentance
and salvation. While there are elements of criticism in these texts (places
where the converts or Apess himself points toward hypocrisy and racism
among white Christians), the book remains heavily implicated in the
broader discourse of colonialism.

Beyond the manner in which its title and publication context demonstrate the book's identification with the missionary system, there are
a number of other, subtle ways in which Apess's first autobiographical
text can be seen as engaged with the colonial legal order and its model
of Indianness. It is striking that in spite of numerous critical gestures
leveled against white society, Apess's understanding of what it means
to be Indian (like Occom's) remains essentially negative here. Throughout his conversion narrative, Apess implicitly embraces two of the key
ideas about subjectivity and identity formation that broadly informed
the legal discourse of Indianness—the teleological, historical myths of
contractarianism and the ideology of assimilationism. For example, early
in "Experience," in his representation of his Indian heritage, Apess advances the contractarian understanding of the state of nature and historical progress. He writes: "My parents were of the same disposition of
the Indians, that is, to wander to and fro. And although my father was
partly white, yet he had so much of the native blood that he fashioned
after them in traveling from river to river, and from mountain to mountain, and plain to plain, on their journey" (120). Such comments, coupled
with frequent use of the phrase "children of the forest" to characterize
Indian people, serve to locate Indian identity in the (preproperty) state
of nature.[30] The pervasive notion that such a state was historically antecedent to present-day civil society (along with the traumatic historical
experience of Apess's tribe, the Pequots) contributes to one of the most
striking aspects of this "Indian" autobiography—its failure to provide
much of a substantive description of Indian life. (Indeed, this aspect of
Apess's text separates it from the work of a writer like Copway, who *does*
provide interesting "ethnographic" observations in his autobiographical
work). In Apess's case, the tendency of the conversion narrative form to
treat external experience merely as a pretext for critical introspection

meshes perfectly with the ideological imperative to induce the Indian to negate himself.

Apess represents himself in the text as increasingly cut off from this past, and consequently from a developed sense of Indianness as a positive entity. He notes that though he is descended from a chief (in later writings, Apess would go so far as to claim descent from King Philip himself), such lineage offers him little. "This [his ancestry] availed nothing with me," he writes. "[T]he land of my fathers was gone; and their characters were not known as human beings, but as beasts of prey" (119). Significantly though, even if he was not willing to accept the characterization of his ancestors as "beasts," as his tone suggests, Apess seems unable to counter it. He is able to articulate his Indian identity as only a negative condition, as a state of privation. Lacking any positive models to put in place of the colonial ones, he is left in a state of profound self-alienation and loss.[31] In the passage above, Apess draws attention to the enormous autobiographical problem he faced as a result. Because of his location within the colonial system and the particular history of imperialism in New England, he suffered from the lack of any sort of "precontact" model of Indianness and was left therefore with the need to construct his identity almost exclusively within the terms of the legal discourse of colonialism.

Apess's ambivalent internalization of the "negative" model of Indian identity standing behind the Indian conversion form likely contributed to his willingness to embrace the second key element of the discourse of Indianness mentioned above—its assimilationist rhetoric. An emphasis on the tractability of Native subjects and the possibility of civilizing them by altering their environmental conditions runs through "The Experience of the Missionary." The very prominence of the term "experience" in the title of all five of its conversion narratives suggests certain broad debts to assimilationist thinking (and to its Lockean roots in particular). Throughout his own particular narrative, Apess echoes late eighteenth- and early nineteenth-century thought in its emphasis on the importance of environment in shaping consciousness. When he addresses young white readers in the hope of securing their sympathetic identification with the Indians' plight, he invokes environmentalism fairly directly: "little children, how thankful you should be that you are not in the same condition that we were" (120). Even though the environmental "condition" into which he was born can be blamed to some degree on the whites (he comments regularly on the pernicious influence of liquor, for example), Apess makes clear that such circumstances constitute a cultural and personal dead-end. Blaming the colonial system does not enable him suddenly to constitute a positive sense of Indian self. Instead, he is placed in the problematic situation where he seems to rely on Euro-American education to help him define his identity.

As the text develops, Apess recounts a relatively happy period spent living with a benevolent white foster family (the Furmans) and begins to explore how the proper circumstances and surroundings led him to moral and intellectual advancement. After a short time with the Furmans, he observes that "[t]hings now began to wear a different aspect; and my little heart began again to be expanded, and I began to be inquisitive about many things" (121). This flowering of both his faith and his intellect derives from the benevolence of his caretakers and the nurturing environment they provided. Seemingly lacking viable indigenous models of identity, Apess emphasizes the importance of this kind of nurture and education for a young Indian like himself, to ensure his passage into the realm of grace. He laments, "In those days, the aged thought the youth were not subjects of grace . . . so there was none to comfort the little Indian boy" (122). Much of the thrust of Apess's narrative, though, is to stress that he was indeed a proper "subject of grace," needing only the proper environment, education, and support to make the leap into a Christian life. In this sense, his spiritual autobiography functions as an argument on behalf of Indian religious education and assimilation and the normative models of identity standing behind such policies.

The two elements I have been tracing thus far—the lack of a developed, positive definition of Indian identity and the related emphasis on both environmentalist theories of self and the importance of education—contribute to the emergence of the dominant theme of "The Experience of the Missionary," a theme that highlights the conversion form's inadequacy for Apess in his attempt to articulate a postcontact sense of Indian identity. Throughout the text, Apess represents his experience of Indianness as the experience of being orphaned. This implicit metaphor of self (the Indian-as-orphan) places much of his focus on the quest for adequate parenting, a quest which takes him further and further away from his Indian roots and into the paternalistic *nomos* of Indian law. Apess recalls that his parents separated shortly after his birth in 1798 and that he was placed in the care of his maternal grandparents. Such care provided little stability for the boy, however, as his grandparents suffered from "fits of intoxication," leading to his mistreatment. During one such fit he was badly beaten, including having an arm broken in three places (an incident that led to his being orphaned again). Apess emphasizes the gap between himself and his grandmother, commenting that it was his inability to speak her language that contributed directly to his beating.

At the same time, he insists that he does not blame her for the act, noting that it was whites who brought "spiritous liquours" first among the children of the forest. Yet the force of such condemnation is qualified by Apess's invocation of the kind of discourse characteristic of Indian law: "We little babes of the forest had to suffer much on its [liquor's] account. Oh white man! How can you account to God for this? Are you not afraid that the children of the forest will rise up in judgement and condemn you" (121). If he does not condemn his Indian grandmother for her acts, Apess nevertheless turns to the figure of the white "parent" with his pleas for better care and treatment of his Indian children. The juxtaposition of "white man" and Indian "babe" here parallels the basic rhetoric of legal paternalism. Thus, Apess's putative "inversion" of the religious discourse of judgment and conversion functions largely as an appeal for adequate protection and parenting *from white Americans.* Such a plea is not particularly subversive of colonialist discourse (though it *may* represent an attempt to claim some form of standing and recognition within a manifestly unequal social system).

After the beating incident, Apess recounts being brought by his uncle before the selectmen in Colchester, Connecticut. At that point, he is taken into a form of foster care, or indenture, quite literally becoming the "ward" of the state, which Indian law had come to designate him. (We should recall that only two years before Apess published "Experiences" in 1833, John Marshall made his famous claim in *Cherokee Nation v. Georgia* that the relation of the Indian to the United States "resembles that of a ward to his guardian.") This moment, when Apess the orphan is taken up by the state, becomes the real beginning of his autobiography as a conventional conversion narrative—the story of his progressive education and opening up to the ways of God. We should recall Apess's claim that his adoption by the Furman family marked the beginning of his expansive experience of Christianity. He does not equivocate about the positive significance of this adoption and the six years of schooling that followed, writing without apparent irony that "the amount of benefit which I have received from this, none can tell" (121). He even deems the punishments meted out by the Furmans to have "weighed well with me, so that forever afterward I was enabled to keep my balance well" (122). Because of the education and discipline provided by his white foster parents, Apess recalls that "the preaching of the Gospel powerfully affected my mind." As the narrative proceeds, he continues to stress the importance of proper guardianship and a basic acceptance of the cultural assumptions of assimilationist ideology. He links the state of his soul directly to the kind of environment in which he finds himself and the degree to which his white "parents" live up to their paternalistic responsibilities. Apess criticizes his second foster father, Judge Hillhouse, for failing to provide for his education, and notes that "this good man did not care much about the Indian boy" (124). In contrast, he offers a generally positive appraisal of his third father, Judge William Williams. He notes that Williams promised "to make me a good boy, but at the same time told me I must obey the heads of his family" (125). This seemed acceptable to Apess, for while living with his new master he had the opportunity to receive religious instruction, attending the Congregational Church and, later on, Methodist meetings. He embraces the paternal yoke, then, since it was being applied for the right ends (i.e., his moral education). "All this [Williams's authority over him] was perfectly right," Apess observes, "and some good, I think, was accomplished."

From the commencement of his regular religious instruction, Apess's autobiography bears its closest resemblance to the conventional conversion narrative, with its self-critical interiority. He remarks upon a growing "conviction" of his own sinfulness and a determination to seek for salvation of his soul. While attending a Methodist meeting, he comes to a sense of saving grace and experiences Christianity as an egalitarian faith. At this point, Apess remarks that he "felt assured that I was included in the plan of redemption, with all of my brethren" (127). Significantly, though, his sense of the nature of that plan underscores both the degree to which his autobiographical act was shaped by his engagement with colonialist discourse as well as the conversion form's tendency to turn him inward against his own Indianness. Though he provides little detailed discussion of these points in "Experience," in his only published sermon, "The Increase of the Kingdom of Christ" (1831), Apess offers a fairly striking example of how the rhetoric of evangelical Christianity often defined the place of the Indian in God's plan. Preaching on John 3:30 ("He must increase, but I must decrease"), he recalls John the Baptist's remarks that "the mighty prophet of the wilderness [John himself] . . . should wane away before a being greater than himself" (O'Connell, On Our Own Ground 101). It is easy to see typological parallels between John and the modern Indian missionary, a point that reinforces the sermon's colonialist subtext. In spite of his criticism of the white man's "oppression" of his "red brother," Apess here displays an understanding of Christian history characterized by a sense of wonder at the inevitable increase and spread of the "Kingdom of Christ on Heaven and Earth" (102). Any line between a purely religious register for the sermon and the form of spiritual imperialism we have seen pervading the legal discourse of New World colonialism collapses when Apess chastises his white audience for the nation's failure to Christianize the Indians: "Have not the great American nation reason to fear the swift judgments of heaven on them for nameless cruelties, extortions, and exterminations inflicted on the poor natives of the forest? We fear the account of national sin, which lies at the doors of the American people, will be a terrible one to balance in the chancery of heaven. America has utterly failed to amalgamate the red man of the woods into the artificial, cultivated ranks of social life . . . When shall the strong, proud, and fleet warriors of the western wilds, the remnants of the powerful tribes, come up to the help of the lord against the man of sin, as strong and bold for Christ as they are in council, and in deeds of arms!" (107). The metaphorical use of equity jurisprudence in this jeremiad is an interesting indication of the degree to which the legal language of Euro-American society was dominating Apess's rhetoric at this point. (The one complication here is the missionary's acceptance of the need to "amalgamate"—through intermarriage—the wild Indian into Christian civilization). Yet when he goes on later in the sermon to adopt an even more strident rhetoric ("It is a noble enterprise to conquer the world for Christ"), the line between colonized and colonizer seems to collapse entirely (108). Overall, then, the sermon's rhetoric seems to suggest that the divine plan is a form of spiritual manifest destiny. Apess's "inclusion" in that plan, along with all his brethren, places his act of self-fashioning in "Experience" squarely within the discourse of Indian law.

On balance, then, Apess's "The Experience of the Missionary" demonstrates a remarkable degree of receptivity to the colonialist rhetoric of Indianness. In doing so, the text provides strong evidence of the importance of socially available models of self for any autobiographical endeavor. Apess's particular location within the colonial system that had cut him off from positive models of Indian identity left him with seemingly little recourse but to draw on Euro-American discourse for rhetorical inspiration. At the same time, his use of what was probably the most readily available autobiographical form, the conversion narrative, provided Apess little room to develop the kind of outward-directed language of self-definition that he needed. Identification with the missionary office and quasi-imperialist vision of Christian evangelism placed him directly in line with the kinds of assumptions behind institutions like Wheelock's manual school. Thus, in his initial autobiography, Apess constitutes "the Indian" as a cultural and social orphan in need of guidance and care. His primary critical move in the text is to castigate his white guardians for failing to properly educate him and to provide for his entrance into the Christian faith. In this sense, there is relatively little in Apess's narrative that can be construed as an "affirmation of Indian pride and autonomy," as O'Connell puts it. His first foray into autobiographical expression finds him firmly situated within the framework provided by the discourse of Indian law and disseminated by the colonial missionary system. At this stage in his career, he reproduces the sort of melancholic self-negation that we saw in the last chapter in our discussion of Ely S. Parker's short autobiography. He asks to be interpellated into the paternalistic institutions of colonial law.

We should remember, though, that "The Experience of the Missionary" was only Apess's *first* foray into autobiography. That he went on to write additional autobiographical texts suggests that the conversion narrative's model of Indianness as a "negative" form of identity did not provide him with a wholly satisfactory basis for self-definition. If the conversion form proved problematic for Apess in his attempt to define his Indianness in positive terms, though, the sense of religious identity he develops in "Experience" would go on to play an important, foundational role in his second autobiography. In *A Son of the Forest* we find him still struggling to articulate a sense of self within the context of colonialism, but coming to a deeper recognition of the social context of both his religious experience and his identity crisis. As he turns increasingly outward and begins to deal more directly with colonial law, Apess develops a more complicated form of autobiographical act rooted in his continuing engagement with legal models of self. In his second autobiography, we begin to see the development of a different rhetoric of Indianness, one centered on a nascent discourse of Indian rights and property.

4 William Apess and
Indian Liberalism

If the tendency to overlook the institutional conjunctions between conversion and assimilationism in early America has shaped readings of William Apess's initial autobiography, the rhetoric of authenticity has sometimes dictated critical responses to his second. As I suggested in the previous chapter, because he underemphasizes the historical conditions of colonial contact, Barry O'Connell's interpretation of "The Experience of the Missionary" makes exaggerated claims regarding that text's subversiveness, claims that might lead us to overlook the shifts in Apess's approach to autobiographical writing in *A Son of the Forest*. Interestingly enough, Arnold Krupat's initial reading of the latter text errs in the opposite direction. In his discussion of Apess in his 1989 book *The Voice in the Margin*, Krupat makes what should seem by now a problematic assumption: he suggests that the process of engagement with the language of the colonizer is automatically an act of self-alienation. Consequently, he treats Apess's second autobiography as a representative example of colonial domination. Krupat argues that "the voice that sounds everywhere in [the text] seems to mirror very closely a voice to be heard commonly in the early nineteenth century, the voice of what I have called salvationism" (*Voice* 144). He subsequently dismisses *A Son of the Forest* from the canon of Native American autobiography, suggesting that "Apes[s] proclaims a sense of self, *if we may call it that,* deriving entirely from Christian culture" [my emphasis] (45). While Krupat rightly focuses on the prominence of religious language in the text here, it seems to me that in this reading he misconstrues the relationship between that language and colonial discourse in Apess's second autobiographical act. The assertion that Apess's "salvationism" means that he has no real "Indian" self grows out of Krupat's linkage of Bahktin's idea of "monologism" with Western domination and individualistic models of self. According to Krupat, then, "the single voice on which the monologist settles is never his or hers alone, but is derived from a social hegemony, as the many voices that the dialogist might represent are always the voices of social others" (160). In the end, the argument he is making in such Bahktinian language is basically one about Apess's lack of cultural authenticity. In Krupat's view, Apess's adoption of religious discourse marks him as fully interpellated by the hegemonic colonial order. *A Son of the Forest* thus becomes significantly less "Indian" than, say, Leslie Marmon Silko's *Storyteller*, which seems somehow less engaged with the monologic language of the oppressor.[1]

As we have seen, some of Krupat's concerns might be applicable to a text like "The Experience of the Missionary," which does suggest in fairly striking ways the rhetorical dominance of colonial norms. Still, to read *A Son of the Forest* as just a longer version of the former text would be to misread Apess's achievement in both cases. The autobiographical dilemma manifest in "The Experience of the Missionary" (i.e., the absence of Indian identity as a retrievable, positive entity) continues to inform Apess's second autobiography.[2] Nevertheless, the latter text presents the "negative" model of Indianness as only the starting point for the autobiographical act, not its endpoint. We find a more pronounced arc of self-definition in *A Son of the Forest* than in "The Experience of the Missionary," and consequently the text provides a more complex example of the communicative dynamic of colonial engagement. Although conversion remains a prominent part of this second autobiography, Apess's scope widens considerably, and his treatment of his religious consciousness begins to address larger legal contexts. As his autobiographical project progresses, then, it demonstrates a powerful shift in self-awareness as Apess develops a new form of Indian rights consciousness. Such a move not only attests to his embeddedness in legal discourse, but also demonstrates how engagement with that discourse provided him, *over time*, with the linguistic resources to develop an oppositional rhetoric of Indian identity in the wake of colonial contact.

Reflecting, perhaps, Apess's ongoing sense of generic constraint, *A Son of the Forest* opens with a pair of odd, yet related, rhetorical moves. Its first sentence reads: "William Apess, the author of the following narrative, was born in the town of Colrain, on the thirty-first of January, in the year of our Lord seventeen hundred and ninety-eight" (3). Though he quickly abandons the strategy, Apess's decision to open his text in the third person suggests a persistent feeling of discomfort with the autobiographical form (and perhaps a recognition that autobiographical writing involves the assumption of a role). It also may serve as a subtle manifestation of the general sense of self-alienation (related to historical and biographical factors) that we saw pervading his earlier conversion narrative. Indeed, when we note the direction the opening paragraph subsequently takes, we receive additional evidence of Apess's attempt to narrate his estrangement from his Indian past. As he continues, Apess advances a claim to being a descendant of the Wampanoag "chief" King Philip (or Metacomet), suggesting that his white grandfather had married Philip's granddaughter. Paradoxically, this claim to being of Philip's lineage, and the details provided in support of it, reveals more about his own uncertainty regarding his Indian identity than his ability to grasp that heritage.

Apess's assertion that King Philip ruled over the Pequot peoples is probably historically inaccurate, which suggests that his link to the great leader was largely an imaginative one.[3] Even as a "symbolic" ancestor, though, Philip emerges as a peculiar and ambiguous kind of figure in *A Son of the Forest*. Apess presents him as a symbol of Indian strength (overcome only by betrayal), but Philip stands even more directly as an embodiment of Indian dispossession and loss:

> . . . it will suffice to say that he was overcome by treachery, and the goodly heritage occupied by this once happy, powerful, yet peaceful people was possessed in the process of time by their avowed enemies, the whites, who had been welcomed to their land in the spirit of kindness so peculiar to the red men of the woods. But the violation of their inherent rights, by those to whom they had extended the hand of friendship, was not the only act of injustice which this oppressed and afflicted nation was called to suffer at the hands of their white neighbors—alas! They were subject to a more intense and heart-corroding affliction, that of having their daughters claimed by the conquerors, and however much subsequent efforts were made to soothe their sorrows, in this particular, they considered the glory of their nation as having departed. (4)

Within the overall context of his autobiographical project, such a description takes on a particular resonance, representing Apess's articulation of a sense of disjunction from his Indian origins. As his symbolic grandfather, Philip (it is noteworthy that Apess uses the name he was given by the English colonists) becomes a metonym for Indian loss, not just of their lands but also of their heritage and cultural autonomy. He emerges as a figure for the void left by colonial domination and warfare. In light of Apess's admission of descent from a white grandfather, equally remarkable is that he associates Philip's defeat with the "affliction" of miscegenation, presumably by rape. As a product of an interracial union himself, Apess would thus seem to become both a soiled product and a representation of the "departed glory" of the Indian past. Taken as a whole, then, the host of associations that arise in this opening paragraph suggest more a melancholy yearning after an absent Indian past than a successful reconstitution of that heritage.

Apess's considerable debt to written sources in his treatment of Philip, both in this opening paragraph and elsewhere, reinforces the general point that such invocations attest to identity lost, not found. Generally speaking, his understanding of his precontact Indian heritage was heavily mediated by the narratives of the colonizers. In the same opening paragraphs where he makes his initial claim to belong to Philip's "royal" line, Apess demonstrates a remarkably "republican" sensibility in dismissing any pretension associated with his pedigree: "This statement is not given with a view of appearing great in the estimation of others—what, I would ask is *royal* blood"—the blood of a king is no better than that of a subject" (4). Even though he overcomes his democratic scruples about claiming royal status, Apess goes on to provide further evidence that his understanding of Philip as a role model is heavily filtered through colonial textual sources. He closes his introductory comments with a reference to the lengthy appendix attached to the autobiography, which contains "general observations on the origin and character of the Indians, as a nation" (52). In the appendix, Apess again addresses Philip's life and legacy, but in doing so draws his arguments almost exclusively *and verbatim* from English sources—David Brainerd's journals, Elias Boudinot's *A Star in the West* (1816), and Cadwallader Colden's *The History of the Five Indian Nations* (1727; 1747).[4] Terms and concepts from Enlightenment moral philosophy, the ideology of civil society, "noble savage" primitivism, and the "Lost Tribes" thesis of Indian origin all color his subsequent discussions of the "Indian character."[5] Even a brief survey of these sources suggests that Apess's invocation of King Philip at the beginning of *A Son of the Forest* represents not an unmediated affirmation of pan-Indian pride, but a much more complicated expression of a crisis of identity. Without even raising obvious questions about the accuracy of his sources, one can make the point that Apess relied heavily on colonial writing for access to his Indian past, a fact with autobiographical implications he no doubt recognized.

Perhaps the most significant point about the elegiac tone of Apess's invocation of King Philip, though, is that it helps to clarify his reasons for making another foray into autobiography. Regrettably, lacking the kind of biographical materials and personal documents (or oral histories) that would provide direct insight into Apess's thinking at the time of composition, we must rely somewhat on conjecture in dealing with the question of motive. The one fact we do have (based on internal textual evidence) is that Apess began writing *A Son of the Forest* almost immediately after completing the text of "The Experience of the Missionary." This point, taken in conjunction with the conversion narrative's formal limitations for early Indian writers, suggests that Apess recognized the need to develop a more complex language of public self-definition if he hoped to oppose colonial domination successfully. It may also suggest that composing "The Experience of the Missionary" failed to provide him with a satisfactory resolution to his personal struggles with identity. Indeed, readers familiar with the earlier text who turn to *A Son of the Forest* receive an immediate reminder of its author's painful awareness of his status as a cultural orphan, cut off from positive models of precontact Indian identity. Even as he tries, imaginatively, to recover his roots, Apess's turn toward them is rendered problematic by the harsh realities of colonialism in New England. In this respect, it is interesting that even as he makes his claim to Philip's line, Apess equivocates on the solidity of such a claim, noting, "I have given the above account of my origin with the simple view of narrating the truth *as I have received it*" [my emphasis] (4).[6] Taken in context, this remark seems to testify not to faith in the power of oral transmission as a mode of history (which we might expect in an Indian autobiography) but rather to Apess's anxiety and uncertainty about such transmission. Apess commences his second autobiographical act, then, as a man ambivalent about his own genealogical roots and cut off from his cultural ones.

Still, in light of the discussion of treaty making offered in chapter 1, it is also interesting to note that Apess's choice to open his second autobiography with a statement of mourning positions the text as a similar act of legal engagement. Rituals of mourning, we should recall, provided the basis for the diplomatic language used by many of the Indian nations of the eastern woodlands. Indeed, as Robert A. Williams Jr. has pointed out, "the plaintive cry for peace from the wood's edge" initiated the Iroquois condolence ritual that undergirded the system of Indian treaty making that dominated the region (*Linking* 54). Again, though it is difficult to determine authorial intention with certainty, it nevertheless seems significant to note that Apess opens *A Son of the Forest* with just such a lament from the woods, the traditional signal for the opening of an act of diplomatic engagement and for the creation of cross-cultural connections and bonds of kinship. In this respect, the role of the King Philip section in the book seems twofold. Apess does more than simply register his own sense of loss, his crisis of identity, and his need to keep struggling to define himself. He also identifies the text to follow as a kind of "treaty," as a linguistic act of engagement (albeit unequal) with the normative universe of meaning that confronted him.

In this context, it should not be surprising that Apess would begin to look toward the dominant American legal model of subjectivity to provide the necessary grounding for his autobiographical act of self-definition. As we have seen, liberal subjectivity informs Indian law by providing the normative standard against which Indian identity is measured. The assimilationist side of Indian law and policy during the eighteenth and nineteenth centuries thus sets as its central goal the transformation of the Indian subject into a generic, possessive individual. At the turn of the nineteenth century, the time of Apess's birth, this basically Lockean model was also widely disseminated through the broader rubric of republican ideology. It is interesting, in this respect, that as Apess's narrative proceeds, he demonstrates a deepening commitment to liberal subjectivity, both in his treatment of his early "republican" education and in his discussion of the role his foster parents played in that education; this is the first place where a reader can note a significant shift between his first and second autobiographies.

Admittedly, as Apess moves from the historical to the biographical register, from Philip to himself, his treatment of personal experience initially reinforces the sense of a self adrift we have been discussing. As in "The Experience of the Missionary," the discussion of early childhood in *A Son of the Forest* stresses his alienation from both parents and grandparents and his subsequent status as an orphan. Apess again relates having been taken up by the state and indentured to the Furmans by authority of the selectmen of Colrain, and he notes that this moment marked the beginning of his only sustained period of education. As he turns to deal with this education, though, *A Son of the Forest* reveals a consciousness characterized by a much more complex form of engagement with the law of colonialism than we saw in "Experience." From the point in the narrative where Apess takes up his education, he manifests broad affinities with republican ideology and its liberal model of subjectivity, affinities that enable him to transform his religious consciousness from an inner-directed form of self-negation to an outer-directed form of self-assertion. These affinities likely grew directly out of his early educational experiences and his immersion in a social institution steeped in legal ideology.

During the decades following the Revolution, a wide range of writers from divergent points on the political spectrum had begun to advocate a national system of secondary education, rooted in the norms of legal subjectivity characteristic of the modern liberal state. Montesquieu's point in *The Spirit of the Laws* that "the laws of education ought to be relative to the principles of government" provided the rallying cry (31). Consequently, the two decades between the Revolutionary War and Apess's years of schooling (he seems to have attended school in Connecticut from 1804 to 1810) saw the first systematic attempts to develop American education along such nationalistic lines.[7] Federalist writers, in particular, were clear in their sense of the nature of the connection between education and government; the primary purpose of schooling was to create good citizens (i.e., legal subjects) for a republican society, rooted in contractarian principles and respect for the rights of property. In his 1786 essay "A Plan for the Establishment of Public Schools and the Diffusion of Knowledge in Pennsylvania," Benjamin Rush contends that "our schools of learning, by producing one general and uniform system of education, will render the mass of the people more homogeneous and thereby fit them more easily for uniform and peaceable government" (qtd. in Rudolph 10). Interestingly, while he was not writing about Indian education per se, Rush's formulation stresses the synergy between religious instruction and civilized norms (a key tenet of Indian legal discourse). He observes that "the only foundation for a useful education in a republic is to be laid in religion," for "a Christian cannot fail of being a republican" (10–11). In Rush's view, this harmony between religious principle and secular knowledge renders it possible "to convert men into republican machines," work that must be done "if we expect them to perform their parts properly in the great machine of the government of the state" (17).

We can find similar sentiments to Rush's in the thinking of Noah Webster, an individual who was even more directly influential in shaping the educational landscape of early America. In a 1790 essay "On the Education of Youth in America," Webster (who authored a number of widely used spellers and textbooks in addition to his "American" dictionary of the English language) argues for a basic link between the norms of the legal and educational systems. "The education of youth is, in all governments," he notes, "an object of the first consequence. The impressions received in early life usually form the characters of individuals, a union of which forms the general character of a nation" (qtd. in Rudolph 44). Indeed, as Webster sees it, education sows the seeds of national legal subjectivity: "Laws can only check the public effects of vicious principles but can never reach the principles themselves . . . an attempt to eradicate old habits is as absurd as to lop off the branches of a huge oak in order to root it out of a rich soil. The most that such clipping will effect is to prevent a further growth. The only practicable method to reform mankind is to begin with children" (63). Here Webster makes clear his sense that punitive legal institutions (though not their norms) enter into the subject-making process relatively late. While the courts can only prune, education does the planting that ensures that the national orchard can grow harmoniously. Probably the most influential voice on the topic in early America, Webster stresses the foundational role of education in developing the kind of liberal individual that composes the body politic of the modern contractarian state: "Our constitutions of civil government are not yet firmly established; our national character is not yet formed and it is an object of vast magnitude that systems of education should be adopted and pursued which may not only diffuse a knowledge of the sciences but may implant in the minds of the American youth the principles of virtue and liberty and inspire them with just and liberal ideas of government and with an inviolable attachment to their own country" (45). The "constitutions" to which Webster refers are the various components of the American legal system, the concrete manifestation of, and support for, the social contract (and the *nomos*, or normative universe, it represents). The integrity of that contract is rooted, in his view, in the "character" of the individuals who compose it, and that character must be implanted on the tabula rasa of young minds by proper education. As Webster notes, quite tellingly in the present context, "a boy, bred in the woods, will be a savage" (61).

Admittedly, essays like those of Rush and Webster represent an ideal standard, one against which most American schools in the late eighteenth and early nineteenth centuries would have failed to measure up.[8] Yet if any state in the union came close to achieving the ideological goals they advanced for centralized "legal" education, it was Apess's Connecticut. During the early decades of the nineteenth century, Connecticut was far ahead of the rest of the nation in developing a universal system of public schooling. In 1795 the legislature passed a law providing a funding mechanism for public education. The state sold all of its lands in the Western Reserve and placed the proceeds ($1,200,000) in a permanent school fund. The interest from this fund, supplemented until 1820 by a local property tax, provided the necessary money for a centralized school system. As Carl F. Kaestle has noted in *Pillars of the Republic* (1983), between the 1790s and the 1820s many American commentators and foreign visitors rated these common schools as "the best in the country" (11–12). Well before the era of widespread common school reform began in the 1830s, then, schools in Connecticut were implementing a "republican" curriculum, centered around three linked principles to be instilled in young pupils—faith in balanced government, support of liberty, and a sense of virtue. Frequently, especially in rural areas, these principles were tied to the ideal of a landed yeomanry. Such a freeholding ideal, the kind most clearly articulated by Hector St. John de Crèvecouer in his *Letters from an American Farmer*, is an almost direct reflection of the legal ideology of possessive individualism and Lockean contractarianism. Even if we cannot establish with certainty that the curriculum Apess was being taught during his years in public school had attained the level of a well-developed system of civic normalization, when we look at his language in *A Son of the Forest*, there is little doubt that he identified, probably through his schooling, with the republican models advanced by men like Rush and Webster. Indeed, Apess's explicit discussion of education shows these links between his developing autobiographical self-consciousness and the norms of civil society.

Apess's compensatory identification with the norms of civil society manifests itself most clearly in two ways. First, in his discussion of education he draws on manifestly Lockean discourse. Second, he characterizes himself initially in the text as an ordinary American child, not as an "Indian" boy. While the rhetoric of "conversion" opens Chapter Two of *A Son of the Forest* ("the Spirit of Truth operates on different minds in a variety of ways"), Apess shifts almost immediately into an explicitly Lockean vocabulary of psychological development. His initial concern with proper religious instruction for "children" thus dovetails with some of the broader assumptions about subjectivity characteristic of republican ideology. He notes, "If constant and judicious means are used to impress upon their young and susceptible minds sentiments of truth, virtue, morality, and religion, and these efforts are sustained by a corresponding practice on the part of parents or those who strive to make these early impressions, we may rationally trust that as their young minds expand they will be led to act upon the wholesome principles they have received" (8). The assumptions about identity behind a passage like this emerge directly from Revolution-era republicanism and Lockean sensationalism (note, for example, the recurrent discussion of "impressions"), with Apess stressing the malleability of the young mind as a blank slate.[9] As we have noted, the appeal that such models held for him likely derived from the fact that his direct sense of his own cultural past had been largely "erased" by colonialism. In such a context, identification with the ideals of American republicanism seems to provide Apess with a way of understanding and articulating his own development and of compensating for the loss of heritage stressed in the early chapters. In this respect, it is not surprising that, in addition to the great deal of republican rhetoric throughout these early passages on education, we find little in this part of the autobiography that marks it obviously as an "Indian" text. It is a powerful index of Apess's application of the norms of American legal ideology to ground himself that references to Indianness (as a form of "otherness") largely fall away here. Throughout his discussion of education, Apess makes repeated references to "the young" or "young people" or "children at an early age," a fact that suggests his desire to identify himself with a generalized Anglo-American model of the child. Apess intimates a process of self-definition centered around a growing consciousness of himself as just another boy in the republic and a yearning to leave behind his orphan past. At this point, Krupat's reading of the text's "monologism" seems apt.

Yet Apess was not just another American child, a fact that was made clear to him even during these early years of education. In Chapter Three, he recalls a key event (in terms of his process of self-definition) that both brought an end to his time with the Furmans and abruptly stripped away any illusions of "normality." Apess describes the sale of his indentures first from Mr. Furman to a Judge Hillhouse and then from the latter to Judge William Williams, noting that a failed act of self-assertion precipitated the first sale. Apess recalls having been led astray by some of his schoolmates, who planted false ideas of freedom and autonomy in the young boy's head:

> At this time it was fashionable for boys to run away, and the wicked one put it into the head of the oldest boy on the farm to persuade me to follow the fashion. He told me that I could take care of myself and get my own living. I thought it was a very pretty notion to be a man—*to do business for myself and become rich.* Like a fool, I concluded to make the experiment and accordingly began to pack up my clothes as deliberately as could be, and in which my adviser assisted. I had once or twice been to New London . . . Thither I determined to bend my course, as I expected that on reaching the town I should be metamorphosed into a person of consequence. I had the world and everything my little heart could desire on a string, when behold, my companion, who had persuaded me to act thus, informed my master that I was going to run off. (14)

The cruelty of the boys seems to be linked to the fact that they reinforced Apess's own youthful sense that he was like them, and that he might act in the way that other "fashionable" boys acted. Striking in this passage is his unselfconscious acceptance of a model of "self-possession"

and his apparent faith in his ability to tread the path of economic independence as a way to wealth and social status. Coincidentally, perhaps,
his account echoes Benjamin Franklin's tale of flight from indentures in
Boston to "consequence" in Philadelphia in his *Autobiography*. Unlike
Franklin, though, Apess's "experiment" meets with frustration, owing
to his status as an Indian ward in the colonial order and his inability to
transcend that status. Indeed, his story culminates with a forced recognition of the fact that the law prevented this *Indian* child from becoming
an incorporated legal subject and from calling his white father to account
for restraining his property rights. At such a moment, Apess suggests
that his consciousness of himself *as an Indian* came back in full force.
It does so, however, in a way that stresses how his engagement with the
basic norms of identity of American society led him to reinterpret that
identity in the wake of colonialism. Unlike at the opening of the text,
where Indianness represents a lost heritage, Apess reveals an emerging
argument that to be Indian was to be *an individual American deprived
of his natural rights of self-possession.* Indianness becomes a layer of
identity built atop a foundation of liberal individualism. This is an important step in the evolution of his rhetoric.

Apess's treatment of his failed flight and of his subsequent years under the authority of foster parents traces the gradual refinement of this
sense of Indianness as a form of legal identity. He notes that Mr. Furman's
response to his futile act of rebellion was to sell his indentures to Judge
Hillhouse for the sum of twenty dollars. Apess clearly saw such an act as
both offensive and contrary to the kind of relationship which should have
pertained between them. Recalling initial stages of the transfer, though,
he makes an odd series of observations: "Of course, after the bargain
was made, my consent was to be obtained, but I was as unwilling to go
now as I had been anxious to run away before. After some persuasion,
I agreed to try it for a fortnight, on condition that I should take my dog
with me, and my request being granted I was soon under the old man's
roof, as he only lived about six miles off. Here everything was done to
make me contented, because they thought to promote their own interests
by securing my services" (14). Apess's tone in this passage, as well as
its content, is intriguing. Opening with the phrase "of course," he suggests that what follows would be "self-evident" to the reader. Tellingly,
what follows is his claim to a considerable degree of independence and
self-possession. Apess suggests that his consent was required for Judge
Hillhouse to make the contract for his services, thus evincing a belief
in his own proprietary control over his person. Intimating that even Mr.
Furman recognized that right on some level, Apess thus characterizes the

transfer of his services as a rational agreement between self-interested, sovereign parties. Following that assumption, he feels entitled to decide, after the fortnight, whether he wishes to return "home." To his great dismay, though, when he makes that decision he is confronted with the inaccuracy of his naive assumptions. "The joy I felt on returning home," he notes, "was turned to sorrow on being informed that I had been *sold* to the judge and must instantly return. This I was compelled to do" (15). At this moment Apess finds himself confronted with his actual legal status as an Indian, much lower than any ordinary indentured servant, and he comes to recognize his powerlessness to prevent the sale. The lesson learned from this encounter with the law was that as an *Indian* boy, he could not be a free man. The legal relationship between white guardian and Indian ward functioned to prevent his full assertion of the individualistic subjectivity that had been fostered within him.

From this point onward in *A Son of the Forest*, Apess suggests that his main problem was to figure out how an Indian like himself might claim his inherent rights as a liberal individual and follow the Franklin model into civil liberty. What is important to recognize is that Apess's struggle with the colonial order and its Indian law is grounded in this regard in an acceptance of the normative legal models behind that law. The rights he begins to assert are individual property rights (the rights of a possessive individual) that are being denied him because he is an Indian. Consequently, much of the rest of the autobiography takes the form of "constitutional" argument, with Apess's articulation of self (the story he wants his readers to accept) implicitly questioning the justice and validity of Indian law. Apess's complex relationship to legal models of self suggested here is what makes *A Son of the Forest* such a striking example of the rhetoric of engagement, in a way that "The Experience of the Missionary" was not. In his second autobiography, the collision between Apess's basically Lockean sense of subjectivity and the restrictions placed on him by Indian law leads to the narrative development of a new model of Indian identity (emerging from the experience of racial discrimination). The sense of Indianness that pervades *A Son of the Forest* represents something different from either precontact "authenticity" (which may no longer have been possible for Apess) or colonialist pacification.

In this context, one of the most interesting manifestations of Apess's developing rhetorical sophistication is his treatment of conversion in *A Son of the Forest*. Contrary to the inward turn of "The Experience of the Missionary," his second autobiography treats his spiritual condition primarily as a social problem, a question of religious liberty denied.

Religious concerns come up gradually in the text, initially growing out of a broader consideration of moral instruction. In the early chapters, Apess's discussion of the role of the Furmans in his moral education initially mirrors his commentary on the proper conduct of republican parents in educating their children. Here again he offers a series of blanket statements dealing not specifically with Indian children, but with children in general. Apess lays considerable responsibility at the feet of parents, noting that "a vast proportion of the misconduct of young people . . . is chargeable to their parents and guardians" (9). Again, like a good Lockean, he stresses that such responsibility for instruction need not involve immediate corporal punishment.[10] As evidence, Apess recalls an incident when, having been caught stealing melons, he received some gentle yet effective instruction from Mrs. Furman.[11] He notes that "Mrs Furman . . . talked seriously to me about it. She told me that I could be sent to prison for it, that I had done wrong, and gave me a good deal of wholesome advice. This had a much better effect than forty floggings—it sunk so deep into my mind that the impression can never be effaced" (11). Apess's references to moral education do not end with this kind of blithe assertion of the need for parents to make good "impressions" on their children, though. His criticism of the failures of adults in terms of moral instruction quickly modulates into a consideration of explicitly religious instruction and the importance of worship.

Throughout the early chapters of *A Son of the Forest,* Apess repeatedly expresses concern about his guardians' attentiveness to his spiritual welfare. He stresses that one of the great virtues of the Furmans (particularly Mrs. Furman) as foster parents was that they provided him with religious instruction and encouraged him to be attentive to the state of his soul. Their attitude and behavior stands in marked contrast to that of his subsequent guardians and even to other members of their own Baptist congregation, who seem little concerned with the Indian boy's spiritual welfare. Of the latter, Apess notes that "they all considered me *too young* to be impressed with a sense of divine things" (13). As we would expect, though, based upon his acceptance of the basic Lockean notions of subjectivity and development, Apess feels differently:

> I have heard a great deal said respecting infants feeling, as it were, the operation of the Holy Spirit on their minds, impressing them with a sense of their wickedness and the necessity of a preparation for a future state. Children at a very early age manifest in a strong degree two of the evil passions of our nature—*anger* and *pride.* We need not wonder, then, that persons in early life feel good impressions; indeed it is a fact, too well established to admit of doubt or controversy, that many children

have manifested a strength of intellect far above their years and have given ample evidence of a good work of grace manifest by the influence of the Spirit of God in their young and tender minds. But this is perhaps attributable to the care and attention bestowed upon them. (8)[12]

Admittedly, stressing the susceptibility of children to religious impressions in this way might be seen as merely buttressing the assimilationist assumptions of missionary colonialism (as we saw in "The Experience of the Missionary"). Yet unlike in the earlier text, Apess's claim here begins to broaden into a different kind of assertion, as Enlightenment models of self, educational theories, and religious concerns converge. Having argued that a child like himself could be impressed by the workings of the Holy Spirit and could benefit from religious education, Apess's treatment of his subsequent foster parents' attentiveness to the state of his soul suggests a burgeoning sense of a *right* to such education (a right enjoyed by all liberal legal subjects).

Following his account of his failed bid for independence, Apess provides an account of his unhappy life with his second foster father, Judge Hillhouse, which focuses largely on the judge's moral inadequacy and failure to provide for Apess's spiritual education. Though his attempt to grasp the ring of social consequence by flight had been rebuffed, Apess continues to reveal a liberal individualist sensibility in discussing his second guardian. He initially represents the judge's failures as a parent as a breach of contract: "to be sure I had enough to eat, such as it was, but he did not send me to school as he promised" (16). In the end, Apess suggests that the judge saw the relationship between them as solely one of economic exploitation. "I believed he fulfilled only one item of the transferred indentures," he writes, "and that was work" (16). Having been confronted already with the difficulties of challenging the judge's legal control over his body and labor, though, Apess turns to a different kind of protest, centered around Hillhouse's failure to fulfill his spiritual obligations. Apess comments critically on the judge's rote devotions and contrasts them with Mrs. Furman's more compassionate instruction, noting, "I could fix no value on his prayers" (15). Even more damning in this context is his point that with the judge he "had not the opportunity of attending meeting as before" (15). This neglect did not destroy the young boy's burgeoning sense of religious identity, though. He notes that "as the divine and reclaiming impression had not been entirely defaced, I would frequently retire behind the barn and attempt to pray in my weak manner" (15). In making this point Apess stresses that when allowed to turn outward rather than inward, his sense of religious selfhood had begun to produce in him a sense of oppositional consciousness. Indeed,

Hillhouse's restraint of his religious liberty provides another catalyst in his reconstitution of a sense of his Indianness.

Chafing under Hillhouse's breaches of contract and his failure to provide moral instruction, Apess continues his pattern of running away. This time, his flight precipitates another sale of his indentures, to William Williams (also a judge and, interestingly enough, later an overseer of the Mashantucket Pequots). Again encountering the repressiveness of the legal order, Apess continues to express his sense that his rightful autonomy and control of his person was being ignored. He notes that "if my consent had been solicited . . . I should not have felt so bad. But to be sold to and treated unkindly by those who had got our fathers' lands for nothing was too much to bear" (16). Still, two failed attempts at flight had unequivocally demonstrated to Apess that a young Indian like himself could not challenge the colonial system's direct control over his body in such a manner. Consequently, in the wake of this recognition, his narrative (unlike the earlier autobiography's treatment of these events) stresses his increasing insistence in challenging that system's control over his soul. Apess recalls being forced by Williams to attend Presbyterian services, which he saw as representative of a religion of meaningless forms. Thirsting for spiritual fulfillment, he begins to sneak away to attend Methodist meetings. He presents his decision to do so as a last-ditch attempt to assert his own freedom and autonomy: "They had possession of the red man's inheritance and had deprived me of liberty; with this they were satisfied and could do as they pleased; therefore, I thought I could do as I pleased, measurably. I therefore went to hear the noisy Methodists" (18). Apess's comments here clearly suggest that he saw his assertion of religious liberty as directly related to his opposition to colonial restrictions on his property rights. His right to free religion exists on the same continuum as his unrecognized right to liberty in his property (both his own property in himself and his rightful share in the land of which his people had been defrauded). Apess's challenge of Hillhouse's and Williams's legal authority to inhibit his spiritual development is therefore based on precisely the same contractarian ideology he felt was being ignored in their abuse of his property rights.

The sense of self behind the kinds of claims we can see Apess making here is rooted, by definition, in a manifestly postcontact kind of Indian self-consciousness. For an Indian like Apess to assert either his prerogative to contract his own indentures or to be Christian in his own way is to lay the groundwork for a broad-based form of liberal subjectivity, rooted in the property paradigm of possessive individualism. As Mary Ann Glendon points out in her 1991 book *Rights Talk*, rights consciousness carries with it certain fundamental assumptions about the identity of the claimant of such rights; to use Glendon's exact phrasing, the "dialect of rights talk encodes an image of the possessor of rights" (47). What the narrative arc of *A Son of the Forest* reveals is Apess's struggle to find the right dialect, to lay claim to an image that would offer some degree of empowerment in the context of colonialism. Once again, John Locke provides us with the most succinct articulation of some of the key ideological assumptions at the heart of the "image" behind Apess's assertion of religious liberty. In his 1689 *A Letter Concerning Toleration*, Locke distinguishes between two spheres of regulation in modern civil society. The "religious" sphere involves regulation of men's lives according to "the rules of virtue and piety," i.e., the care of the soul (13). Within that sphere, churches have the right to craft ecclesiastical law directing their own affairs and rules for obtaining membership. At the same time, the choice of the citizen to join or not join a church must be free. The sphere of civil government is concerned with protecting man's civil interests—life, liberty, and most importantly property. In the state of nature, the choice to form a civil society was also entered into voluntarily, though Locke assumes that in the present the choice to live in a territory stands as tacit consent to abide by its law. In his view, though, the civil magistrate *cannot* be the steward of the individual soul in the way that he is in the case of an individual's property rights. This inability is rooted in the modern liberal conception of the nature of identity and subjectivity, and certain limits consequently placed on the law of the state.

The basis of Locke's theory of civil government is the possessive individual's capacity and rational willingness to alienate some of his sovereignty to that government in order to preserve his property rights. As we saw earlier, the inevitability and "rationality" of this act provide the major basis for the kind of normative assumptions and assimilationist mechanisms deployed by Indian law. In matters of faith, though, Locke sees a relationship between the individual and God that cannot be mediated in that way. He argues that the "care of souls" cannot be "committed to the civil magistrate . . . because no man can abandon the care of his own salvation as blindly to leave it to the choice of another" (19). In effect, Locke argues (as the modern liberal nation-state holds) that the sovereignty of the possessive individual over his soul is limited, for control of the soul cannot be alienated to another. Contractarian theory establishes religion as a zone of negative liberty, where autonomy is protected by law. Significantly, in *A Letter Concerning Toleration* Locke takes care to extend this point to address the context of New World colonialism, noting that "neither pagans there, nor any dissenting Christians here, can with any right . . . [have] any civil rights to be changed or violated upon account of religion" (51). Admittedly, in the United States, the legal principle of toleration has been inconsistently applied. As we have seen, the fusion of Christianization and civilization policies toward the colonized Indians, where it took on a manifestly coercive tone, represents a willingness to overlook the religious liberties of these "pagans." Nevertheless, a sense of religious liberty informs the Constitution itself in the so-called "establishment clause," suggesting at least a theoretical commitment to such rights at the heart of the American legal system, especially for members of various Christian sects. Indeed, in Apess's own time men like Daniel Webster were actively engaged in articulating a national mythology on the foundation of the religious dissent of the Puritan forefathers. (Public addresses like "The First Settlement of New England," delivered at Plymouth on December 22, 1820, and the first "Bunker Hill Monument Address," delivered on June 17, 1825, provide representative examples.) Apess's burgeoning rights consciousness seems rooted in his appreciation of the power of this kind of discourse and in his developing sense that the liberal models of identity (accessed through the language of conversion) could also potentially provide him with a viable, oppositional rhetoric of Indianness. Consequently, his account of his religious struggle in *A Son of the Forest* becomes the story of a "conversion for liberty."

Throughout Chapter Four of *A Son of the Forest*, Apess's chief concern is to attest to his state of spiritual turmoil, his yearning for a conversion experience, and his rage at the injustice of Judge Williams's restraint of his religious liberty (interfering with his attendance at Methodist meetings). His re-engagement of some of the conventions of the conversion narrative serves a complex legal purpose here, as part of his insistence on his civil right to care for his own soul. Reinforcing the sense of spiritual imperative and trial characteristic of the conversion form adds emphasis to Apess's suggestion that his ability to seek salvation must not be restrained because he is Indian. He observes that "[m]y distress finally became so acute that the family took notice of it. Some of them persecuted me because I was serious and fond of attending meeting. Now, persecution raged on every hand, within and without, and I had no one to take me by the hand and say, 'Go with us and we will do thee good.'" (20). In this context, Apess's struggle with his diabolical "adversary" becomes less a point of focus than his guardians' oppression of his liberty to worship as he pleased. Judge Williams's "conclusion that it was advisable for me to absent myself entirely from the Methodist meetings" appears an unjustifiable abridgment of the young boy's religious freedom as a liberal subject (22). Apess recalls being beaten for sneaking off to meetings, as well as numerous other occasions where he was flogged "unjustly." Most interestingly, though, is his characterization of the nature of this persecution. He notes that "the abuse heaped on me was in consequence *of my being a Methodist*" [my emphasis] (22). Recognizing that his past protests as an "Indian" regarding his property rights generally had not registered within his colonial context, Apess here foregrounds his identity as an individual "Christian" as the foundation for making his oppositional claims. His situates himself within the context of liberal "toleration" as he claims the right of any member of civil society to assert his or her proprietary freedom to choose religion. In doing so he invokes a broader legal authority than that of the Indian law which had heretofore stymied him. He claims his rights as a civilized *Christian*, without abrogating his identity as an Indian. Such an act represents a significant step forward in carving out a new space for Indianness within the framework of the colonial legal order.

The emergence of the form of liberal rights consciousness we have been tracing carries over directly into Apess's renewal of some of his earlier claims, providing evidence of the overall rhetorical strategy of the text. After his assertion of spiritual liberty, Apess turns in Chapter Five to deal with his participation in the War of 1812. There, he revisits his protest against breaches of contract with Indians. (In this case he is concerned with the fact that he enlisted in the American army as a drummer but was subsequently made into a rifleman.) The main thrust of the chapter, however, is to stress his participation in and embrace of "American" civilization. Recalling his involvement in the Battle of Plattsburgh, Apess notes that "the adjacent shores resounded with the alternate shouts of the sons of liberty and the groans of their parting spirits" (30). The (mildly ironic) identification by this "son of the forest" with the "sons of liberty" becomes clear later in the paragraph: "This was indeed a proud day for our country . . . On land we had compelled the enemy to seek safety in flight. Our army did not lose many men, but on the lake many a brave man fell—fell in defense of his country's rights" (30). Apess's subsequent outrage at the failure of the government to pay its Indian soldiers attests to his sense of the legitimacy of his full participation in all the rights and institutions of "civilized" life. He notes, "I could never think the government acted right toward the 'Natives,' not merely in refusing to pay us but in claiming our services in case of perilous emergency, and still deny us the right of citizenship; and as long as our nation is debarred the privilege of voting for civil officers, I shall believe that the government has no claim on our services" (31).

If such a moment suggests Apess's belief that the problems of the Indian are those of a lack of incorporation into the political and social order, comments in the next chapter provide the final piece of evidence regarding his broad-based engagement with liberal models of subjectivity. His ability to develop a strategy for resisting religious oppression and other areas of colonial domination are both firmly embedded in the dominant legal ideology. Coming on the heels of his account of the mistreatment and lack of incorporation of the Indians participating in the War of 1812, Apess opens Chapter Six with a suggestive echo of the kind of rhetoric we saw used earlier by Samson Occom:

> No doubt there are many good people in the United States who would not trample on the rights of the poor, but there are many others who are willing to roll in their coaches upon the tears and blood of the poor and unoffending natives—those who are ready at all times to speculate on the Indians and defraud them out of their rightful possessions. Let the poor Indian attempt to resist the encroachments of his white neighbors, what a hue and cry is instantly raised against him . . . Suppose an overwhelming army should march into the United States for the purposes of subduing it and enslaving the citizens; how quick would they fly to arms, gather in multitudes around the tree of liberty, and contend for their rights with every drop of blood. (31)

Eliding the "rights of the poor" and the plight of the "poor Indian" here, Apess renews his claim that the Indian's problem is one of a failure to acknowledge and respect his fundamental rights of property (especially over himself). The echo of revolutionary rhetoric is quite explicit and suggests a continued attempt to link his model of identity with the *nomos* of American liberalism. Apess's sense of outrage and injustice seems to emerge from a belief that civilized whites have failed to incorporate the Indian into the social contract and protect his fundamental rights in the way they would expect their own to be defended. He suggests that Indianness is being deployed as a false, racist, legal construct to deny a segment of the population their God-given and constitutional rights. At this point his autobiographical act obviates any sense of difference by which a prejudicial system of Indian law could restrain his liberty *as an American.*

All this is not to claim, of course, that there is no "Indian" self in *A Son of the Forest.* The text acknowledges at least two basic forms—the precontact Indianness associated with King Philip and the postcontact model Apess develops within the text. Apess's autobiographical narrative suggests his sense that the former could be (and probably had to be) transcended in favor of the "liberal" Indian subjectivity he subsequently articulates. In Chapter Seven, he notes that "great objections have been raised against efforts to civilize the natives" but insists that the apparent failure of assimilationist policies has more to do with the "sinister motives" of some whites rather than the intractability of the Indian (33). In his view, the idea that Indians are "not susceptible of improvement" had been disproved by numerous instances of conversion in Canada and the West. Significantly, such a comment draws our attention back to the ways that Apess's invocation of conversion rhetoric in *A Son of the Forest* takes place within a larger colonial context. His representation of religious identity (of himself as a Christian Indian) stands here as the foundation for full participation in civil society. Getting rid of the sense of inferiority and loss associated with his orphaned past provides him with a basis for forceful self-assertion of a wide range of rights.

It is no coincidence that Chapter Seven (which begins with an emphasis on Apess's travails during his youthful conversion) closes with a discussion of an attempt by a white man to defraud Apess of wages owed him and to treat him "as he would a degraded African slave" (37). He recalls that this employer, a Mr. Geers, "took a cart stake in order to pay me, but he soon found out his mistake, as I made him put it down as quick as he had taken it up. I had been cheated so often that I determined to have my rights this time, and forever after" (37). Not only does Apess counter force with force in this situation (a moment that anticipates Frederick Douglass's defining confrontation with the slave-breaker, Covey, in his 1845 *Narrative of the Life of Frederick Douglass*), he expresses a plain determination to have his property rights. The tonal change in such a passage draws our attention to the process I have been trying to expose in discussing the shift from "Experience" to *A Son of the Forest*—the move from an inward-looking conversion experience to a burgeoning consciousness of religious liberty as a civil right and to a more aggressive assertion of other property rights. Both of these aspects reflect Apess's ongoing engagement with legal discourse in his articulation of identity. They also trace his development into a more effective force of opposition, in the long term, than his "ancestor" King Philip.

Admittedly, the emergence of Indian rights consciousness we have been following did not lead to an easy end to Apess's struggle to define an oppositional rhetoric. The extremity of the colonial experience that inspired his autobiographical endeavors ensured a continuous and manifest instability in his acts of self-definition. Throughout *A Son of the Forest*, Apess stresses constant backsliding in his religious struggle, a battle with what may have been an alcoholic addiction to rum, and a recurrent sense of alienation.[13] In Chapter Eight, the bulk of which focuses on the fact that his heart was "susceptible of good impressions" and on his increasing immersion in the Methodist religion, Apess includes one of the most intriguing symbolic moments in the text. Immediately after his baptism in 1818, having obtained a certificate of standing in the Episcopal Methodist Church, Apess recalls undertaking a journey to visit his Indian family in another part of Connecticut. On the way to see his biological father, he loses his way in the forest. Apess presents the incident in the allegorical register typical of spiritual autobiography; being lost in woods and swamp becomes a form of spiritual trial. "I was now amazed," he writes, "what to do I knew not; shut out from the light of heaven . . . this was the hour of peril" (42). For a "son of the forest," though, this symbolic moment takes on dimensions beyond the religious ones, representing a recurrent anxiety that his attempt to engage with legal discourse had not ended his struggle to define himself. Having just been baptized and incorporated into the Methodist "society" (which, we have seen, was for him the foundation of incorporation into civil society), Apess becomes lost in what theoretically should have been familiar countryside. Even the fact that God delivers him from his peril and enables him to find his way to his family for a visit does not suggest a complete resolution to Apess's identity crisis or an escape from the recurrent sense of loss that his immersion in liberal ideology seems likely to have precipitated.

If Apess's account of his conversion experience in *A Son of the Forest* becomes a tale of conversion for liberty, then, there clearly were costs associated with claiming freedom in that way. Nevertheless, in his second autobiographical act he does seem to have articulated a viable, oppositional model of Indian selfhood; this is not the collapse of Ely S. Parker's personal narrative. Granted, Apess does not provide readers with an ethnographically illuminating account of "traditional" Indianness, but this may be due in large measure to his appreciation of the fact that such a story, in the early nineteenth century, would do little to assist him in his attempt to assert his rights. Were he writing in the legal climate of today, of course, matters might be different. Yet simply to deem *A Son of the Forest* "inauthentic" because it fails to satisfy prior assumptions about "Indian" identity would be to misconstrue Apess's achievement. Engagement with the dominant American legal ideology and its identity models grounds the assertiveness of *A Son of the Forest* and distinguishes it from Apess's previous autobiography. Furthermore, the model of identity manifested here subsequently enabled Apess to plunge into his most direct confrontation with the colonial order. During the Mashpee Revolt of 1833–34 Apess was a central figure in the first successful example of civil disobedience in Native American history. Turning, then, to *Indian*

Nullification (1835), his account of the events in question, we can see some of the practical applications of his model of self developed in *A Son of the Forest*. At the same time, we can consider the complex ways Apess's rhetoric of Indianness continues to be politically significant in contemporary America (an issue I will explore in relation to the legal struggle of the Mashpee in the late 1970s to re-achieve legal recognition as an Indian tribe).

Apess's longest work, *Indian Nullification*, is not the same kind of "autobiography" as the two earlier works we have been discussing. First of all, unlike "The Experience of the Missionary" and *A Son of the Forest*, *Indian Nullification* was not produced wholly independently. As Barry O'Connell has suggested, William Joseph Snelling (author of *Tales of the Northwest* [1830]) may have served as an editor of the text, and perhaps even wrote some of the narrative material connecting the various public documents included within it.[14] Whatever Snelling's role, though, the text is bound together primarily through first-person narrative that, based on its rhetorical style, was quite obviously written by Apess. This fact makes me willing to consider the text in conjunction with Apess's earlier works. The more interesting difference between *Indian Nullification* and the earlier texts is structural. While the later book does contain considerable stretches of first-person narrative (where Apess deals with details of his personal involvement in the Mashpee Revolt), the majority of it is made up of those aforementioned documents (newspaper editorials, letters, petitions, etc.). The text is thus a combination of conventional autobiography and legal memorial, seeking both to establish the Mashpee community's own legal rights and to justify and explain Apess's personal conduct.

In a profound sense, this fusion of manifestly autobiographical material and public documents represents a logical culmination of the process of engagement we have been tracing in this chapter—i.e., Apess's progressive articulation of Indianness as a form of civil selfhood, articulated largely in a public language of rights. Over time, his engagement with legal discourse led Apess to articulate an almost exclusively "public" identity, a form of individualist self-consciousness wholly residing in the public sphere of the modern liberal state. *Indian Nullification* links narrative accounts of individual experience, treatments of the social realities confronting all Indian subjects, and a range of "colonialist" writing into a manifesto of rights consciousness and postcontact Indianness. Perhaps the most accurate designation for the book, then, might be to call it a rhetorical performance of Indianness where Apess's engagement with law leads him to fuse completely the personal elements of his earlier autobiographies with a public language of legal opposition. *Indian Nullification* functions simultaneously as an autobiographical act of self-construction and as "evidence" in support of individual and collective legal claims growing out of the Mashpee Revolt of 1833–34. In this sense, it demonstrates the degree to which legal models had come to influence Apess's formulation of Indian identity just six years after he wrote his first autobiography.

Belying the almost hysterical reaction from political authorities in the state of Massachusetts, the so-called "Masphee Revolt" was not an armed uprising at all, but rather an attempt by the Mashpee Indian tribe of Cape Cod, largely through petition and public remonstrance, to assert their right to choose a minister and to stop white neighbors from despoiling their lands. When Apess arrived in Mashpee in 1833 he encountered an Indian community of 315, similar in some respects to the Pequots of Connecticut, languishing under the domination of colonial law. The Mashpee plantation dated from 1660, when Richard Bourne had secured a grant of land on Cape Cod for the use of Indian survivors of colonial conflicts and disease, and their descendants. This "praying town" was initially overseen by English proprietors, starting with Bourne himself. Over time, though, the legal relationship between the tribe and Massachusetts changed drastically, becoming increasingly restrictive. In 1788, the state legislature created a three-person board of overseers with broad powers to regulate the plantation, ostensibly for the Mashpee's protection. In religious matters, the Mashpee similarly lacked a voice in their own affairs. A missionary fund established in 1711 by Daniel Williams and entrusted to Harvard College provided the means of support for official (Congregationalist) missionaries appointed to serve the tribe. Phineas Fish, who was the missionary when Apess arrived in 1833, began his tenure in 1807 and enjoyed a comfortable income from tribal resources; the Harvard trustees paid him a generous salary, and he was allowed to sell wood from his parsonage lands at Mashpee to supplement his income. Fish's concern with the orderly practice of religion led him to forbid any non-Congregational worship in the Mashpee meeting house, a fact that, combined with his failure to minister to the tribe, effectively meant that the Indians were turned out of their own church building. In terms of both their secular and religious affairs, then, the Mashpee in the early nineteenth century found themselves firmly in the grip of colonial domination. Plagued by alcoholism, poverty, high mortality, transience, and apathy, their reservation was, as Donald M. Nielson has pointed out, a "rural slum."[15]

Apess heard about the Mashpee while preaching in Connecticut in

1833 and set out in May to visit Cape Cod. Upon arriving, he attended one of Fish's services in the meeting house and was appalled to find the congregation to be almost entirely white. Fish's antagonistic response to his questions about this arrangement led Apess to call a public meeting and subsequently to organize the Mashpee and help them articulate their grievances. On May 21, the tribe sent a memorial to Governor Levi Lincoln and his council, signed by 102 persons. The Mashpee signatories demanded that the overseers be eliminated and that the tribal treasurer, Obed Good-speed, turn over his books. They further insisted that they would control their own lands and property from that point onward. Subsequently Apess led a group of Indians in unloading the carts belonging to whites cutting wood on tribal lands. At this point the conflict exploded into the newspapers. John Fiske of the governor's council was sent to mediate the dispute and held a mass meeting attended by many members of the tribe, some bearing muskets. As the press began to speak of "war" on the Cape, Fiske had Apess arrested and convicted of inciting a riot. Though the arrest had its desired immediate effect of quieting the Mashpee, Apess was quickly bailed out of jail by the former treasurer of the tribe, Lemuel Ewer, who was sympathetic to their cause. At this point the conflict passed on to the legislature, turning into a war of words and a campaign of public relations. (The Mashpee's principal defenders were their attorney, Benjamin Franklin Hallet, editor of the Boston *Daily Advocate,* and William Lloyd Garrison's *Liberator.*) Finally, in 1834 the crisis was resolved in a special joint session of the Massachusetts legislature. Mashpee was incorporated as a district (one step away from full township status), and the Indians were granted the right to elect their own selectmen. Though it took until 1846 to get rid of Reverend Fish, the Mashpee were well on their way to full incorporation into the political fabric of Massachusetts. In 1870, after a close vote, the tribe opted to become a town. With the elimination of restrictions on land sale and the assumption of individual, fee simple land title, the Mashpee became full citizens.

Apess's account of the Mashpee Revolt provides us with considerable insight into the process of legal engagement that led to Mashpee self-determination, a process that he seems to have been instrumental in instigating. Indeed, when we consider the overall character of a text like *Indian Nullification* as a sort of manifesto of Indian rights and identity, the parallels in narrative structure between its autobiographical elements and those in *A Son of the Forest* suggest deep continuities between both texts. In a real sense, Apess's "history" of the identity claims of the Mashpee replicates the story of his own arc of self-development; the oppositional consciousness he develops in the earlier text stands clearly behind his representation of the Mashpee's own struggle for self-determination. He presents the 1833 conflict as rooted in the same issues of religious liberty and failed educational responsibilities that emerged in *A Son of the Forest*. Apess's indictment not only of Reverend Fish's failure to minister to his Indian charges but also of his use of their meeting house to preach to whites demonstrates his continued sense that such spiritual issues are also the kind of property issues that most intimately concerned him as a liberal individual. As he presents it, "these pale men were certainly *stealing from the Indians their portion of the Gospel,* by leaving their own houses of worship and crowding them out of theirs" [my emphasis] (171). Apess is clear that this "theft" of salvation being perpetrated is part of the same legal order that denies the Indian basic rights of property and sovereignty. "The law," he notes, "allowed them to do so," and it seems clear that the failure to properly educate the Mashpee had contributed greatly to their lack of effective resistance to colonial domination (171). Recognizing what seems to have been a paucity of such knowledge, Apess recalls "[holding] forth upon the civil and religious rights of the Indian," an act that by all accounts helped to galvanize the Mashpee community to protest and agitate for such rights. In effect, he called upon his Mashpee brethren to undergo fully the same kind of awakening of rights consciousness that he had undergone himself. Of course, to teach the Mashpee what their rights were was, in a profound sense, to move them toward the dominant American legal models of identity—and toward Indian liberalism. In this respect, Apess suggests that he sought to guide them through the same process of engagement we saw in *A Son of the Forest*. We can see more evidence of the parallels Apess draws in *Indian Nullification* between his own autobiographical self-consciousness and the Mashpee's struggle when we consider the language of the series of resolutions sent soon after his arrival to the Corporation of Harvard College demanding control over the choice of minister and castigating Reverend Fish for denying the tribe access to the sacrament. The Mashpee assert their sense of religious liberty, arguing that they "have as good a right to the table of the Lord as others" (176). This petition demonstrates again how the renewal of tribal consciousness and oppositional identity takes place in a way that mirrors the legal nomos of the colonial power being opposed.

The manner in which *Indian Nullification* alludes, both directly and indirectly, to broader issues and conflicts further reinforces the reader's sense that the model of Indian identity stressed in the text is one rooted in engagement with American law. On several occasions in the text, Apess refers to the Cherokee removal crisis, suggesting his sense that the Mashpee's struggle under his influence and leadership resembled what had been happening to their fellow Indians in Georgia and North Carolina during the preceding decade. Though the primary thrust of many of these references is to tweak the consciences of the citizens of Massachusetts (imploring them not to become another Georgia), they also function to situate the identity claims of the Mashpee firmly within the ideology of the U.S. Constitution and liberal contractarianism. At the time Apess wrote, the Cherokee provided the most striking and far-reaching example of a Native American tribe attempting to engage with the Anglo-American legal models to redefine themselves and their communities in the wake of colonial contact. Indeed, the Cherokee had gone so far as to adopt a constitution modeled on that of the United States and to put their claims to sovereignty before the Supreme Court in the famous "Cherokee Cases."[16] Though the Cherokee lost their struggle with the government, the lesson Apess seems to have drawn from their experience involved the central role of American law in regulating colonial contact and providing a discourse of opposition. Apess notes that the failure of either the governor or the Harvard Corporation to respond favorably to the Mashpee petitions led the tribe to hold its own constitutional convention on June 25, 1833: "We now, in our synagogue, for the first time, concerted the form of a government suited to the spirit and capacity of freeborn sons of the forest, after the pattern set us by our white brethren. There was but one exception, viz., that *all* who dwelt in our precincts were to be held free and equal, *in truth* as well as in letter. Several officers, twelve in all, were elected to give effect to this novelty of a government . . . Having thus organized ourselves, we gave notice to the former board of overseers and the public at large, of our intentions" (179). In Apess's account of this convention, the "spirit" of these sons of the forest appears congruent with contractarian thinking (albeit with something of a Jacksonian edge). The "proclamation" that follows explicitly claims that the Masphee "acted in accordance with the spirit of the Constitution" in moving to "nullify the existing laws" that denied them their rights of self-determination.

In using the language of "nullification," Apess and the Mashpee invoke another national legal issue in making their claims, alluding directly to the Nullification Crisis of 1831–32. Though the background of that conflict dated back to the controversy surrounding the Alien and Sedition Acts of the 1790s, the primary issue in 1831–32 was South Carolina's opposition to the Federal Tariff Acts of 1828 and 1832. The most radical positions being taken by Carolinians involved claims that the people of the state did not permanently surrender their sovereignty when the Constitution was adopted and therefore could, as a sovereign body, secede from the Union. A less extreme claim came to the fore, though, whereby the legislature of South Carolina declared only a specific law (the Tariff Act) to be null and void. President Jackson's response was to threaten military force to collect the tariff revenues, but also to push Congress to lower the rate, thereby diffusing the crisis. (The constitutional questions surrounding state's rights would persist for decades, however, particularly with regards to the issue of slavery.)[17] While the specific details of South Carolina's conflict with the federal government do not come up in *Indian Nullification*, it is nevertheless clear that Apess intended to frame both the Mashpee protests and his account of it as a "constitutional" argument regarding the unlawful usurpation of authority by a central government (in this case a state government) over sovereign selves. Significantly, in doing so, Apess moves beyond the kinds of arguments made, unsuccessfully, by the Cherokee. Where they had sought only to invoke treaty rights (their rights as a collective, foreign nation) to sovereignty, Apess and the Mashpee make a claim for full incorporation and the protection, albeit through a corporate structure, of what are *individual* rights. (We should recall that they agitated to organize the Indian plantation of Mashpee into an independent township.) Indeed, according to one of the newspaper articles Apess includes in his text (taken from the December 4, 1833, issue of the *Boston Advocate*) the key identity claim being made by the Mashpee is that "they are capable of organizing societies, and taking care of their own concerns, as well, to say the least, as any equal number of persons in the Commonwealth, for they feel more strongly interested for themselves than others can be for them" (204). *Indian Nullification* thus approaches the issues of identity and sovereignty from a perspective that stresses the embeddedness of Indian *individuals* within the legal ideology of the American state.

In an "open letter" that fronts *Indian Nullification*, Benjamin Franklin Hallet, the tribe's attorney, clarifies the nature of the Mashpee's claims in a way that further emphasizes the emergence of the kind of postcontact identity that we traced in our discussion of *A Son of the Forest*. Hallet justifies Apess's conduct in the case, comparing him to the patriots of the revolutionary era. He notes that in the events leading up to his arrest, Apess was "as justifiable in what [he] did, as our fathers were, who threw the tea overboard" making him a modern-day son of liberty (a point echoed in Apess's discussion of the War of 1812 in *A Son of the Forest*) (167). Consequently, Hallet stresses that the text to follow will tell the story of "liberty" unjustly denied. His point that "our laws have denied all rights of property" to the Mashpee clearly foreshadows the way Apess's representation of himself and his brethren would engage with the root assumptions of the liberal state. Indeed, Apess's own entry into *Indian Nullification* in his "Introduction" frames the entire text to follow as a kind of "evidence" (a term he uses) in support of a series of rights claims, claims that must, by definition, be rooted in an individualist model of legal identity. He notes that the treatment of the Mashpee is inconsistent with his belief "that God has given to all men an equal right to possess and occupy the earth, and enjoy the fruits thereof, without any distinction" (168). This "belief" is, of course, part of the foundation of contractarian thought; we should note that Apess does not say that men should share the world in common, but that based on their labor all men have the right to take possession of the earth (enjoying the fruits).

If a commitment to legal rights as a manifestation of Indian individualism dominates Apess's claims on behalf of the Mashpee in *Indian Nullification*, those elements of the text that represent more personal autobiographical assertions of his own identity further show his deep rhetorical commitment to legal models. Because of his adoption into the community, of course, every claim Apess makes on behalf of the Mashpee implicitly includes him. At the same time, Apess's treatment of that "adoption" is revealing of his legal consciousness in other ways. Setting the tone for the text to come, *Indian Nullification* begins with an open letter "to the white people of Massachusetts" signed by "three selectmen of the Marshpee [sic] Tribe" (Israel Amos, Isaac Coombs, and Ezra Attaquin). The authors, as official representatives of the Mashpee (we should note how their offices mirror familiar governmental structures in other Massachusetts towns), claim to have written the letter for the "benefit" of their "brother Apess," to legitimize the role he had played in the conflict. If the writers chose somewhat inflammatory language in doing so, the letter serves its primary purpose of verifying Apess's legal status to petition governmental authorities during the conflict (i.e., it gives him the status on which to base the claims to follow).[18] In this respect, it stands in conjunction with another document that appears a few pages later in the text—an official statement of his adoption into the Mashpee tribe. In discussing that adoption, Apess reveals the degree to which his rhetoric of Indian identity had come to center around a civic or legal consciousness. He recalls comments made at the first mass meeting after his arrival at Mashpee: "I began by saying that, though I was a stranger among them, I did not doubt that I might do them some good and be instrumental in procuring the discharge of the overseers and an alteration of the existing laws. As, however, I was not a son of their particular tribe, if they wished me to assist them, it would be necessary for them to give me a right to act on their behalf by adopting me, as then our rights and interests would become identical" (173). Ironically, the end of Apess's "orphan" status seems to come with his "legal" adoption into a governmentally recognized Indian community (one that was, in fact, a product of colonial exploitation). The key point to note here, though, it that Apess acknowledges the prime importance of establishing his *legal status* as a Mashpee "citizen" before he can even begin to make other claims or share their "interests." While one might think that as an Indian, Apess would share "interests" with the Mashpee regardless of tribal affiliation, he suggests here the pervasiveness of the ideology we saw in *A Son of the Forest* and the signal importance of property in his model of Indianness. Being Indian, for Apess, was to be a liberal man unjustly denied his property rights. His particular rhetoric of "pan-Indian" rights consciousness demanded that he be under the same oppressive law denying such rights (in this case the law of the Commonwealth of Massachusetts) in order to make his claim for shared identity with the Mashpee.

If Apess's concern with establishing his legal status as a Mashpee "citizen" reveals the degree to which the model of Indian identity he articulated (and which motivates his entire orchestration of the Mashpee protest) was engaged with "legal" models, we can see a final bit of confirmation when we consider one last level of meaning in *Indian Nullification.* Throughout his involvement in the "revolt," Apess was forced to defend himself against accusations against his character and questions regarding his legal right to represent the Mashpee position. In this sense, the text stands as a kind of autobiographical justification of self to such critics and to the legal system that had him jailed for inciting a riot. Yet Apess's consciousness of "reputation" went even beyond a sense of the need to prove his Mashpee affiliation. As he notes in the text, in the wake of claims not just that he was an interloper but that he was a drunken debaucher, Apess undertook a libel suit against some of his accusers. In this sense, *Indian Nullification* emerges as a personal autobiographical document tied to his legal attempt to assert proprietary control over his reputation and over the writing of his history—to own himself in every possible sense that modern legal ideology allows.

We should recall in this context that the legal notion of libel developed in the early eighteenth century, hand in hand with the modern notion of copyright. The rise of a sense of authorial rights in a text, representing a blend of liberal property discourse and a nascent discourse of original genius, stood behind the 1710 Statute of Anne, the world's first copyright law. For the notion of literary property as a kind of freehold to make sense, though, required a consequent development of a notion of individual authorial "style" or original genius as the mark that establishes one's "ownership" of a text. This move led in turn to a metaphorical linkage of personality and text, with a literary work being increasingly seen as an objectification of the writer's self. This "legal fiction" of a linkage between selves and texts fuels the modern conception of libel—the idea that an "attack" on someone in writing can be seen to cause harm to their person and the related notion that reputation is a form of property protected by law. Apess closes his text with an observation and address to his white readers that resonates with such a legal context and its assumptions regarding identity: "For troubling my readers with so much of my own affairs, I have this excuse. I have been assailed by the vilest calumnies, represented as an exciter of sedition, a hypocrite, and a gambler. These slanders, though disproved, still continue to circulate. Though I am an Indian, I am at least a man, with all the feelings proper to humanity, and my reputation is dear to me; and I conceive it to be my duty to the children I shall leave behind me, as well as to myself, not to leave them the inheritance of a blasted name. In doing so, I humbly presume to think, I have not exceeded the moderation proper for a Christian man to use" (274). As a "Christian man," oppressed by society because he is also an Indian, Apess justifies both his text and his lawsuit by suggesting that his name (and the identity it represents) stands as a kind of property, the value of which must be defended if it is to be bequeathed to the next generation. In this sense, he re-emphasizes his broad identification with liberal ideology and its legal models of identity. Apess's defense of his reputation as an Indian involved in the Mashpee Revolt rests on his sense of his rights as a possessive individual to preserve the value of that reputation. Both oppositional and engaged to the end, then, this last piece of autobiographical writing embodies the complex form of self-definition that grew out of his contact with colonialism and the legal discourse of early America.

In the previous two chapters, I have tried to emphasize how the communicative dynamic of colonial engagement, centered around legal language and institutions, inevitably complicates our reading of autobiographical texts like "The Experience of the Missionary," *A Son of the Forest*, and *Indian Nullification*. In my view, the failure to appreciate the complexity of colonial contact and to fall back on problematic notions of "authenticity" has led many critics to misconstrue Apess's overall achievement. The implications of such misunderstandings extend well beyond the formation of an autobiographical canon, though. Probably the best example of this appears in the Mashpee's unsuccessful legal struggle during the late 1970s to obtain recognition from the federal government as an official tribe. In "Identity at Mashpee," his tremendously provocative account of the trial and its significance, anthropologist James Clifford notes that the Mashpee's defeat was rooted in the federal district court's adherence to a rigorous standard of cultural authenticity.[19] Indeed, during the trial Clifford observed a familiar process whereby "stories of cultural contact and change have been structured by a pervasive dichotomy: absorption by the other *or* resistance to the other" (344). As I have suggested elsewhere, such dichotomies also characterize much contemporary criticism of Native American writing, especially autobiographical writing. As I see it, based both on the assumptions used by the court in determining whether or not the Mashpee exhibited a continuous sense of "Indian" identity and on some of the conventional critical interpretations of his work, had Apess's autobiographies been read into the court record they probably would have been used as evidence *against the tribe.* Indeed, in their failed bid for tribal recognition, the Mashpee's earlier move to incorporate as a township (a movement initiated under Apess's leadership) was seen as proof that they had assimilated into American culture, giving up their Indian identity. I will not enter here into a detailed discussion of the 1977 case of *Mashpee Tribe v. New Seabury et al.;* the facts of the case are too complicated and the issues too important to allow for quick and easy pronouncements. In closing, though, I would simply suggest that the preceding discussion of Apess's autobiographical acts supports Clifford's call for a "history of hesitations" in conceptualizing the process of colonial contact we see reflected in Indian autobiography. At the end of "Identity at Mashpee," Clifford echoes my earlier critique of spatial metaphors of contact by wondering "what if identity is conceived not as a boundary to be maintained but as a nexus of relations and transactions actively engaging a subject?" (344). Such a "what if" stands directly behind my reading of Apess's texts. The fact that I have challenged certain literary and legal orthodoxies regarding Indianness suggests that those orthodoxies have failed to do justice to the language of self-definition that his texts offer to the reader.

5 *Charles Eastman and the Discourse of Allotment*

If William Apess stands apart as the most prolific and innovative Native American autobiographer of the antebellum period, Charles Alexander Eastman (Ohiyesa) casts a similarly long shadow at the end of the nineteenth century and the beginning of the twentieth. In this respect, it is of particular interest (in the context of the present study) to note the striking resemblance between the shapes of these two writers' autobiographical careers. As was the case with Apess, Eastman's prolonged engagement with the discourse of Indian law led him, over time, to redefine himself in a manner not adequately captured using the critical lens of "authenticity." Yet while the *process* of self-definition revealed in his autobiographies resembles that of his predecessor, Eastman's final model of Indianness differs in important ways from Apess's. As I have been arguing throughout this book, the explanation for this difference should be sought in the contrasting discursive contexts of each man's autobiographical acts. By addressing those contrasts, the readings to follow will further support the general theory of autobiographical engagement I have been advancing, providing another illustration of the complex, performative nature of Native American autobiography during the first century and a half of American colonialism.

What most distinguishes the dynamic of colonial contact in Eastman's era from that of the early national period is the rise of a potent federal bureaucracy, the emergence of which was part of a larger national process of "incorporation," to use Alan Trachtenberg's term. Writing on

the development of the Bureau of Indian Affairs (BIA) during the late
nineteenth century, historian Paul Stuart has observed that the evolution of Indian administration paralleled the political modernization and
bureaucratization of the country as a whole. Following and expanding on
the work of sociologist Max Weber, Stuart further notes that this process
involved the replacement of traditional, customary relations with increasingly formal and hierarchical systems and structures. In the specific case
of the BIA, such changes centered on the development of new discursive
mechanisms and a body of administrative law designed to transform Native American identity. Eastman's autobiographical career, as we shall
see, was shaped by his lifelong engagement with precisely these bureaucratic apparatuses (which flowered during the so-called allotment period
of U.S. Indian policy). Eastman's first autobiographical act, suggestively
titled *Indian Boyhood,* more or less adopts the legal model of Indian-as-
child at the heart of the discourse of allotment. In contrast, his second
autobiography, *From the Deep Woods to Civilization,* represents a more
complex, critical form of engagement. Over time, Eastman seems to
have found a way, within the institutional framework of allotment-era
Indian law, to develop a new language of self that was centered on a very
modern conception of the rights of personhood. In this sense, his autobiographical acts of self-definition move beyond the property-centered
rights consciousness that dominated Apess's writings toward a focus on
more broadly defined civil rights. In the end, it is Eastman's ability to
make such innovations within his discursive context that makes him a
major figure in the history of Native American autobiographical expression. Working simultaneously in the realms of literature and politics,
his writings advance a historical—we might say dialectical—process of
discursive engagement.

   To understand the process of legal engagement as it plays out in
Eastman's writings, however, we must first consider the origins and distinctiveness of allotment-era Indian law (and the way some of his contemporaries responded to that law). Generally speaking, the genesis of
the allotment policy coincided with the creation of the massive reservations in the western territories of the United States, a process that was
initially conceived in the early decades of the nineteenth century. Only
after the Civil War, though, as the reservation policy took off in earnest,
did a full-fledged bureaucratic apparatus capable of casting a meaningful
legal shadow on Indian self-consciousness truly emerge. The Bureau of
Indian Affairs had been established by Secretary of War John Calhoun in
1824, and in 1832 Congress ratified the existence of the office, placing
its administration under the newly created position of commissioner of

Indian affairs. However, in its early years, the BIA lacked the overwhelming power and authority it would eventually enjoy. The responsibilities of the Indian commissioner, whose bureau was transferred to the Department of the Interior in 1849, were confined for a long time to the creation of advisory reports on the "Indian problem" and to the administration of Indian trade in accordance with the various incarnations of the Trade and Intercourse Act. After the Civil War a number of events would contribute to a change in this situation.

Prior to 1867, relations with the Indians in the West had been seen primarily as a military matter. In that year, though, concerned about the cost (both in lives and money) of conflict with the western tribes, President Grant created the Indian Peace Commission to come up with alternative approaches to the Indian "problem." In its initial report of 1868, the commission initiated a process of change by recommending that the Trade and Intercourse Acts be revised to reinforce the assimilationist policies increasingly circulating in the BIA, policies designed to "educate and instruct in the peaceful arts—in other words, to civilize the Indian" (qtd. in Prucha, *Documents* 108). Significant outbreaks of violence on the plains during the 1870s retarded the progress of these initiatives and led to a spirited debate over who was best suited to administer Indian affairs (military men or civilians). Nevertheless, by the late 1870s philanthropic and assimilationist ideals had become the dominant force in Indian policy. Military officers continued to serve in administrative posts within the BIA (and federal troops were called out with some regularity to deal with various signs of Indian unrest), but the more idealistic assumptions of the so-called "friends of the Indian" came to dominate Indian law during this period.[1] These reformers would argue vigorously for a period of twenty years in favor of a stronger bureaucracy to protect and nurture the nation's Indian wards.

Ironically, though, the key event in the development of the discourse of allotment and the BIA's administrative power was a high-profile legal case where Indian plaintiffs were victorious in making a claim against the government—i.e., in a "successful" act of legal engagement. In 1879, the removal of a group of Ponca Indians from their ancestral lands to another reservation and the subsequent challenge of that removal in *Standing Bear v. Crook* (1879) refocused national debate around questions of Native Americans' rights and problematic lack of legal status. The dispute in *Standing Bear v. Crook* enabled the creation of enduring national reform organizations and administrative structures. In doing so it triggered the final proliferation of the legal discourse of allotment, which would provide the dominant model of Indian identity for the next fifty years. The legal issue at the heart of *Standing Bear v. Crook* was the question of wrongful arrest and the right of Native Americans to obtain a writ of habeas corpus nullifying such an arrest. In 1877, in what seemed a violation of an 1858 treaty, the federal government moved the Ponca from their tribal lands in the Dakota territory to an area in the Indian Territory, in present-day Oklahoma, as a result of their having agreed in another treaty to settle several bands of Sioux on the Ponca's original lands. Once in the Indian Territory, the Ponca rapidly began to decline (largely from illness and hunger); 158 of the 581 Indians who were removed died within a year. In 1878 a tribal leader, Standing Bear, informed the agent that he would lead a group of his people back to their Dakota lands so that they "might live and die in peace, and be buried with [their] fathers." During their attempted migration, the band of Ponca were arrested and imprisoned by federal troops under the command of General George Crook. Subsequently, they brought suit in the U.S. Circuit Court in Nebraska, seeking a writ of habeas corpus from Judge Elmer S. Dundy, who decided the case in their favor.

The opening phrases of Dundy's decision in *Standing Bear* make manifest both the unequal and paternalistic relationship between whites and Indians implicit in U.S. Indian law and the ability of the Ponca and their attorney to engage with that discourse in making their claim. Noting that in fifteen years on the bench he had never decided a case which "appealed so strongly to [his] sympathy," the judge characterizes the parties in the dispute in this way:

> On the one side, we have a few of the remnants of a once numerous and powerful, but now weak, insignificant, unlettered, and generally despised race; on the other, we have the representative of one of the most powerful, most enlightened, and most Christianized nations of modern times. On the one side, we have the representatives of this wasted race coming into this national tribunal of ours, asking for justice and liberty to enable them to adopt our boasted civilization, and to pursue the arts of peace, which have made us great and happy as a nation; on the other side, we have this magnificent, if not magnanimous, government, resisting this application with the determination of sending these people back to the country which is to them less desirable than perpetual imprisonment in their own native land.

In defining the parties in the case (the Indian *relators* and the *respondent*, General Crook—the embodiment of state power), Dundy makes clear certain operative assumptions about the nature and destiny of the Ponca people. The opening of the decision sets up a familiar tragic tableau; one can sense another drama of inevitable decline about to unfold.

In deciding in favor of the Ponca, though, the court seems to undercut those assumptions by recognizing the Indians' claim of the right to be incorporated in American society and to enjoy certain legal protections. Perhaps thinking back to previous appellate and Supreme Court decisions, Dundy argues that it is law, not sympathy, that can provide the remedy to the current dispute.[2] To put this another way, he argues that the case could only be decided based on the ability of Indians to constitute themselves as (liberal) legal subjects and to make legal claims based on that subjectivity.

Judge Dundy prefaces his decision with a summary of the divergent identity claims made by the parties involved in the case. The Ponca's petition asserts that they had severed their tribal relations, had adopted the ways of the whites, and were endeavoring to be self-sufficient (possessive) individuals before they were wrongfully arrested. Clearly, from the vantage point of Standing Bear and his attorneys, living in a "civilized" manner offered a more secure foundation for claiming legal protection than being a "wild" tribe of Indians. General Crook's counsel concedes that point, noting that the relators were "*individual* members of the Ponca Tribe" (emphasis added). The argument in the case then turns to whether the *individual* Indians were citizens and thus had the right to bring their suit. Judge Dundy rejects the question as irrelevant to the proceedings, holding that the right to sue on a writ of habeas corpus belonged to any "persons" wrongfully imprisoned, not any "citizen." Pointing out that foreign nationals are protected by law from wrongful arrest, the judge turns to a dictionary definition of personhood to make his point: "Webster describes a person as 'a living soul; a self-conscious being; a moral agent; especially a living human being; a man, woman, or child; an individual of the human race.' This is comprehensive enough, it would seem, to include even an Indian." According to this "lowest denominator" definition, the judge upholds the court's jurisdiction to decide the case, validating the Indians' legal standing to bring their suit. From the relator's perspective, so far so good. The real question for the judge then becomes a relatively simple question of law: were the Ponca wrongfully arrested?

Once he enters into a discussion of the suit's central issue, however, Dundy's opinion becomes somewhat muddled. Despite his claim that the Indians' legal status (as citizens or foreigners) was a non-issue, in explaining his decision regarding the law in this case, Judge Dundy returns to the issue of Standing Bear's band's alleged abandonment of tribal identity. Directly posing the question of "whether or not an Indian can withdraw from his tribe [. . .] for the purpose of making an independent living and adopting our civilization," the judge defends the inviolable and God-given "right of expatriation, "a central principle in American constitutionalism since the revolutionary era. In this sense, his opinion seems intended to buttress the assimilationist ideology of Indian law as a whole—its imperative that Indians give up tribal selfhood in favor of an individualistic model. Having made that point, Dundy goes on to address the question of the legality of detaining the Ponca. Here he defends the paternal authority of the government to protect Indians on reservations from violators of law (both whites and Indians) whose actions jeopardize their peace and welfare. He insists, however, that due process was not followed in detaining the Ponca without charging them with such violations and suggests that his review of extent treaties and statutes provides no basis for any such charges. In conclusion, the judge recognizes the right to habeas corpus held by the Ponca as persons, deems their arrest unlawful, and orders them freed. Significantly, though, the decision leaves open the possibility that statutes or treaties that could justify actions like Crook's *might* come into being. In this sense, it does little to protect Indian tribal sovereignty or rights. In the end, the only legal principle which appears inviolable (besides the right to sue on the writ of habeas corpus in the first place) is the right of assimilation—the right to give up being an Indian in order to become a liberal subject and U.S. citizen.

In spite of Judge Dundy's position on habeas corpus, many saw his decision as evidence that the Indians' fundamental lack of legal status would continue to lead to rampant injustice perpetrated against them. In this way, the real impact of the court's opinion was to provide the kind of strong legal imperative and argument for the establishment of an administrative regime to administer the "sundering" of tribal bonds and the incorporation of individual Indians into the body politic of the United States. The year 1879, then, saw the real beginning of the national Indian reform movement that would provide much of the impetus and political clout needed to establish a far-reaching, modern, and bureaucratized BIA.[3] *Standing Bear v. Crook* made the paternalistic goal of forced assimilation (all for the laudable purpose of protecting Indian rights) a national priority and a humanitarian cause. Two influential books dealing with the plight of the Indian, Helen Hunt Jackson's *A Century of Dishonor* (1881) and former Indian commissioner George W. Monypenny's *Our Indian Wards* (1880), were published and widely read soon after the case was decided. The sentiments contained in such works also found active expression in the formation of a number of reform organizations. After the Ponca story broke nationwide, Mary L. Bonny of Pennsylvania began organizing Christian women in support of Indian reform; her efforts culminated in a petition to Congress in 1880, signed by 13,000 people, and eventually in the formation of the Women's National Indian Association in 1883. Other influential organizations formed at this time as well. In 1882, Herbert Welsh, later a friend and supporter of Eastman, founded the Indian Rights Association, with the stated goals of helping Indians attain civil rights and citizenship and bringing U.S. law to the reservations. In 1883 the Lake Mohonk Conference of the Friends of the Indian began meeting in New York. This annual event (and organization), which Elaine Goodale Eastman attended long before she met her husband, was also primarily concerned with Indian citizenship and suffrage, though there was much disagreement on the proper pace of the acculturation process. From 1879 onward, then, organizations like these were in the vanguard of U.S. Indian policy.[4]

Generally speaking, a broad consensus existed both within the Indian reform movement and federal policy circles that the basis for Indian rights lay in rights of property, especially real property. In this respect, driven by an act of legal engagement on the part of the Ponca, white philanthropists in the late nineteenth century came to conclusions much like those that William Apess had drawn more than a generation earlier. Consequently, from 1879 until 1887 (when the General Allotment Act was finally passed) a series of far-reaching allotment measures, designed to make individual property owners out of Indians, began making their way to Congress. *Standing Bear v. Crook* generated the ideological foundation for a new era of U.S. Indian law, centered on two related ideas: (1) the sense that Indians' rights needed more explicit legal definition, and (2) the belief that such rights should be understood as essentially individual property rights. Together, these notions undergirded the emergent policy of assimilation through allotment. That this policy turned on the familiar identity model of the "Indian-as-child," however, ensured the perpetuation of legal paternalism in the supervisory bureaucracy that would oversee the assimilation process. Thus, *Standing Bear v. Crook* and the national reform movement it engendered spurred the creation of a more powerful, paternalistic discourse of Indian law, with a series of significant legal events during the 1880s advancing the process. These included the creation of the Court of Indian Offenses (1883), the appellate decision in *Ex Parte Crow Dog* (1883), the passage of the Major Crimes Act (1885), the Supreme Court's decision in *U.S. v. Kagama* (1886), and finally the passage of the General Allotment Act, or Dawes Act (1887).

In one form or another, the first four of the events listed above involved the expansion and empowerment of the BIA bureaucratic machine that would be responsible for imprinting the normative model of identity behind the Dawes Act directly onto reservation Indians. In 1883, the BIA sought to increase the power of reservation agents to force assimilation by creating special courts to regulate Indian cultural practices. In practice, the courts served as a means of extending BIA administrative law over Indians and increased factionalization between "progressive" and "traditional" groups. As with the prior formation of the Indian Police in 1879, no statutory or constitutional basis existed for this new model of institutional authority. A manifestation of the new move toward institutionalization and bureaucratic power, the courts were created by administrative order from the secretary of the interior, Henry M. Teller. Arguing that "many of the agencies are without law of any kind," Teller saw the Courts of Indian Offenses as a tool to destroy tribal law and customs in order to accelerate the assimilation process. In his view, traditional practices carried out by "a few non-progressive, degraded Indians" provided the means "to exhibit before the young and susceptible children all the debauchery, diabolism, and savagery of the worst state of the Indian race." Consequently, Teller authorized reservation agents to define offenses that a tribunal, composed of three "progressive" Indians chosen by the agent, would punish. All this would serve as a means of "bringing the Indians under the civilizing influence of law" (qtd. in Prucha, *Documents* 160).[5] Though the courts were not always effective (indicating tribal resistance), the establishment of these arms of administrative law was a key link in the chain of events during the 1880s whereby an increasingly potent BIA bureaucracy took greater and greater control over the lives of Indian subjects.

In the same year the courts were formed, another high-profile legal case, this time involving the murder of a "progressive" Sioux, Spotted Tail, by another reservation Indian, Crow Dog, provided additional momentum for increased bureaucratic control over western Indians. On the surface, *Ex Parte Crow Dog* appeared to be a vindication of Indian sovereignty rights; in the case, the plaintiff, Crow Dog, who had been sentenced to hang by the district court of Dakota for the murder of Spotted Tail, was granted a writ of habeas corpus by the Supreme Court, which deemed that the district court lacked jurisdiction. *Crow Dog* had been cultivated as a test case by the BIA, though, as a means of extending its administrative and legal control over reservation Indians. As with Dundy's decision in *Standing Bear v. Crook,* the Supreme Court's decision made it clear that any direct legislative attempt to bring Indians under the rule of law would probably meet with a sympathetic judiciary. Though the court saw no extant legal basis for placing Crow Dog's offense under federal authority, the opinion characterized the crime in question as a case of "red man's revenge" and an example of primitive law, which to civilized whites was really a form of lawlessness. No attempt was made to understand the nature of the Native American legal forms underlying the events in question.[6]

The Indian agents and other advocates of bureaucratic control of the Indian took notice of the Court's language in *Crow Dog*. After the decision had been rendered, the BIA was joined by the Indian Rights Association in calling for an extension of federal jurisdiction over serious crimes committed on reservations. An IRA pamphlet, "The Indian Before the Law" (1883), advanced the paternalistic logic that Indians needed to be protected (from themselves, in part) and held responsible under U.S. law in order to prepare them for eventual citizenship. The furor over *Crow Dog*, then, quickly overshadowed the limited legal victory enjoyed by Indians in the case. The most significant result of the case was not therefore Crow Dog's release, but rather the subsequent passage of the Major Crimes Act of 1885, whereby Congress made seven crimes committed by Indians (murder, manslaughter, rape, assault with intent to kill, arson, burglary, and larceny) federal matters.[7] This was a major encroachment of the tribal sovereignty seemingly upheld just four years earlier. *United States v. Kagama*, the test case for the Major Crimes Act, dealt with a murder case on the Hoopa Valley Indian Reservation in northern California. In its decision on the case, the Supreme Court upheld the law, offering up in the process the first statement of the so-called "plenary power doctrine," the final key plank in the development of late-nineteenth-century legal paternalism. *United States v. Kagama* did not overturn *Ex Parte Crow Dog*; it allowed for the existence of Indian sovereignty. However, the Court argued that such sovereignty only exists where Congress has not acted to limit it. The "plenary power doctrine" held (and still holds) that congressional authority and power over Indian affairs was, finally, unlimited by treaty rights of tribal sovereignty. The Court's decision here, then, provided absolute legal sanction for the policy of forced assimilation that would become a matter of statutory law one year later with the passage of the Dawes Act.

The Dawes Act marked the final step in a process of crafting a potent discourse of Indian law centered on paternalistic notions of forced assimilation. As such, this statute serves as the central legal text dealing with Indian identity from its passage in 1887 until the granting of citizenship to Native Americans in 1924 (nominally the end of the allotment/assimilation era). The language of the General Allotment Act made clear, at the outset, that Indians occupied reservation lands upon the sufferance of the government and also that the transition from savagery to civilization would be carefully orchestrated and controlled. The law authorized the president to divide up reservation territory and allot the lands in severalty to Indians as individual landholders "whenever in his opinion any reservation or any part thereof of such Indians is advantageous for agricultural or grazing purposes" (qtd. in Prucha, *Documents* 171).[8] Any "surplus" lands would be sold off to white settlers, a provision that demonstrated the pervasive assumption that part of what kept Indians in a precivilized state was their failure to properly and efficiently use their lands. The allotments were designed to undermine any collective or communal sense of identity among the Indians affected. Lands were granted to (male) heads of families (the precise determination of which would later become an issue for the government), to single adults over eighteen, and to orphans. In this way, the law sought to establish the individual, not the band or tribe, as the dominant political and social unit among the Indians. The language of the law made clear that Indians would be shepherded into their new models of identity, in a manner fitting their status as political wards. The act stipulated that Indians be allowed to choose their allotments wherever possible, but the secretary of the interior (or a special agent) was authorized to make selections for eligible Indians who did not make a selection within four years of the presidential order to allot a particular reservation. Once patents for allotted lands had been issued, the U.S. government would hold said lands in trust for a period of twenty-five years in order to provide sufficient time for the Indians to become self-sufficient and "civilized." After the twenty-five-year tutorial period, title to the land would be granted in fee simple. At this point, finally, the individual Indian would theoretically pass from a state of wardship into full participation in American society. The granting of land title would bring Indian allottees completely under the civil and criminal laws (including taxation) of the state or territory in which they resided, ushering them into full citizenship. The federal government pledged itself to provide the necessary assistance and education to help its wards to make the transition from savage to civilized life.

Commissioner Thomas J. Morgan, who had charge of the BIA during the initial years under the Dawes Act, summed up the assumptions and implications of the allotment policy in this way: "The logic of events demands the absorption of the Indians into our national life, not as Indians, but as American citizens . . . the relations of the Indian to the government must rest solely upon the full recognition of their individuality. Each Indian must be *treated like a man* [my emphasis], be allowed a man's rights and privileges, and be held to the performance of a man's obligations. Each Indian is entitled to his proper share of the inherited wealth of the tribe, and to the protection of the courts in his 'life, liberty, and pursuit of happiness'" (qtd. in Prucha, *Documents* 177). As Morgan and his contemporaries understood it, assimilation based on allotment fully codified the image of the Indian-as-child. At the same time, it reinforced the archetypal possessive individualist model of American citizenship and selfhood. These two models of self were intrinsically linked in the allotment policy of assimilation. In the words of the famous Indian educator and founder of the Carlisle School, Captain Richard H. Pratt, the law aspired to "kill the Indian, and save the man." Thus, the discourse of allotment deployed a complex paternalistic regime of control over "wild" Indians on reservations and sought to regulate and engineer their "growth" into civilized manhood. Not surprisingly, both of these models of Indian subjectivity had a profound impact on the autobiographical writings of Native Americans.

A brief consideration of the work of one of Eastman's near contemporaries, Sarah Winnemucca Hopkins, can help to foreground some of the intense pressures placed on Indian writers by late nineteenth-century colonialism. In some respects, Winnemucca's 1883 autobiography, *Life among the Piutes*, resembles the earlier subgenre of missionary conversion narratives discussed in chapter 3. If the conversion narratives of Indian preachers often served to situate their authors within a church-centered set of colonial institutions, though, Winnemucca's text speaks directly to her difficult position as an interpreter for the U.S. Army during the period of Grant's Peace Policy.[9] As its subtitle (*Their Rights and Claims*) suggests, the dominant theme of this autobiography is the injustices suffered by Winnemucca's Piute people as a result of their vulnerable legal and military position. Often written in a distinctly sentimental style designed to appeal to the emotions and sympathies of middle-class readers, *Life among the Piutes* chronicles discrete incidents of mistreatment of Indians by white settlers as well as larger, "historical" events, such as the Bannock War and the fraudulent relocation of the Piutes to the Yakima reservation in Washington. Throughout her discussion of these incidents, Winnemucca stresses her own difficulties as a mediator between whites and Indians and defends her personal reputation against a variety of accusations. (It is not insignificant that the text concludes with an appendix consisting of a range of testimonials—mostly letters from military officers and employees of the BIA—addressing her character and veracity.) In this respect, much of the emphasis of her autobiographical narrative is on offering an apologia for her work as a paid employee of the U.S. Army, one who nevertheless kept her people's best interests in constant focus. Defending herself from accusations of bribery, Winnemucca states simply that she "never did get anything from the government, or government officials" (222).

In a manner reminiscent of Samson Occom's *Narrative*, though, the ambiguities and difficulties of Winnemucca's cultural position seem to have rendered it difficult for her to write an autobiographical text that simultaneously defended her own job performance and radically challenged the system of U.S. colonialism. This is reflected in the central "metaphor of self," to use James Olney's phrase, in the narrative. The dominant trope in *Life among the Piutes* is that of filiopiety, loyalty to fathers. Offering a somewhat dubious portrait of Piute society as strongly patriarchal (and, interestingly enough, under the leadership of her own family), Winnemucca implicitly buttresses the attempts of the government to elevate individual male chiefs to positions of absolute authority. She thus creates a picture of Piute society that is congruent with the model of Indian politics most desired by the United States. On a more personal level, Winnemucca dramatizes her early sense of the tension between assimilationism and traditionalism in terms of her conflicted loyalties to her grandfather (known by whites as Captain Truckee) and father, Chief Winnemucca. This issue of choosing "fathers" subsequently becomes central to the overall structure of *Life among the Piutes*, carrying over into the book's discussion of Indian policy and reservation life. Winnemucca offers positive testimonials of the military officials for whom she worked (and who, at times, had charge of her people), while offering strong critiques of the Christian agents with whom she had dealings. "Can you wonder, dear readers," she writes, "that I like to have my people taken care of by the army?" (93). In the end, both Winnemucca's strong indictment of the corruption of the Indian bureau and her attacks on the "savagery" of white settlers on the frontier is thus balanced by her strong support of the Indians' "soldier-fathers." This is not to say, of course, that (given her choice) Winnemucca would have wished for military-supervised reservation life instead of the traditional life of the precontact Piutes. It is certainly clear, however, that her sense of the rhetorical possibilities for protest within her autobiography was constrained by harsh political realities. What Winnemucca chose to do in her autobiographical act was to adopt the paternalistic language and model of self that undergirded preallotment Indian policy and to work within that framework to try to argue for the best possible "father-protectors" (i.e., military officers) for her people. She also hoped to obtain financial support for the project to which she devoted the last decade of her life, the creation of residential Indian schools (employing Indian teachers).

The passage of the Dawes Act (which also included a provision requiring Indians to be educated in English-speaking boarding schools) effectively crushed both of these efforts.

As Winnemucca's experience (and also the discussion of Ely S. Parker in chapter 2) suggests, engagement with the colonial institutions of the late nineteenth century was a difficult matter. Both in political and autobiographical terms, it was not easy for Indian mediators to achieve what they wanted (for themselves and for their communities). For this reason, Gretchen Bataille and Kathleen Mullen Sands characterize Winnemucca's text as "heavily biased by her acculturated and Christianized viewpoint" (21). It would be more accurate to say, however, that Winnemucca's particular subject position in the colonial bureaucracy rendered it difficult (as it would be for any writer in her position) to find a voice of protest and a way of rhetoric of Indianness that could withstand the pressures of Indian law. Reading *Life among the Piutes* in this light makes the rhetorical sophistication of Charles Eastman's autobiographical acts seem all the more impressive. For much like William Apess in the early nineteenth century, Eastman worked through the constraints that thwarted his contemporaries to produce texts that engaged the legal discourse of his time in innovative ways. In the remainder of this chapter, I will consider the first stage of that process of engagement—Eastman's initial autobiographical act, *Indian Boyhood*.

In 1893, when Charles Eastman began working on the sketches that would eventually become his first autobiography, *Indian Boyhood*, he had just moved his family from the Pine Ridge Reservation (where he was employed as the agency physician) to St. Paul, Minnesota. The relocation was not wholly voluntary. Conflicts earlier that year with Pine Ridge's military agent over irregularities in remunerations paid to the Wounded Knee massacre survivors had precipitated Eastman's temporary resignation from the Indian bureau.[10] In his first entry into a dispute with the Bureau of Indian Affairs (an agency whose goals he had heretofore supported), Eastman found himself marginalized by erstwhile supporters and frustrated by an inability to protect his brethren from graft and government corruption. At precisely such a moment, having come into direct conflict with the institutional apparatus of federal Indian law, he commenced writing a series of autobiographical sketches, addressed to a predominantly white audience. In all, six articles were serialized in *St. Nicholas: An Illustrated Magazine for Young Folks* between December 1893 and May 1894.[11] These pieces later became incorporated into the text of *Indian Boyhood* when it was published in 1902 (by which time Eastman was again working for the BIA as the agency physician at the Crow Creek Reservation).

Reflecting both his long-standing immersion in the bureaucracy of colonial domination and his desire to act as a cultural mediator between whites and Native Americans, Eastman's *Indian Boyhood* is a complex and intriguing work.[12] Like a number of his contemporaries (writers such as Winnemucca, Zitkala-Sa, Luther Standing Bear, and Francis La Flesche), Eastman set out to interpret Indian culture and identity for the benefit of his (hopefully sympathetic) white readership. Consequently, *Indian Boyhood* contains a great deal of ethnographic material, seemingly intended to suggest the possibility and desirability of assimilating all Native Americans into the cultural and political mainstream of the United States (while implicitly validating the old ways against derogatory accusations of savagery). At the same time, Eastman also frames his work as an autobiography, a sincere attempt to record, organize, and make sense of his own individual memories of the process of becoming "civilized."[13] What is most interesting about *Indian Boyhood* is the complex way these personal and collective narratives intertwine. I would suggest that this blending is notable not merely as evidence of Eastman's literary sophistication, but also as an index of his embeddedness in the colonial institutions of his time. Both the ethnographic and autobiographical aspects of *Indian Boyhood* take shape around a familiar legal model of self: the paternalistic identity model of the Indian-as-child, which buttressed the federal government's allotment policy. But the book's complexity derives from its author's specific engagement with the hegemonic legal discourse of allotment on the western reservations during his adult life. Looking back on his childhood, Eastman produced a text that established him as a national spokesman and authority on Indian affairs, naturalized the process of cultural assimilation, and legitimized the ideology of allotment. In doing so, he also provided subsequent generations of readers with a stark example of the extreme pressures felt by Native American mediator figures during the early decades of the twentieth century.

If most Native Americans at the turn of the century were forced to grapple with the ideological assumptions and institutional power of allotment law, few had as much direct experience with, and understanding of, the colonial bureaucracy as Charles Eastman. Though he spent his first fifteen years living the traditional life of a Santee youth in the woods of Minnesota and on the plains of Western Canada, for most of his adult life Eastman was known to white Americans as one of the best exemplars of the Indian's ability to assimilate into modern society. He came to the public's attention by rapidly progressing through the Indian educational system and subsequently making a career for himself in the Indian service. Eastman attended the Santee Normal School from 1873–76 and later studied at Beloit College, Knox College, Dartmouth College, and Boston University (where he received his medical degree in 1890). While studying in the east, he also established friendships with influential philanthropists committed to the cause of Indian reform. Mr. and Mrs. Frank Wood of Boston, trustees of Wellesley College, extended both personal and financial support to Eastman and arranged for him to present a paid lecture at Wellesley in 1882, which brought him to the attention of a larger community of reformers in the east. Connections like these were instrumental in subsequently securing him various positions in the Indian service, including his first appointment as physician at Pine Ridge. At the same time, they also provided Eastman with a first-rate, albeit informal, legal education. The Woods kept him informed of pending legislation and shifts in Indian policy; he was even consulted about various provisions of the Dawes Act (which he supported) as it worked its way through Congress in 1887.[14] This kind of involvement in legal reform and policy development would continue throughout Eastman's career. In 1911, for example, he was a founding member of the American Indian Association, later called the Society of American Indians (SAI), and he frequently contributed to the society's journal, the *American Indian Magazine*. Between his organizational affiliations, personal ties, and professional involvement in the Indian service, then, Eastman experienced an unusual degree of immersion in the legal discourse of Indianness.[15]

Eastman's views on the allotment policy remained fairly stable throughout his career as a lecturer and public servant; he consistently affirmed the principle of Indian assimilation into the social and political fabric of the United States, and he viewed the allotment policy as a major stepping-stone to full citizenship. Interestingly enough, he also showed a willingness to tolerate, for a time at least, some of the paternalistic elements of U.S. Indian policy, provided that those elements would give way, in time, to individual autonomy and political equality. Perhaps Eastman's most direct and detailed endorsement of the ideology of allotment appears in a 1915 article, "The Indian as Citizen," which appeared in *Lippincott's Magazine*. This essay also provides some interesting insights into his typical rhetorical strategies, strategies that also appear in his autobiographical writings. Eastman opens the piece deferentially, using the passive voice and acknowledging the Indian's need for assistance in the transition to modern life. "After due protest and resistance," he notes, the Indian "is found to be easily governed by civilized law and usages" and "is capable of sustaining a high moral and social standard, when placed under wise guidance" (70). As the essay continues, Eastman presents exemplary accounts of assimilation, such as William Duncan's Christian Indian community of Metlakatla, Alaska, and the Sioux citizen community at Flandreau, South Dakota (where Eastman's father took him at age sixteen). For Eastman, the essential lesson provided by these case studies is the following: "who can say that civilization is beyond the reach of the untutored primitive man *in a single generation?*" [my emphasis] (72). With this as his keynote, then, Eastman uses the rest of his essay to argue in support of the basic mechanisms of the allotment policy (rapid assimilation and cultural change through altered legal and property relations). He notes that the Dawes Act opened the "door to American citizenship," comments approvingly on the fact that more than half of the nation's 330,000 Indians have been allotted lands in fee simple, and criticizes the Burke Bill of 1906 for slowing down the process. Commenting also on his own work in revising the allotment rolls among the Sioux (an issue I will take up again shortly), Eastman places himself firmly in the pro-allotment camp, affirming the notion that after a period of transitional "wardship," Native Americans will blend into the fabric of American society. Indeed, he reflects positively on the fact that the "bands of citizen Sioux with whom I am acquainted, are becoming more and more identified with the general farming population of Nebraska and the Dakotas" (72).

Bearing in mind the details of his biography and such evidence of his philosophical commitments, we should not be surprised that Eastman's initial autobiographical act would evince a broad identification with the ideology behind the allotment policy. Confronted with the discursive power of allotment law and needing to negotiate his way through a complex modern world, Eastman seems to have been committed early in his career to defining himself (indeed, to defining Indianness) in terms of the law's paternalistic model of Indian identity. Assuming the identity model of the Indian-as-child in *Indian Boyhood,* Eastman worked to establish himself as a mediating voice within the colonial legal order by providing his white readers with a reassuringly familiar and acceptable image of the Indian. This emphasis appears from the outset of the book in his adaptation of generic conventions taken from the Euro-American literary tradition. The fact that *Indian Boyhood* is a book about Eastman's own childhood roots draws immediate attention to its author's familiarity with assumptions about identity formation characteristic of modern non-native autobiography. As H. David Brumble III has pointed out, a distinguishing characteristic of precontact Native American autobiographical expression was its lack of interest in early childhood memories. Coup tales (stories of valor), tales of hunting prowess, and accounts of actions that earned the performer a new name might be told, and such tales might indeed delve back into earlier experience.[16] However, childhood itself, as an area of intrinsic interest in dealing with the origins of adult identity, does not emerge as a subject with the same prominence that we see in Western autobiographical discourse (especially since Rousseau). Eastman's initial conception for his autobiographical text thus shows his engagement with conventions familiar to his white readers. In this respect, his work resembles that of a number of other contemporary Native American writers, such as Zitkala-Sa and Francis La Flesche, who were also active both as cross-cultural interpreters and activists on behalf of Native peoples.[17]

Still, *Indian Boyhood* is much more than a generic coming-of-age story. Eastman also frames his account of childhood experience in accordance with the conventions of a particularly popular form of contemporary American writing about childhood—the late nineteenth-century "boy book." When we recall that the chapters of *Indian Boyhood* were initially serialized in a youth magazine, it should probably not surprise us that the text would share certain affinities with popular works like Hamlin Garland's *Boy Life on the Prairie* (1899) or Mark Twain's *Huckleberry Finn* (1884), texts that obliquely invoke Indianness as part of a romanticized atmosphere of youthful adventure. As Marcia Jacobson points out, the American "boy book" of the turn of the century was characterized by its primitivist nostalgia for a life before the restraints and responsibilities of modern (i.e., commercial and industrial) adult life. Jacobson also notes that the image of childhood developed in the literature was deeply influenced by the so-called "recapitulation theory" of psychological development, popularized in America by G. Stanley Hall. According to that theory, the individual's progression from childhood to maturity re-enacts the historical progression of the human race from savagery to civilization.[18] A boy's "natural" inclination to "savagery" (an inclination represented in part by his affinity for outdoor activities like hunting and fishing) thus represents a necessary prelude to his development of a higher moral consciousness and eventual integration into the adult life of modern Western society. It is here that we begin to see how Eastman's engagement with the literary conventions of white America also marks an engagement with its legal ideology vis-à-vis Native Americans. The resemblance between the "boy" of recapitulation psychology and the colonialist fantasy of the "white man's Indian" is deep; both turn on a particularly paternalistic, teleological identification of ontogeny with phylogeny—the common assumption being that individual and cultural development proceed along parallel trajectories. In penning the sketches that would become *Indian Boyhood*, then, Eastman was responding not only to the tradition of boy books, but also to a powerful cultural consensus about the nature of Indian identity.

In a sense, the assumptions behind recapitulation psychology (and Indian law) provided Eastman with a rhetorical blueprint for pursuing his goal of cross-cultural mediation. *Indian Boyhood* presents its readers simultaneously with a story of individual and cultural identity, identifying Eastman's personal experience with the collective experience of his people, the Santee Sioux. Throughout the book, he refers to "Indian children" and "Indians" almost as frequently as to himself in the first person. The opening of the chapter called "Life in the Woods" provides a representative example: "The month of September recalls to every Indian's mind the season of the fall hunt. I remember one such expedition which is typical of many" (183). Of course, following the work of critics like Hertha Wong and Arnold Krupat, we might argue that the association of personal and collective experience in Eastman's autobiographical act represents a gesture toward preserving traditional forms of Native American self-narration, what Wong refers to as "communo-bio-oratory."[19] Such a hypothesis seems questionable, though, when we also consider the kind of narrative structure Eastman imposes on such experiences in the text. If he suggests that his personal story is also a representative one, Eastman's primary intent in doing so does not seem to have been to challenge the dominant Western paradigm of the individual self. Rather, he foregrounds the teleology of allotment law, rooted in the Euro-American emphasis on growing out of boyish "savagery" into a more "mature," civilized form of identity.

One of the first places we see hints of Eastman's privileging of the teleological, assimilationist ideology of the allotment era is the way he positions himself as the narrator of his life story. It is a commonplace among many critics of autobiography (most notably Philippe Lejeune) that a part of what constitutes the genre, on a formal-linguistic level, is the simultaneous temporal separation *and* sense of connection between the autobiographer as author of his or her story and as the subject of that story.[20] This sense of similarity and difference is generated both formally and functionally through the use of verb tense (usually past tense) and the first-person pronoun. In this context, it is interesting that throughout *Indian Boyhood*, even where he is talking about himself (as opposed to "Indian children" generally), Eastman frequently discusses his experiences in the third person. In the opening pages of the book, he actually shifts between two modes of expression, enacting at the pronominal level a fairly radical sundering of the bonds between childhood and adult selves. Relating some of his earliest recollections of childhood, Eastman notes that at birth he "had to bear the humiliating name of 'Hakadah,' meaning the pitiful last" (4). Immediately after making this observation, though, Eastman the narrator begins to refer to Eastman the child as "the babe," or "Hakadah," terms which he uses from that point on at least as frequently as he uses "I." Part of what is going on at a moment like this, of course, is Eastman's attempt to dramatize the fact that he left his birth name (Hakadah) behind when he was later renamed Ohiyesa ("the winner"). Recalling Wong's discussion of naming practices among the Plains tribes as "serial, but non-linear autobiographical acts," we can read such a gesture as evidence of Eastman's debt to traditional identity models.[21] Yet there also seems to be something more drastically disruptive (rather than constitutive) in Eastman's pronominal shifts here, especially when we compare his authorial stance with that taken by Winnemucca (who consistently uses the first-person pronoun in *Life among the Piutes*), or when we take note of other biographical details. Eastman's work in revising the Sioux allotment rolls between 1903 and 1909 provides particularly striking evidence that he appreciated the significance of being renamed as a central element in the assimilation process. During the period immediately after the publication of *Indian Boyhood*, working under the supervision of author and Indian activist Hamlin Garland, he renamed close to 25,000 individual Sioux. Eastman describes this labor in *From the Deep Woods to Civilization*, remarking that his responsibilities included "the revision of the Sioux allotment rolls, including the determination of family groups, and the assignation of surnames when those were lacking." He notes that "originally, the Indians had no family names" leading to "difficulties and complications in the way of land inheritance, hence my unique commission" (182).[22] The claim that the Sioux lack family names is true from a Western legal perspective, but it overlooks the complex ways that Siouan languages define kinship relations on a number of levels.[23] Eastman's willingness to engage in the work of renaming on behalf of the federal government and his characterization of that work in his second autobiography highlight the degree to which his experience had taken him away from the traditions of his youth. In light of such details, the shifting, disjunctive use of pronouns in *Indian Boyhood* seems more suggestive of his rhetorical commitment to allotment-era legal models of assimilation than to enduring traditional notions of serial identity.

The role that third-person point of view plays in suggesting a sense of distance from the Indian past appears even more striking in a chapter called "Hakadah's First Offering." Here, more than anywhere else in the book, Eastman works in a particularly literary (one might even say "fictional") narrative mode. "Hakadah" appears to the reader very much as a character; were one to take this section out of its larger context in the book, it would be impossible to tell that he and Eastman are the same person. In the chapter, the narrator tells the reader that when Hakadah was eight years old, his grandmother insisted that he offer his most prized possession to the Great Mystery as a sacrifice. We are told that the boy realized that this prized possession was his beloved hunting dog, but still committed himself, reluctantly, to the sacrifice. The chapter then shifts to a surprising, speculative digression (clearly outside of the autobiographical mode) where the narrator imagines Hakadah's grandmother nearly relenting in her insistence that the boy sacrifice his beloved pet. (This odd addition to the autobiographical narrative seems addressed primarily to some members of Eastman's middle-class audience, who may have found the entire scene distasteful.) The sacrifice proceeds, though, and the chapter ends with grandmother praying to the Great Mystery to accept the offering and make Hakadah "a warrior and hunter" as great as his father and grandfather (96). At this moment, the narrative collapses beneath a final irony, for the reader knows that Hakadah will become the physician Charles Eastman, and not a great Santee warrior.

Eastman's exclusive use of third-person narration in the chapter reinforces this ironic sense of discontinuity between his present (adult/civilized) and past (childhood/Indian) selves. The tale offers no hint of a consciousness of serial identity, and little even of the nostalgia of a boy book. (Even if we are to read this moment as a celebration of a Siouan ethos of sacrifice, there is something unsettling here.) In the end, the divide only becomes more clear when we recall Eastman's observation earlier in the book that he had been renamed Ohiyesa during an intertribal lacrosse contest *when he was age four,* four years before Hakadah's offering is said to have taken place (32). Even if we bear in mind the initial serialization of the chapters of *Indian Boyhood,* such a narrative discrepancy suggests an unusually large gap between Eastman's adult self-consciousness and childhood self. There are a number of ways to read this inconsistency. One might infer that Eastman's discomfort with the recollection of participating in this sacrificial rite was so great that the vicissitudes of memory entered in and disrupted his sense of chronology. Alternately, one might read this apparent narrative "slip" as an intentional rhetorical strategy, suggestive somehow of the radical discontinuities of Eastman's life. Intentional or accidental, though, the impact of the discrepancy remains the same; it further stresses that "Charles Eastman," the adult autobiographical narrator, and "Hakadah," the child-protagonist of this part of the autobiographical narrative, have fundamentally different identities.

The phenomenon I have been tracing in Eastman's use of narrative technique can best be explained as an attempt to represent, through language, the legal fiction of a rapidly crossable divide between Indian life and civilized life. Eastman's engagement with legal models of identity in *Indian Boyhood* is suggested by much more than pronoun usage alone, though. The dedication appearing opposite the book's title page provides further evidence of his rhetorical engagement with the telos of allotment law. Repeatedly referring to *the* Indian in the past tense, and thus again blending the collective and personal dimension of the book, the dedication invokes dominant legal assumptions about the historical trajectory of Native identity. Noting that the "North American Indian was the highest type of pagan and uncivilized man," Eastman situates his book as a specific kind of *bequest* to his son. Eastman, the father, is looking back both on his own "Indian boyhood" (and on a vanished Indian past) from the perspective of his adult (civilized) life. He leaves his own child a form of written knowledge of the way of life now lost to him, since he [the son] "came too late to behold the drama of savage existence." Eastman's language here echoes the cultural mythology of the vanishing Indian, a mythology that had been explicitly integrated into the body of Indian law in Chief Justice John Marshall's opinion in the 1823 case of *Johnson and Graham's Lessee v. William McIntosh* (as we saw in chapter 1). As a communicative act addressed to his son, then, the dedication to *Indian Boyhood* seems not only to acknowledge the child's natural identification with Indianness, but also to suggest implicitly a historical trajectory to personal and cultural maturation. In framing his autobiographical writing in such a way, Eastman foregrounds the root assumptions inherent in the legal discourse underpinning the reservation system and the allotment policy.

These practices of distancing his present self from his past and suggesting an inevitable and necessary progression beyond Indian boyhood appear in other ways throughout the text, most noticeably in Eastman's manner of rationalizing and demystifying his own experiences of Indian culture. As noted earlier, as a part of his act of self-definition as a civilized Indian, Eastman sets himself up in the book as an interpreter of the Indian to his white audience; he does so, however, with a surprising mix of nostalgia and condescension. Owing to his role as cultural interpreter, Eastman adopts explanation by analogy as one of his dominant rhetorical modes in *Indian Boyhood*. A representative moment finds him describing a midsummer festival by comparing it to a state fair. Admittedly, such

analogical translation need not always involve condescension or the imposition of cultural hierarchies. Indeed, at times it highlights pleasurable
and desirable aspects of Indian culture (for the benefit of his non-Indian
readership). Frequently, though, Eastman's interpretive acts go further
than this, imposing "rational" models upon Indian cultural practices and
either explain away their mystery or dismiss them as superstitious relics.
In a later chapter, for instance, Eastman recounts a visit to a storyteller,
Smoky Day, who utters the following remarkable pronouncement: "Well,
this time I will tell you one of the kind we call myths or fairy stories.
They are about men and women who do wonderful things—things that
ordinary people cannot do at all. Sometimes they are not exactly human
beings, for they partake of the nature of men and beasts, or of men and
gods. I tell you this beforehand, so that you may not ask any questions,
or be puzzled by the inconsistency of the actors in these old stories"
(108). Considering the centrality of stories and storytelling to the social
orders and the worldviews of all Native American peoples (not just the
Santee Sioux), it seems peculiar to read of an elder suggesting that his
stories are mere fairy tales (and to suggest that sacred stories should *not*
be inconsistent and/or provoke critical thought).[24] For Eastman's late
nineteenth-century readers, such a label would have placed these tales
firmly in the realm of the child's bedroom, diminishing their complexity and power. It is particularly striking in this regard that Smoky Day
goes on to tell the "Stone Boy" narrative, one of the most important
myths of Siouan-speaking peoples. Eastman's "translation" here frames
his representation of Santee orality by explaining away its mystery and
its spiritual significance—turning sacred, performative discourse, in effect, into amusing folklore. Such a gesture both increases the sense of
distance between Eastman the author and subject of his autobiography
and indicates his acute awareness of the expectations of his white readers.[25] While he *is* able to preserve something of the culture of his youth
here, then, he does so in a way that does not radically challenge the
dominant discourse of Indianness.

Perhaps the most significant example of this pattern of pseudo-scien-
tific distancing from traditional Indian life appears in a late chapter, "The
End of the Bear Dance." There Eastman deals with a traditional healing
ritual—a telling choice of subject, considering his subsequent medical
training and employment by the BIA as a physician (a functionary seen
by the Indian bureau as a key figure in the cultural war against traditionalists on the reservations).[26] He begins by noting that "it was one of the
superstitions of the Santee Sioux to treat disease from the standpoint of
some animal or inanimate thing" (145). As a whole, the chapter centers

on his recollection of a sick friend, Redhorn, whom Eastman retrospectively diagnoses as having had tuberculosis. According to Eastman, Redhorn placed excessive faith in his grandmother, who falsely pretended to be a great "medicine woman" when in fact she merely "conjured" the sick. Eastman characterizes the healing arts taught him by his own beloved grandmother as a form of herbalism; he sets her natural science (the knowledge of the medicinal properties of plants) against Redhorn's grandmother's superstition. The chapter goes on to describe Redhorn's insistence on giving a bear dance to cure himself (at his grandmother's urging). Providing only limited details of the proceedings, Eastman's main purpose seems to be to debunk the ritual. When one of the participants falls down, Eastman recalls, the people felt sure that this was a bad omen. Confirming their suspicions, both Redhorn and the man who fell during the ritual later perished. Eastman gives no clinical explanation for the death of the second, but he does close the chapter noting that "to the people, another Indian superstition had been verified" (152). This phrasing implies that the educated Charles Eastman does not accept the pseudo-science of this native practice. His reluctance to offer a detailed discussion of the ritual and insistence on criticizing Native culture only add to the sense that this facet of Indianness is a form of childishness that *Dr.* Charles Eastman has left behind.

Interestingly enough, a passage like the bear dance chapter, where Eastman seems to be playing the role of amateur anthropologist, demonstrates with particular clarity the dominant influence of legal ideology (as opposed to other discursive frameworks) on *Indian Boyhood*. Following H. David Brumble's insights in *American Indian Autobiography*, one might first be inclined to read Eastman's interpretation of the bear dance as evidence that evolutionary anthropology—and not law—provided the primary ideological framework for the autobiography.[27] Indeed, most readers would acknowledge that the book's thematic organization (with chapters like "Games and Sports," "An Indian Sugar Camp," and "A Midsummer Night's Feast") does give it a somewhat ethnographic feel. Nevertheless, the teleological elements we have been observing in the autobiography mark it as more directly engaged with legal, rather than anthropological, discourse. While Lewis Henry Morgan's evolutionary model of primitive cultures (appearing in his 1851 work *Ancient Society* as well as in his 1871 book *Systems of Consanguinity and Affinity*) placed the Indian at a point of development well beneath (and historically behind) that of the civilized white man, evolutionary anthropology did not accept the possibility of rapid or forced cultural change.[28] According to Morgan's classificatory scheme, generations would be required to move the Indian from the state of savage barbarism to that of civilization, and such movement would derive more from internal pressures (or miscegenation) than external coercion. Consequently, federal policies of forced assimilation (like allotment) were rejected by many evolutionary anthropologists (including Morgan) as being foolishly utopian and unscientific. The notion of an abrupt transition between cultural stages, then, is more properly a legal one—rooted in the contractarian legal fiction regarding the progression from the state of nature to civil society. To the extent that it documents, both in terms of narrative structure and content, its author's transition from his traditional culture to modernity in the span of a few years, then, *Indian Boyhood* embraces a *legal* discourse of the Indian-as-child. The root assumptions behind Eastman's narrative posture in "The End of the Bear Dance" have a closer resemblance to Locke's *Second Treatise of Government* or a BIA policy document than to Morgan's ethnographic work.

If Eastman's emphasis on the Indian's capacity for rapid cultural development is rooted in legal discourse, legal engagement also explains his intimation that such development should be encouraged. In another broad appeal to allotment-era thinking, Eastman provides his readers with subtle suggestions about the desirability of using external pressure to forcefully accelerate progression in a section titled "Early Hardships." There he discusses various sufferings he endured while living on the plains in the 1860s and offers the following summary remarks on the Indian's way of life: "Such was the Indian's wild life! When game was to be had and the sun shone they easily forgot the bitter experiences of the winter before. Little preparation was made for the future. They are the children of Nature, and occasionally she whips them with the lashes of experience, yet they are forgetful and careless. Much of their suffering might have been prevented by a little calculation" (15). Eastman's characterization of his people as thoughtless children provides yet another example of the dissociative mode operative throughout his text. The use of the impersonal "they" in presenting this personal memory adds to the sense of distance, but the elision between past and present tense is also interesting ("they *are* the children of Nature.") With such a gesture, he moves subtly from an autobiographical statement about the suffering he and his own band of Santee Sioux experienced during the 1860s to a broader generalization about present-day reservation Indians. The wild nature of the Indian, the passage argues, is tied to a kind of cultural inefficiency and to a deficient memory, precisely the assumptions buttressing the legal discourse of allotment. The text implies that, in much the same way nature had sought to discipline her children when they roamed the plains, the austere measures of the law of assimilation would be justifiable on the reservations to prepare Indians to integrate into the modern economic order. As Indian Commissioner Thomas J. Morgan had stated in his 1889 report to Congress, "He [the Indian] is not entitled to be supported in idleness" (qtd. in Prucha, *Documents* 177). Eastman's comment about the efficacy of a little "calculation," especially coming in the context of a discussion of the unreliability of game as a food source, reads like a subtle endorsement of the allotment policy's project of aggressively transforming Indians into landholders and farmers.

Not surprisingly, having addressed the need to induce Indian traditionalists to adopt the white man's approach to economic self-sufficiency, Eastman also takes up the issue of means. He does so through a wide-ranging discussion of education that, once again, demonstrates his deep engagement with the legal ideology of his time. The importance of having a national system of Indian education to supplement the allotment policy of forced assimilation had been articulated by the Lake Mohonk Conference (to which Eastman was connected through friendship with philanthropists like the Woods) as early as their second annual meeting in 1884.[29] Indian education, as the attendees of the conference saw it, required industrial, educational (especially language-related), and moral/religious components. Commissioner Morgan's report to the gathering a few years later (in 1889) indicates how thoroughly this educational theory was integrated into the legal discourse of allotment. The government-sponsored system of Indian education over which he presided was theoretically intended to support the property-distribution component of the allotment policy in bridging the gap between savage and civilized life. Morgan noted that the education of the Indian involved a "comprehensive system of training and instruction which will convert them into American citizens" (qtd. in Prucha, *Documents* 178). The system he discussed was to be universal, completely systematized, and, if necessary, compulsory. Its curriculum would stress both industrial training and "that general literary culture which the experience of the white race has shown to be the very essence of education" (179). English language instruction was paramount. As for the overall intent of the system, Morgan was quite explicit: "That which is fundamental in all this is the recognition of the complete manhood of the Indians, their individuality, their right to be recognized as citizens of the United States, with the same rights and privileges which we accord to any other class of people . . . Education should seek the disintegration of the tribes, and not their segregation. They should be educated, not as Indians, but as Americans" (179–80). Adulthood (gendered male), individuality, citizenship, and rights all emerge as linked, overlapping categories here. As a whole, Morgan's point that education could and should usher Indians into a kind of civic manhood resonates with the legal ideology of the wild Indian-as-child. At the same time, it holds out the promise that such education could lead to the end of legal domination, an idea that held great appeal for educated Indian elites like Eastman.

By the time *Indian Boyhood* was published in 1902, Eastman's familiarity with the theoretical and practical aspects of the Indian education system had been broadened well beyond his experiences from his days as a student. His wife and collaborator, Elaine Goodale Eastman, had worked as the superintendent of day schools at Pine Ridge and continued to be actively involved in Indian education. Beyond this, during 1899 and 1900, Eastman worked as the "outing agent" for Captain (later Colonel) Richard Henry Pratt's famous Carlisle Indian School, coordinating a program whereby Indian students lived with white families for a time to further their assimilation into civilized ways. His treatment of the theme of education in *Indian Boyhood* thus reflects an increasingly keen sense of the relationship between education and assimilation during the allotment era. In a chapter called "The Boy Hunter," he opens with the following reflection: "It will be no exaggeration to say that the life of the Indian hunter was a life of fascination. From the moment he lost sight of his rude home in the midst of the Forest, his untutored mind lost itself in the myriad beauties and forces of nature" (73). The link made between Indian, hunter, and child duplicates key assumptions about Native identity underpinning late-nineteenth-century Indian law. Framing his discussion of his own childhood experiences as a hunter in such terms, Eastman again places a gap between that past self and his current incarnation as civilized physician, a gap mediated by a legal discourse defining the passage from the state of nature to civil society. The Indian's "natural" state, at the same time, is interpreted broadly through the lens of Lockean sensationalism, which had, as we have seen, provided the philosophical foundation for assimilationist policies of educational conditioning since the Revolutionary War. The passage characterizes the childlike Indian as one who remains caught in passive responsiveness to sense impressions (as soon as he enters the forest he is "fascinated" and loses himself in the immediacy of nature), having failed to progress to the more mature mode of active reflection. Though there is a mild sort of romantic appeal regarding some form of immediate experience, Eastman's use of terms suggests the importance of being "tutored," (a key word, taken up from Alexander Pope, used frequently in the history of missionary education among Native peoples). The idyll must come to an end and, thus, some form of education would seem to be in order to help the "untutored mind."

Eastman addresses the link between education and assimilation even more directly in a chapter called "An Indian Boy's Training." He opens that chapter again acting as cross-cultural interpreter, with a pointed statement that Indian custom was indeed a form of systematic education. Through these traditional practices, young Ohiyesa learns about his people's cosmology and his immediate family and kinship groups. Here Eastman evinces a more appreciative sense of his past than in the sections dealing with traditional healing practices, but his point is not only to present precontact Indian culture to his readers in a positive light. He also stresses the Indians' capacity both to learn and change in order to challenge the notion of an essential, static Indian self. Eastman notes, "It seems to be a popular idea that all the characteristic skill of the Indian is instinctive and hereditary. This is a mistake. *All the stoicism and patience of the Indian are acquired traits,* and continual practice alone makes him master of the art of woodcraft" [my emphasis] (43). If all "Indian" characteristics are learned, though, a key implication of this comment, in the overall context of this book, is that they could be unlearned, and that "civilized" practices could come to replace them. From such a perspective, the issue of identity formation becomes one of evaluating and internalizing models and ways of life. Eastman's emphasis on the adaptability of the Indian reassures his white readers about the potential for assimilation. It may also suggest something about his own attempt to rethink what Indianness might mean in a postcontact environment.

In light of Eastman's quasi-Lockean comments about education, it is striking to note how much of *Indian Boyhood* suggests the value of impressing onto the Indian-child the models of self encoded in the white man's law. In many respects, the opening lines of the book encapsulate the overall thrust of the narrative, building on dissociative language to invoke the assimilationist assumptions that Indians can, and should, change their identity. Here again, the conventions of the boy book provide Eastman with his starting point: "What boy would not be an Indian for a while when he thinks of the freest life in the world? This life was mine. Every day there was a real hunt. There was real game. Occasionally there was a medicine dance away off in the woods where no one would disturb us, in which the boys impersonated their elders, Brave Bull, Standing Elk, High Hawk, and Medicine Bear, and the rest. They painted and imitated their fathers and grandfathers to the minutest detail, and accurately too, because they had seen the real thing all of their lives" (3).

Linking the Indian way of life with boyish pleasure, Eastman reiterates that Native American identity is a stage in the progression from childhood to adulthood (the phrase "for a while" looms large). While doing so, he also stresses the importance of the universal, childish affinity for acting and role-playing in the process of identity formation. Describing his recollection of Indian boys "impersonating" their elders, Eastman suggests that, as with any child, his process of becoming fully a part of his culture involved a kind of mimicry of others. If an Indian boy like himself grew into an Indian man primarily by "impersonation," the door is likewise opened for such a boy to assume new masks once exposed to other models of self. There is a bit of the primitivism of the "boy book" at work here, of course; Eastman appeals to his white audience by painting Indian life as a sort of pleasurable idyll for a civilized child.[30] At the same time, though, his representation of the Indian's playful capacity for learning counters any tendency toward essentialist arguments about the "nature" of the Indian, arguments that could be used to consign Native peoples to inevitable extinction.

In this context, it is instructive to juxtapose a pair of related observations that Eastman makes elsewhere in the book. He notes both that "The Indian Youth was a born hunter" and that "Indians are born imitators" (73, 59). The first comment, taken from the section cited earlier where Eastman describes the "fascination" nature held for Indians, stresses how an Indian boy's birth initially ties his identity to a specific anterior stage of cultural development—the state of nature predating contractarian society. The second statement works in a slightly different register. It relates more directly to Eastman's assumptions about education and acculturation, reinforcing the environmentalist idea that an Indian's identity, like that of any child, is a function of imitation and modeling, not essence. Overall, *Indian Boyhood* presents an image of the Native American (especially the young) as extraordinarily malleable and impressionable (in the Lockean sense). Thus, while Eastman's recollections of the many ways in which figures like his grandmother Uncheedah, his Uncle Mysterious Medicine, and the storyteller Smoky Day impressed upon him a sense of self can (and should) be read as positive treatments of Native life, they also cut in another direction, suggesting both the past-tense nature of traditional Indian culture and the ability of Indians to rapidly learn new ways of living. It is instructive that as evidence of his skill as a child "mimic," Eastman describes not only playing "medicine dance," but also "white man" (59). "We painted two or three of our number with white clay," he recalls, but also notes that he and his playmates quickly focused on imitating the commercial practices of the "white shirts." He informs the readers that the "merchandise consisted of sand for sugar, wild beans for coffee, dried leaves for tea, pulverized earth for gun-powder, pebbles for bullets and clear water for 'spirit water.' We traded for these goods with skins of squirrels, rabbits, and small birds" (60). Equally able to learn the ways of modern and traditional life, Eastman's Indian boy emerges from such scenes as a paragon of adaptability. To be "Indian" is to be able to change.

In the end, what may prove most striking about *Indian Boyhood* to modern readers is that Eastman offers little apparent challenge to the dominant colonialist discourse of his time. Yet his engagement with the legal model of the Indian-as-child in the text is understandable, both in terms of his unusual biography and the pressures of his position as a cultural mediator. If Eastman gives his readers back a reassuring portrait of the white man's Indian, he does so in part because that was the public life he had come to lead. Educated in white schools, married (happily for a time) to a patrician reformer from New England, and praised as an example of the Indian's capacity for achievement, Eastman defined himself using the rhetoric of allotment-era legal discourse, at least in the early years of his career. Writing an autobiography dominated by the legal model of the Indian provided him with a way of reinforcing this public persona. At the same time, Eastman seems to have recognized the limits of white charity and benevolence and thus to have seen the need to establish himself as a national voice if he hoped to be an effective advocate for Indian interests. Having learned firsthand the difficulties faced by even an "exemplary" Indian in directly and aggressively challenging the Indian bureaucracy, Eastman divined the importance of making the right kind of appeal to white America. For a Native American leader at the turn of the century, engagement often meant assuming one's status as a "ward," or cultural child, who desired the support needed for a successful transition into modern life.

Still, in offering white readers an image of Indian life congruent with their understanding of childhood, Eastman may not simply have been capitulating to colonial power. To the extent he was able to bring a picture of America's Indian "children" into the public consciousness, Eastman was possibly trying to tap into legal structures beyond the discourse of allotment. By the late nineteenth century, discussions of the responsibilities of the government to its Indian wards could sound at times remarkably like the changing discourse of custody law. At that time, the custodial powers of parents began to be seen not as simply a form of property right inviolably vested in a biological father, but rather as a kind of trust linked to his responsibility as a guardian. Family law in the nineteenth century thus opened up a greater degree of judicial discretion, as "fatherhood" in particular was redefined as a transferable form of trusteeship, regulated under law. Native Americans occupied, not surprisingly, a sort of ambiguous middle ground in this legal landscape. On the one hand, the government's restrictions of Indian sovereignty seemed an embodiment of earlier notions of absolute paternal authority over, and "ownership" of, the child. At the same time, the legal culture's emphasis on parental authority as a form of trusteeship subject to public oversight (a view similar to that taken by benevolent eastern reformers with regards to Indian policy) theoretically circumscribed such authority under the rubric of the "best interests of the child."[31] Even as other legal avenues were closing for Native Americans, this broad shift in thinking about the legal status of children opened up the possibility that the courts (and the court of public opinion) might be used as venues for making claims. Admittedly, Native Americans won few legal battles during this period. Nevertheless, many members of the national intellectual elite, like Eastman, believed that the struggles of the foreseeable future would be legal ones where Native peoples would have little opportunity to *demand* rights or restitution.[32] Calling for equitable trusteeship became, for some, the most viable form of resistance. In this respect, being "Indian for a while" provided Eastman with the rhetorical and political foundation to make appeals to white America.

The nature of these appeals would change, of course, as Eastman's career as a writer and activist continued. This highlights the final point I would like to make regarding Eastman's initial autobiographical act. In foregrounding the idea that Indian identity was in a process of change (owing to the historical pressures of colonialism), Eastman's autobiography reveals his own struggle to redefine himself in dialogue with the American vision of modernity. In time, it became clear to him that the paternalistic shield of allotment could not protect Indian peoples from colonial domination and exploitation. Much like Apess before him (confronting the limitations of the discourse of conversion), Eastman would be forced to re-evaluate his rhetorical strategies and definition of Indian identity. Though he never rejected his basic commitment to engagement with the legal discourse of the United States, in the latter stages of his career Eastman sought to change the terms of that engagement, in subtle but significant ways. To see that process, however, we must turn to his second autobiography, *From the Deep Woods to Civilization,* which I will take up in the next chapter. There we can consider Eastman's rhetorical turn away from his Indian "boyhood" and toward the "rights of character."

6 Charles Eastman and the Rights of Character

Speaking of Charles Eastman and his literary contemporaries, Robert Allen Warrior has noted that "this generation was the integrationist legacy of post–Wounded Knee existence" (*Tribal* 7). Confronted with the prospect of "total dispossession," Warrior argues, "these figures believed strongly in . . . abandonment of Native traditional government structures and full participation in mainstream U.S. life" (7). Read against such a background, Eastman's writings become "highly sentimental accounts of his childhood in which he portrays Natives as needy for, worthy of, and ready for inclusion in mainstream civilization" (8). Reflecting his own commitment to the diversification of Indian intellectual history, of course, Warrior refuses to condemn Eastman for his rhetorical position. "Simply to label [Eastman and his contemporaries] misguided, brainwashed, self-hating collaborators," he notes, "misses the point" (8). Still, Warrior maintains, there are "perturbing implications" in these works, implications he sees in need of consideration. As the preceding chapter should indicate, I agree with Warrior's general assessment of the condescension and antagonism toward Native "traditionalism" found in some of Eastman's work; the previous discussion of *Indian Boyhood* focused on such moments in great detail. Yet it is also important, I would suggest, to look more closely at the full arc of Eastman's career before concluding that his was *always* a fundamentally sentimental and paternalistic rhetoric. Indeed, when we look closely at his ongoing autobiographical engagement with the discourse of Indian law, we may see a more sophisticated position emerging underneath the often "perturbing" textual surface.

Throughout his adult life, Eastman's ongoing engagement with the institutions of colonialism had a major influence on the shape of his autobiographical career. After the publication of *Indian Boyhood*, Eastman initially continued to support the General Allotment Act and became increasingly active in various Indian reform organizations (such as the SAI, which he helped found in 1911). He also devoted much energy to lecturing and writing on behalf of a range of reformist causes (including the push to grant Indians full citizenship, which culminated in 1924). Nevertheless, by the time *From the Deep Woods to Civilization* was published in 1916, Eastman had witnessed and experienced several major disappointments through his contact with the discursive system of allotment. Not surprisingly, then, his second autobiographical performance demonstrates both the persistent influence of legal models of identity found in *Indian Boyhood* and some important shifts in his rhetoric of self-definition. The autobiographical act in *From the Deep Woods to Civilization* moves past the acceptance of paternalistic models into a more assertive and innovative form of rights consciousness—one that foreshadows ideas appearing in the works of many Indian writers later in the twentieth century. The book's narrative structure reflects such a shift, breaking down into two fairly distinct components. For roughly the first two-thirds of the text, Eastman continues the theme of progress to civilization that dominated *Indian Boyhood*. In this portion of the autobiography, he maintains a language of self-definition more or less consistent with the discourse of allotment. In its concluding sections, though, *From the Deep Woods to Civilization* develops a different rhetoric of Indianness, one centered around Eastman's growing disillusionment with the ability of the Indian bureaucracy to protect and advocate for its wards. This second dimension involves a transformation, not merely an internalization, of many of the ideological assumptions of allotment-era Indian law. Significantly, owing to his considerable involvement in the formation of national Indian policy, this evolution in Eastman the autobiographer is also connected in a larger sense to his role in changing the legal status of Native Americans in the United States. Again, as with Apess, we see in Eastman a figure endeavoring to combine autobiographical engagement with new forms of political action.

The basic model of identity that dominates *Indian Boyhood* re-emerges in the early chapters of *From the Deep Woods to Civilization*, though the latter book uses a slightly different rhetorical mode. As noted earlier, *Indian Boyhood* manifested the assumption that Indianness is a form of childhood *both on a formal linguistic level and in terms of content,* thus creating a kind of autobiography of dissociation. *From the Deep Woods to Civilization* functions differently as an autobiographical act. No longer representing a civilized Indian looking back on his "wild" past, this book instead primarily presents a civilized Indian looking at his past *civilized* life. Owing at least in part to this greater sense of affinity between the narrator and the self as character, the later book looks more like a traditional Western autobiography, structured chronologically and lacking (with only one brief exception) the kind of third-person distancing we saw before. Building on this conventional narrative structure, the first section of the text stresses the integration of Eastman's self into civilized life in a way that belies the real trauma involved in such a shift. His father, Many Lightnings, serves as the crucial figure in this portion of the text and enables such an orientation.

Similar to his role at the end of *Indian Boyhood,* throughout the early chapters of *Deep Woods,* Many Lightnings symbolically naturalizes the assimilationist assumptions informing allotment-era law and policy. The text records how, shortly after their arrival at the citizen-Indian settlement at Flandreau, South Dakota, he insisted that his son begin school to learn the ways of civilization. Eastman recalls his father's testimony not only of the inevitability but the seeming justification of the ascendancy of the white man's ways. The older man tells him: "Our own life, I will admit, is the best in a world of our own, such as we have enjoyed for ages . . . But here is a race which has learned to weigh and measure everything, time and labor and the results of labor, and has learned to accumulate and preserve both wealth and the records of experience for future generations. [. . .] It is true that they have subdued and taught many peoples, and our own must eventually bow to this law; the sooner we accept their mode of life and follow their teaching, the better it will be for all of us. I have thought much on this matter and such is my conclusion" (8). Difficult though the initial adjustment to school proves for young Ohiyesa, his father's personal example and authority prove decisive for him.[1] Yet it is not only his declaration of the need to pursue civilization that makes Many Lightnings a central, authoritative figure. The manner and context in which such claims are made are also subtly suggestive of his role in the book. As a paternal figure speaking on behalf of the white man's ways, Many Lightnings seems to exceed the authority that would normally accrue to him under Santee kinship structures. Eastman suggests as much when he discusses the conflict between his father and grandmother over his education. Recalling his own evolving "desire" to "follow the new trail to the end" and remarking on his father's remarkably "deep and sound conceptions of a true civilization," Eastman comments on his grandmother Uncheedah's contrasting sense of their new life. Having accompanied her son and grandson back to Flandreau, she makes clear her disdain for civilization, calling it a "sham" and a "made-up life" (27–28). Eastman rejects her authority, though, observing: "Ah Grandmother! you had forgotten one of the first principles of your own teaching, namely: 'When you see a new trail, or a footprint that you don't know, follow it to the point of knowing.'" Eastman's characterization of his grandmother's resistance to the white man's ways suggests his acceptance of his father's view regarding the need for receptiveness to the new; this position is entirely consistent with the manner in which Indian identity is presented in *Indian Boyhood* (and, to a lesser degree, in Winnemucca's *Life among the Piutes*). If his father's example is any indication, Eastman intimates, following the civilized path to the "point of knowing" will lead to a sense of its inevitability and appropriateness for a new age.

By placing his father's example and teachings against those of his grandmother (the dominant influence throughout his Indian boyhood), Eastman demonstrates the influence of colonial contact on his understanding of family and authority in another way. He implicitly undercuts the traditional kinship structures that grounded his precontact Santee life.[2] Many Lightnings's overt conflict with Uncheedah also represents a breakdown of the system of deference that we would expect in traditional Sioux culture; it suggests a patriarchal model of familial authority, emphasizing the absolute dominance of the male head of household. This is precisely the model recognized by "civilized" America at the turn of the century and, significantly, encoded in the very language of the Dawes Act itself (which allotted lands to male heads of families whenever possible). The conflict between father and grandmother thus would seem to represent, on a deeper level, the struggle between traditionalism and assimilation (and their models of identity). As an exemplary, civilized, "citizen Indian," Many Lightnings's assertion of his paternal authority and insistence that the family had "entered upon this life and there is no going back" mark him both as a civilized patriarch and a metonym for the "fatherly" pull of civilization itself. Uncheedah's authority and teachings seem limited and bound up with the world of Ohiyesa's childhood, while Many Lightnings's knowledge and authority speak to Charles Eastman's civilized future. When Ohiyesa subsequently cuts his hair and begins to attend the white man's school, he is obeying not merely a traditional imperative to respect his father, then, but the teleological imperative to embrace civilization. Naturalizing the process of assimilation into civilized life through an image of paternal authority, Eastman shows his continuing engagement with the legal discourse of allotment.

When Eastman subsequently articulates the nature of the civilized life toward which he was moving, we see further evidence of this same process of engagement. In keeping with central assumptions behind allotment-era Indian policy (such as the linkage of "civilization" and "rights" with the idea of real property), Eastman invokes the agrarian freeholding ideal as the embodiment of the appeal of modernity. Recalling his initial journey to Alfred Riggs's famous Santee School in 1873, he notes having observed a farmer hammering a plow into shape on a forge. Eastman identifies with the "manly way in which he handled the iron," noting that "he looked not unlike a successful warrior just returned from the field of battle" (38). Drawing an analogy (a familiar rhetorical strategy for him, as we have seen) between the quintessential legal archetype of the freeholding American citizen (the image of Crèvecoeur's American farmer) and the masculine warrior-ideal typical of Plains tribes, Eastman reinforces the reader's sense of the pull and appeal of civilized life he felt as a young man. Significantly, as he recalls it, experiencing the hospitality of the farmer and observing his way of life marked a turning point for Eastman. He notes that "then and there I loved civilization and renounced my wild life" (38–39). Later, as he completes his journey to Riggs's school he observes the farmhouses spread "as far as the eye can see." They, too, signify "the way of civilization, the basis upon which it rests." Eastman concludes the scene with the simple assertion that he "desired to know that life" (39–40).

Eastman's dramatization of his ongoing engagement with the allotment model of Indianness continues in his subsequent discussion of his formal education. He paints the reader a picture of his natural and willing entry into the kind of individualistic, development-oriented nomos envisioned by Indian policymakers. The religious elements of the Santee school's curriculum receive due attention, of course, but Eastman recalls being particularly fascinated by his introduction to civilized "economy," which he claims he and his fellow Indian students saw as totally reasonable. Based on Eastman's account, Benjamin Franklin's "The Way to Wealth" would seem to have been the secular Bible of Indian education. He writes: "Economy is the able assistant of labor, and the two together produce great results. The systems and methods of business were of great interest to us, especially the adoption of a medium of exchange" (47–48). In stressing the rational appeal of the economy of civilized life, Eastman's autobiography anticipates other autobiographical texts by "modernizing" Indians, most notably Luther

Standing Bear's *My People, the Sioux* (1928). (One of the more intriguing chapters of that work focuses on young Standing Bear's employment at John Wannamaker's Philadelphia department store, a position obtained through the intercession of Richard Henry Pratt of the Carlisle School).[3] At the same time, he aligns himself with the dominant social ethos of the late nineteenth century, where Andrew Carnegie's explicit echoes of Franklin in his *The Gospel of Wealth* (1888) proclaimed the spirit of American capitalism. Building on the twin principles of frugality and a strong work ethic, Eastman suggests that his education introduced him to "the principles of true civilization," central among which seems to have been a consciousness of self as an autonomous liberal individual. He also naturalizes his development of a competitive, individualistic ethos, suggesting that he had always contained the potential for this kind of self. Eastman notes that Riggs "strengthened and developed in me that native strong ambition to win out, by sticking to whatever I might undertake" (48). Overall, Eastman seems to say, within every Indian there is a Franklin waiting to emerge.

As revealed in these early chapters of *From the Deep Woods to Civilization,* the model of civilized identity toward which Eastman was moving represents a combination of self-reliance, individualism, and competitiveness in the service of an ethos of development. He recalls an emerging sense "that I might progress faster where I was not surrounded by my tribesmen," a feeling that led him to leave the reservation school to continue his education at Beloit College in 1876 (58). Alluding to the fusion of classroom and manual learning under the regime of allotment, Eastman suggests that the opportunity to work at farming during that summer added to his understanding of the value of Christian civilization. He writes that he "saw it [civilized life] as the development of every natural resource," an insight that becomes further reinforced later during his journey east to attend Dartmouth College (57). In his account of that trip, Eastman subsequently stresses his "delight" at the proliferation of farms and villages, which denoted for him "the presence of an earnest and persistent people" and the "progress of civilization" (64). Finally, he ties this individualistic ethos of progress and development to a contractual model of labor, recalling with pleasure how during his summer working for wages on a farm "treaties were kept on both sides" (57). In the context of a discussion of his successful engagement with the norms of liberal contractarianism (becoming one capable of alienating his labor for wages), Eastman's allusion to treaties here stands as a subtle testimonial to his continuing commitment to the process of legal engagement, to his willingness to adapt to the nomos of American liberalism. The developing self he presents initially in *From the Deep Woods to Civilization* thus seems to be another exemplary model of what the policy of allotment was intended to achieve. Not surprisingly, then, when he comes to describe the end of his education (his graduation from Boston College in 1890), Eastman expresses his support for the government's "new and permanent plan of educating the young Indians preparatory to admitting them to citizenship" (74).

Yet despite such remarks in the early stages of the text (indicating his general acceptance of the allotment policy's goals), as the book progresses Eastman's broad commitment to legal engagement reveals him beginning to develop a different form of self-consciousness from that seen in *Indian Boyhood*. The first emergence of a more critical language in Eastman's autobiographical writings comes at the end of his account of his formal education. Eastman's discussion there of his entry into government service (along with his comments about the massacre at Wounded Knee in 1890) marks a key turning point in his autobiographical narrative. Admittedly, the muted form this criticism takes attests to his continued rhetorical investment in assimilationist discourse. Initially, Eastman takes care to continue to separate himself from "traditional" Indian cultural practices and to reinforce the idea that the majority of Indians want to do as he had done (move into modernity). He points out that most Indians were not caught up in the ghost dance religion, and even though he expresses understanding for those who were "groping blindly after spiritual relief in their bewilderment and misery," Eastman recalls his belief that "the craze would die out of itself before long" (88). He also writes sympathetically of "friendly" chiefs, like American Horse, who sought to turn Indians from the dance and to avoid bloodshed and conflict. Finally, Eastman makes clear his conviction that in the event of trouble it was his "solemn duty to serve the United States Government" (96). In this way, he continues to carefully identify himself with the colonial bureaucracy and with its goals.

Still, in looking back on the events of 1890 twenty-five years later, Eastman begins to acknowledge that the Indians had many "grievances and causes for discontent." He maintains that the central problem was one of fraud and administrative mismanagement—the failure of the government bureaucracy to adequately provide for its wards. Eastman does not completely reject the basic assumptions of legal paternalism at this stage of his narrative, but he does express concern over the failure of white Americans to live up to their trustee responsibilities on behalf of their Indian children. He goes on to argue that the solution to the problems which led to the massacre could have been found in "humane and conciliatory measures" (99). He suggests further that government mismanagement of its own policies had put barriers in the way of the Indians' natural inclination toward entry into civilized life. In doing so, though, Eastman begins to draw attention to the continued precariousness of the legal rights of Native Americans during the allotment era. This suggest that his years of experience with the BIA between the publication of *Indian Boyhood* and *From the Deep Woods to Civilization* had begun to teach him that the movement to devise institutional mechanisms to protect the nation's Indian-children in the wake of *Standing Bear v. Crook* had not been wholly successful. We begin to sense (along with Eastman the narrator) that a new language for articulating Indian rights (and identity) was needed. Significantly, in the second half of his autobiography Eastman begins to work toward developing such a language.

After the initial hints of discontent with the legal discourse of allotment in his account of the Wounded Knee massacre itself, in his discussion of its aftermath Eastman offers his readers a series of more explicitly critical comments about the BIA. In a chapter called "War with the Politicians" he recalls his legal dispute with Pine Ridge agent Captain George Leroy Brown over the payment of restitutions to survivors. This dispute, we should recall, had immediately preceded his commencement of the sketches for *Indian Boyhood.* No longer content with merely establishing his public voice by assuming the role of model Indian, though, in *From the Deep Woods to Civilization* Eastman begins to address this experience directly. He recalls that in 1891, Congress appropriated $100,000 for reparations to "non-hostile" Indians who had lost property or livestock during the so-called "uprising" at Wounded Knee. Commissioner Morgan, partly on Eastman's own recommendation, placed Special Agent James A. Cooper in charge of distributing the money. Eastman explains that Cooper asked him to be one of three witnesses present at the distribution of the cash payment, but that his busy schedule prevented him from doing so. Subsequently, according to him, numerous Indians began approaching him, claiming that they had not received the proper sums. Rather than reporting the irregularities to Brown, the acting military agent, Eastman wrote to Washington and to others outside of the reservation, precipitating a conflict. Eastman, Brown, and Cooper all gave varying accounts of what had happened both during and after the distributions of the claims. Brown purported to have thoroughly looked into the matter, finding no irregularities and most of the Sioux satisfied. Eastman challenged both the agent's right to conduct the investigation and many of his statements of fact. As a power struggle ensued, influential figures in the Indian policy community took sides—Commissioner

Morgan and Senator Dawes supporting Eastman, Herbert Welsh of the IRA and Theodore Roosevelt supporting Brown. A second independent investigation, which found that $10,000 had gone missing, was tabled by Secretary of the Interior James Noble, and eventually Eastman was removed from his position at Pine Ridge. Rather than accept a transfer, he resigned for a time from the Indian service.[4]

In *From the Deep Woods to Civilization*, Eastman recalls these events as having been a turning point in his life. He describes his initial naiveté in believing that fraud could be corrected simply by being exposed to the Indian's benevolent trustees. Following this observation, his characterization of the movement from "the deep woods" to "civilization" takes on new dimensions. In the later chapters of the autobiography he explicitly characterizes it as a transition into a complex and corrupt world of bureaucratic law. Evincing a growing sense of unease with the complicated legal and political mechanisms surrounding his people, Eastman sums up the lessons he and his wife gleaned from their conflict with colonial institutions. He notes that they were "utterly disillusioned and disgusted with these revelations of Government mismanagement in the field, and realiz[ed] the helplessness of the best-equipped Indians to secure a fair deal for their people" (134–35). At such a moment, Eastman overtly acknowledges what was only subtext in his first autobiography—the precarious legal status of the Indian-child on the allotment-era reservation, living totally at the mercy of officials and bureaucrats without the legal standing to challenge fraud and injustice (to get a "fair deal"). Significantly, in making such an overt acknowledgment, he places the relationship between models of self and claims of justice at the heart of his new autobiographical act.

The balance of *From the Deep Woods to Civilization* represents Eastman's simultaneous reassessment of his earlier political commitments and attempt to redefine himself in relation to the discourse of allotment. In doing so, he begins both implicitly and explicitly to challenge the ideological assumptions behind a number of earlier Native American autobiographies, texts such as Apess's *Indian Nullification*, his own *Indian Boyhood*, and (at least parts of) Sarah Winnemucca Hopkins's *Life among the Piutes* (1883). As we have seen, the process of legal engagement had led Apess to a commitment to self-definition and oppositional claims based on rights of property, an approach whose limitations had been exposed by the failures and corruption of the allotment era. Winnemucca's book, produced with the editorial assistance of Mrs. Horace Mann, is similar in many respects to *Indian Boyhood* in its acceptance of legal paternalism as a basis for making claims. She manifestly places her own and her people's story against the background of the struggle within the U.S. government between civilians and the military for control of Indian policy. Winnemucca makes clear throughout her autobiography that her people inevitably suffered under the administrative authority of civilian agents who failed to civilize them, instead lining their own pockets. However, as we have seen, her discussion of "wrongs and claims" situates her firmly within the overall framework of legal paternalism—hers is a plea to place Indians under the authority of their "soldier fathers" instead of their "Christian fathers" (agents appointed by missionary societies) in order to ensure that they will be properly protected and civilized. The "rights" invoked in her text are still those of being properly treated as a ward of the state, a precarious form of self-definition, to say the least.

Eastman's entry into the realm of claims in *From the Deep Woods to Civilization* differs from both Apess's and Winnemucca's in fundamental ways, most notably in the nature of Indian "rights" as he comes to articulate them. He gradually moves beyond both the "real property" basis for rights (which stands behind the allotment policy) and a meek submission to paternal authority. Instead, Eastman develops a rhetoric of grievance grounded in personal civil rights and a rejuvenated emphasis on a distinctive Indian cultural identity (which Eastman argues can and should coexist with full citizenship). As the book progresses, he reassesses the dissociative impulse of *Indian Boyhood* and begins to move into a recovery mode, seeking to rearticulate elements of precontact Indianness. Initially, Eastman's autobiographical account of his experiences after his resignation from the BIA in 1890 show his continued investment in the idea that traditional models of Indian identity needed to give way to something new. However, he also demonstrates an awareness that a process of assimilation rooted in the possession of property alone presented crippling challenges to Indians whose lands were being rapidly alienated. As a result, his "rights talk" gradually moves beyond his earlier embrace of the freeholding ideal.

In his discussion of his next major conflict with the Indian legal system—his advocacy on behalf of the Santee in Washington—Eastman begins by continuing to invoke the kind of land-oriented rights talk of the allotment policy. He writes of having been employed (beginning in 1896) by one faction of Santee Sioux to serve as their legal agent in Washington, appearing before the president, the Indian bureau, the Court of Indian Claims, and the Congress. Eastman recalls entering into a contractual relationship with his tribe (a significant point considering that he later was involved in a conflict between factions and another group of representatives over compensation) and then "urging our rights." The rights in question are essentially rights of property, validated by past contracts (treaties) between the Sioux and the U.S. government.[5] Seemingly rejecting (or at least overlooking) Congress's assertion of its plenary power to abrogate treaties, Eastman includes a fairly lengthy discussion of the various agreements with the Santee Sioux entered into by the U.S. government during the nineteenth century. In a strong indication of his commitment to the ideal of legal engagement as the basis for asserting Indian rights (as well as his retreat from the individualistic emphasis of the allotment period), Eastman cites treaties signed in 1824, 1837, and 1851 involving land sales. The 1851 treaty concerns him most, for it involved the establishment of a trust fund from which payments would be made to the Santee on a yearly basis. The failure of the government to make these payments in 1860 and 1861 was one of the causes of the Minnesota Uprising of 1862, which was so significant in Eastman's early life. Following the defeat of the Sioux, Eastman explains, the annuities were confiscated as punishment, an act that he presents as a breach of contract. The attempt to get these annuities restored was one of his primary concerns during his time in Washington as a self-proclaimed "lobbyist."[6]

While discussing this direct activism on behalf of the Santee annuity claim, Eastman also recalls having testified before Congress in support of the allotment policy and greater economic self-determination for Indians. He reproduces the following testimony for his readers: "We desire to learn business methods . . . and we can only do this by handling our own property. You learn by experience to manage your business. How are we as Indians to learn if you take from us that wisdom born of mistakes, and leave us to suffer the stings of robbery and deception, with no opportunity to guard against its recurrence? I know that some will misuse this privilege, and some will be defrauded, but the experiment will be worth it at all costs" (159). Such a statement reflects Eastman's general concern over control of property and would again seem to place him firmly within the contractarian ideology and rights talk of nineteenth-century America. Sounding rather like Apess here, he intimates that private control of property is necessary to provide not only the means for advancement, but the basis for political security and rights. At the same time, he argues on behalf of a will theory of contractual relations, stressing the freedom to make a bad bargain (caveat emptor) characteristic of modern American individualism.[7] At this point in the text, then, Eastman seems still to suggest that the platform from which Indians might provide for themselves and claim their rights is full citizenship along contractarian principles—essentially Apess's position and the position of the late-nineteenth-century Indian reformers. The model of identity being advanced appears basically consistent with assimilationist discourse. Tellingly, in spite of his concerns about the Burke Bill, which sped up the pace by which Indian allottees might be declared competent to alienate their lands, and his experience with bureaucratic corruption, Eastman notes that "during this phase of my life, I was brought face to face with a new phase of progress among my people the Dakotas," growing out of the allotment of reservations in severalty. He suggests, perhaps too optimistically, that Indians who were granted citizenship through allotment would develop political power in the west where candidates for office would need to seek their favor during elections. Overall, then, he continues to present the process of legal and political assimilation of Indians, and the Sioux's progress in becoming "entrenched . . . in the warfare of civilized life," as the classic American tale of property securing individual rights.

Yet Eastman's account of his work as an advocate before Congress on behalf of Indian property rights functions within the text in a more complicated way than merely reinforcing the discourse of allotment. In reality, he was only marginally successful in his attempts to draw on treaty law and the discourse of property to advance Indian rights claims. By the mid 1910s, the manifest failures of the allotment policy were becoming readily apparent, and judicial action had rendered treaty rights precarious. Native Americans were losing lands to speculators at an alarming rate and falling deeper and deeper into poverty, without many visible means of redress (as Eastman was learning firsthand). Eastman also was beginning to find himself increasingly at odds with his own people. During this period, he began a long litigation against the Santee, attempting to force them to honor their contractual obligations to him (including payment) as their legally designated agent. This legal action, he concedes, particularly distressed and embittered him. In light of these manifest failures, both in political activism and self-definition, Eastman's account of his commitment to a discourse of property rights draws attention to a dead end in his relationship with colonial institutions and the discourse of allotment, suggesting the need for a new stage of legal engagement and a new model of self-definition. This, perhaps, explains why the final chapters of *From the Deep Woods to Civilization* reveal a broader understanding of rights, indicative of a new stage in Eastman's developing legal consciousness.

In a remarkable change of direction, Eastman presents himself at the end of his second autobiography as a man whose primary objective, both as an author and a lecturer, had been "to present the American Indian in his true character before Americans" (187). What this portrait has shown, he claims, is a people whose "barbarous and atrocious character" dated only from the transition period and their contact with whites. With this dramatic act of self-revision, Eastman tries to redirect his readers away from the predominantly assimilationist ideology of both *Indian Boyhood* and the earlier chapters of *From the Deep Woods to Civilization.* In contrast to that earlier rhetoric, Eastman offers a new assertion that the "democracy and community" of the "original American" is nearer the ideal than that of the present-day white man. Such a statement represents an intriguing attempt to blend the best of American political discourse with an anti-assimilationist celebration of precontact Indianness. In making that attempt, Eastman moves away from the purely property-centered rights consciousness of the allotment era and toward a hybrid blend of liberalism and ethnically grounded self-awareness (something characteristic of twentieth-century Indian civil rights talk). Reflecting on the kind of rights he now wishes to assert, Eastman writes: "It was not until I had to a degree established these claims [about the precontact ideal] that I consented to appear on the platform in our ancestral garb of honor. I feel that I was a pioneer in this new line of defense of the Native American, *not so much of his rights in the land as of his character and religion*" [my emphasis] (188). This statement suggests that as he continued to take up the mantle of the representative Indian from the 1910s until the end of his life, Eastman no longer "represented" the inevitability of assimilation and an unequivocal embrace of the liberal model of self. Instead, he sought to embody a fusion of an essentially "Indian" character and American liberalism set in opposition to the pernicious aspects of modernity. The emergence of this new model of self signals the major evolution in Eastman's autobiographical and political career. It is also precisely the model embodied within the twentieth-century discourse of Indian civil rights.

Unlike claims rooted in the "contractual" obligations of treaty law and the liberal discourse of property rights, Indian claims for *civil* rights require a foundation built on full citizenship and access to the Bill of Rights. Prior to 1924, of course, there had been a number of particular statutes granting citizenship to specific groups of Indians. In each case, though, such citizenship came with significant strings attached—compulsory and total assimilation being the most significant. The citizenship component of the General Allotment Act, as we have seen, followed precisely this model. Within such a framework, clearly, the only kinds of rights claims that an individual Indian seemed able to make would be property claims based on a full acceptance of the ideology of Anglo-

American law. This provided little aid in resisting the pressures of assimilation.

By the early twentieth century, though, some Indian policy reformers (particularly those who were actually *Indian*) came to recognize that a bill granting full citizenship (without the assimilationist component of the Dawes Act) might, in fact, provide a foundation for a different form of advocacy and rights talk. The passage of the Citizenship Act of 1924 (a law actively supported by writers such as Eastman and Zitkala-Sa) sought to accomplish this end, naturalizing all Indians born within the territorial limits of the United States and granting them the full privileges of citizenship at both the state and federal level. The most crucial effect of the 1924 act was to grant Indians access to the protections of civil rights guaranteed in the Bill of Rights, especially the First Amendment guarantees of freedom of religion (which were made applicable to state governments by the Fourteenth Amendment in 1868).[8] This, when combined with earlier decisions by the Supreme Court that held tribal citizenship and U.S. citizenship to be compatible, created a new, unique space for "Indian" identity within the legal system.[9] It allowed, theoretically at least, for a blended language of selfhood to be recognized within the legal system. It allowed Indian people, for example, to reassert the validity of their spiritual traditions, while accepting certain other adaptations demanded by assimilationist discourse.

When we consider the changed nature of the legal discourse of Indianness in the wake of the 1924 Citizenship Act, it seems important to notice that Eastman's writings in 1916 seem to prophesy key elements of the new order. His own discourse may thus be read as an attempt to lay the foundation for a new set of legal fictions governing Indian identity and rights. By this time in his career, Eastman's engagement with the discourse of allotment had led him to begin to reformulate his autobiographical model of self and to agitate to have that model recognized by law. In this context, we might consider the rhetoric of self-definition with which he closes *From the Deep Woods to Civilization.* The modern capitalist economy that Eastman earlier claimed so enthralled him now appears as its own form of "primitive savagery." Based on what he had already written in the autobiography, this change in perspective would seem to derive from a growing belief (one shared by many disenfranchised or marginalized persons in our democracy) that such an economy and its law (now increasingly bureaucratic) was insufficient to meet his and his people's needs. Eastman maintains that he "stands before" his own people "as an advocate of civilization," due both to his continued recognition that the old ways are gone and to his sense that the failures of

Christian society to live up to its ideals do not constitute a refutation of the ideal. This said, though, at the end of *From the Deep Woods to Civilization*, Eastman's advocacy is greatly altered. He writes: "I am an Indian; and while I have learned much from civilization, for which I am grateful, I have never lost my Indian sense of right and justice; I am for development and progress along spiritual and social lines, rather than those of commerce, nationalism or material efficiency. Nevertheless, as long as I live, I am an American" (195).

In this constitutive statement, we can see the evolution of a complex form of self-definition, rooted in some of the same assumptions dominating *Indian Boyhood* but changed into a new and powerful form of civil rights talk. Foregrounding his "Americanness," Eastman both implicitly reminds the reader of his people's distinctive aboriginal status and asserts membership as a citizen in the national order. He aligns Indianness with the essence of American democracy, claiming, in effect, that he is a closer embodiment of republican ideals than the modern capitalists. In doing so, he concedes the need for change and development, thereby recognizing that Indian culture and identity will not be static in the future. Yet in the process, Eastman stresses the existence of factors that can (and should) limit "progress" understood in purely commercial or economic terms—the terms that had heretofore provided the sole basis for the assimilationist policies of Indian law. The main limiting factor is a reconstituted Indianness, understood as a culturally and *spiritually* specific form of selfhood with its own sense of "right and justice." Eastman's final act of autobiographical performance in *From the Deep Woods to Civilization*, then, reintroduces a notion of an *essential* religious identity that is distinctly Indian but can coexist with (and challenge) modernity.[10] This he sets forth as a platform from which to make oppositional claims against an exclusively individualistic and property-oriented legal discourse. "I am an Indian," he says, reversing the distancing we saw in *Indian Boyhood*. No longer just an Indian "for a while," the older and more experienced Eastman begins to reclaim his own heritage, both as a *right* and as a means of challenging some of the materialistic assumptions of allotment-era definitions of Native American identity. He becomes, in his own way, a pioneering voice for Indian civil rights, foreshadowing some of the ways those rights would be claimed later in the twentieth century.

The ending of *From the Deep Woods to Civilization* offers a model of self-definition that was to become a major thread running through Eastman's writings from the 1910s to early 1920s (and which informed the next phase of U.S. Indian policy). During this period, in a number of books and journalistic pieces, Eastman began to utilize a new, more essentialist rhetoric of pan-Indian identity and consistently to assert the form of civil rights consciousness based on that model of self. In *Indian Scout Talks* (1914), for example, he offers practical instruction in Indian woodcraft and lore, while continuing to act as an interpreter of Indian ways to a broader audience. Admittedly, there is still a clear sense of distancing at play in the book (reminiscent of *Indian Boyhood*), as Eastman does not treat traditional practices with the full reverence of a "native" participant. The modern reader will also quite likely be struck by his willingness to encourage whites to "play" Indian; Eastman offers the Sioux system of regalia to the Boy Scouts as an honor system, describing ceremonies they might use, and he even provides instruction on how to make an imitation peace pipe.[11] Nevertheless, in the book's last essay, "The School of Savagery," Eastman offers evidence of his changing sense of the ways in which Indian identity (defined as something ethnically distinctive) might form the basis for counterclaims against colonial domination. Indian ways, he argues, cultivate individuality and initiative, but not selfish individualism. His subsequent discussion of Indianness sounds as much like an invocation of the revolutionary-era ideal of republican citizenship as a reassertion of traditional practice: "Happy, rollicking boy man! Gallant, patriotic, public-spirited—in the Indian is the lusty youth of humanity [. . .] Most of all he values the opportunity of being a minute-man [. . .] let us have more of this spirit of the American Indian, the Boy Scout's prototype, to leaven the brilliant selfishness of our modern civilization" (190). At a moment like this, Eastman again assertively blends his definition of essential Indianness with the rhetoric of republican citizenship. Such a gesture serves not simply as an act of historical or cultural recovery, but also as an attempt to carve out and legitimize a model of Indianness with a claim to recognition that extends beyond issues of personal property rights. Since the "brilliant selfishness" of modern civilization (epitomized in the laissez-faire individualism and property-centered discourse of rights) had proven inadequate both to the Indian's and the nation's needs, Eastman begins to present *the* Native character as a recognizable birthright essentially in harmony with the national legal order. The individual Indian's Indianness, and not his land, becomes the basis for new claims to recognition, legal protection, and respect. Apess's Indian liberalism is evolving into something new here.

This kind of statement on behalf of the Indian's "right of personhood" also informs Eastman's 1911 book *The Soul of the Indian: An Interpretation.* In perhaps his most explicit articulation of pan-Indian spiritual identity, Eastman sets up that text as an attempt to "paint the religious life of the typical American Indian" before contact with whites (ix). In doing so, he does provide a strikingly romanticized portrait of Native life (opening with quotes from Sidney Lanier, Thomas Campbell, and Samuel Taylor Coleridge), one that emphasizes the symbolic nature of Indian religious rites and practices. Yet if Eastman continues to make Indianness extremely palatable and appealing to his white audience, he also articulates a model of self that stresses spiritual distinctiveness. Eastman offers a quasi-primitivist discussion of precontact Indian virtue, setting up the Native "Soul" as a foil to the corruption of the modern world. According to him, Indian spirituality and the essence of true Christianity are as one, and both are irreconcilable to the materialism of the modern world. In this way, Eastman is able to address a key problem alluded to in *From the Deep Woods to Civilization*, the need to balance his sense of the validity of the kind of ideals found in Christianity with his growing sense of the inadequacy of the material basis of white civilization to bring justice to his people. Once again, though, the critical thrust of this text's treatment of identity is to assert the validity and need for Indianness in the modern world. That *The Soul of the Indian* makes its claim in terms of religion, a uniquely privileged realm under the establishment and free exercise clauses of the First Amendment, is not insignificant. In writing the book, Eastman implicitly acknowledges and cultivates an assertive discourse based on the personal, civil right to spiritual and cultural distinctiveness.

As noted earlier, in his shift from self-definition based exclusively on the internalization of paternalistic models and property rights to an increasing emphasis on pan-Indian spiritual identity and civil rights, Eastman anticipates major changes in Indian policy (and in Native American autobiography), changes that he personally helped engineer. These extended well beyond the 1924 Citizenship Act into broader reform within the BIA. Eastman's activities as a lecturer, writer, and reformer were instrumental in changing federal policy in the late 1920s and 1930s. When it had become universally accepted (in the early 1920s) that the Dawes Act had failed to achieve its stated goals, he became a participant in the famous Committee of One-Hundred, which met in 1923 to discuss potential changes in Indian policy. The committee's recommendations served later as the groundwork for the extremely influential Meriam Report of 1928, which provided the basis for Indian policy during the next era (the so-called Indian New Deal).[12] Besides recommending an end to the allotment policy, the Meriam Report sought to provide increased support for Indian education, to secure greater tribal autonomy, to protect Indian lands, and to support Indians' civil rights to engage in traditional cultural practices. The language of the report is striking in this regard. It claims that "care must be exercised to respect the rights of the Indian. This phrase 'rights of the Indian' is often used solely to apply to his property rights. Here it is used in a much broader sense to cover his rights as a human being living in a free country" (qtd. in Prucha, *Documents* 219). It is important to recognize, of course, that the thinking in such a passage does not imply a total abandonment of governmental paternalism. (Indeed, Indian claims to civil rights still take place within the broader context and ambiguities of U.S. Indian law.) The Meriam Report and the policies that flowed from it (like the 1934 Indian Reorganization Act) did not advocate full autonomy for Native Americans, nor did they involve a complete shift from the general assumption that Indians must somehow confront and adapt to modern civilization. The authors of the report stressed that the goal of Indian policy should be to "fit them either to merge into the social and economic life of the prevailing civilization [. . .] or to live in the presence of that civilization at least in accordance with a minimum standard of health and decency" (qtd. in Prucha, *Documents* 220–21). The supervisory impulse comes through clearly here in the persistent assumption that since contact has produced corruption and degradation among Indians, even those who choose not to enter in the political economy of civilized America "must be aided in the preservation of themselves."

If allotment-era paternalism did not give way to recognition of absolute Indian sovereignty, though, it did yield a less aggressive paternalism and, perhaps more significantly, the beginning of an acknowledgment of Indians' rights *as Indians,* not as property holders. Such a change marks one of the beginnings of the rise of a modern discourse of Native American civil rights. It hints at a new emphasis on Indian religious liberty, rooted in the idea of the rights of personhood. It is probably not a coincidence, then, that the next major phase of Native American autobiography would be dominated by rhetorically conflicted "ethnographic" works (often "as-told-to" stories) that focus on traditional Indian spiritual and cultural practices. Texts like Frank B. Lindeman's *Pretty Shield: Medicine Woman of the Crows* (1932), Paul Radin's *Crashing Thunder* (1920), and, of course, John G. Neihardt's *Black Elk Speaks* (1932) reflect *both* the rise of paternalistic Boasian "salvage" ethnography and a new era of Indian policy and civil rights consciousness. Yet even these heavily mediated texts present a new literary model of Indianness, the emergence of which was at least partly a product of the experience of colonial contact during the allotment era.

It would seem then that Eastman was correct in his assessment of himself as a pioneer. His engagement with the colonial system moved him toward a surprisingly modern form of self-definition, one formed through lifelong contact with the discourse of Indian law. His redefinition of the enduring vitality of Indianness anticipates major changes in Native American literature and autobiography during the early decades of the twentieth century. Understanding the intricacies of Eastman's autobiographical career, then, can help us to understand how the rhetoric of Indian identity changed, in broader terms, as a result of colonial contact. At the same time, though, Eastman's example shows us how the process of engagement over time has also had a discernible impact on colonialist discourse and institutions themselves. The model of self and rhetoric of opposition that Eastman (and others like him) developed in the latter part of his career clearly played a role in the policy shift during the 1920s away from allotment and toward greater acknowledgment of Indian sovereignty and cultural distinctiveness.

In highlighting these progressive elements of Eastman's literary career, of course, there is a temptation to overstate his achievements and successes. In truth, Eastman did not live out the final years of his life enjoying a sense of political triumph. After a separation from his wife, he gradually disappeared from public life, "retiring" to Canada to hunt and fish. He died there in 1939, living in a tepee near Detroit, estranged from some of his own children. Such details would seem to suggest that Eastman finally gave up on engagement after three and a half decades of painful struggle for Indian rights. These facts also seem to suggest that he felt a sense of disillusionment regarding his own career as a writer and activist. It is impossible to judge the mind of the man at this stage of his life, especially as he left no written record of his reasons for returning to the woods. Yet even if Eastman felt, in the end, that his literary and political activities had been unsuccessful, there is no reason we cannot offer a more generous assessment. The struggle for Native American rights has continued to be vexed, but this should not diminish our sense of Eastman's literary achievements. Quite to the contrary, understanding the shape of Eastman's career allows us to appreciate both the subtle (and often painfully slow) nature of the legal struggle against colonialist institutions of self-fashioning and the way that autobiographical writing contributed to that struggle. Read in this light, his work offers us a truly impressive example of autoethnographic engagement with the discourse of Indian law, not just a lamentable case of lost authenticity.

Conclusion:
Toward Self-Sovereignty

The story this book has told includes at least two distinct components. On the one hand, I have sought to present the history of a discourse—the colonial discourse of Indianness. In doing so, I have tried to suggest that such a history should be a narrative about the dynamic of engagement in the colonial contact zone. The readings in this study have been designed to show that such engagement functions as a kind of communicative circuit. This circuit was shaped, clearly, by hierarchical power relations. Yet to characterize the linguistic situation in question by using terms like "transmission" is clearly to both oversimplify the nature of colonialism and underestimate the inventiveness of Native American writers. Drawing implicitly on the indigenous paradigm of treaty making, Indian autobiographers in the nineteenth century did more than merely lose their authenticity. As I have tried to show, they shrewdly developed a rhetoric of Indianness that enabled them to push back against the institutions of colonial domination—sometimes to good effect.

Beyond its discursive history of Indianness, though, this book has also been intended to provide readers with the first phase of a new kind of literary history of Native American autobiography. I have sought to develop a narrative that traces a developing autobiographical tradition during the period from the late eighteenth to the early twentieth centuries. In saying this, of course, I do not mean to suggest a line of *direct* influence between writers such as Apess and Eastman. (It is clear, however, based on references in *From the Deep Woods to Civilization*, that

Eastman was at least familiar with Samson Occom. We also know that Ely S. Parker had read William Apess.) At the same time, I feel quite comfortable in suggesting the existence of a broad pattern of continuity. Positing the existence of "linear" developments in Native American writing intertwined with shifts in U.S./Indian relations does not require us to prove a writer's direct exposure to earlier texts. The "tradition" is there, I would maintain, whether or not individual writers would have perceived it that way.

In the end, it is my hope that these two histories (discursive and literary) will provide a framework for future inquiry into the connections between law and Native American autobiography. In closing, then, I would make a few broad comments on how the current study might be extended further forward into the twentieth century. As I mentioned at the end of chapter 6, the next major phase in Indian autobiography coincides with the rise of the so-called "salvage" ethnography (driven largely by the work of Franz Boas and his students). In the wake of Boasian anthropology, collectors (both academically trained and amateur) set out across the nation to "gather" the traditional narratives (and artifacts) of Indian peoples. What this led to, in the realm of autobiography, was a torrent of as-told-to narratives that aimed to record and preserve the "old ways" before they were lost to history. The "ethnographic" autobiographies collected by individuals such as Paul Radin and Frank Linderman embody a range of ideological tensions, of course. They represent an implicit commitment to the "tragic" narrative of the "vanishing Indian" that has soothed the consciences of colonialists since the time of Columbus. They also frequently encode problematic assumptions about cultural authority and authenticity that tend to misrepresent or undervalue Native Americans' adaptation to colonial contact. Radin's editorial intrusions in *The Autobiography of a Winnebago Indian* (1920), for example, range from laments about Natives' inability to "give a well-rounded and complete account of [their] culture" to concerns that the emerging, hybrid peyote religion had compromised the purity of Winnebago society in lamentable ways. Yet such texts can also be understood as a further development in the history of colonial engagement. Even mediated works like Radin's are an index of the increasing interest in the idea of the *distinctive character and traditions* (especially religious) of Native Americans (of both genders—a departure from the male-dominated canon of the nineteenth century). They also reveal a clear retreat from literary dominance of assimilationist discourse, and thus implicitly, albeit slowly, advance the kind of rhetoric of Indian identity and civil rights that Charles Eastman and his contemporaries were developing at the end of the allotment era.

A text such as John G. Neihardt's *Black Elk Speaks* (1932), I would suggest, is very much in the tradition of *The Soul of the Indian*. And the development of that tradition, we should note, continued to inform U.S. Indian policy during the years preceding World War II.

The ethnographic autobiographies of the 1920s and 1930s served to validate Indianness at precisely the same time that the so-called Indian New Deal (under the auspices of Indian Commissioner John Collier) sought to reinvigorate tribal organizations and undo some of the damage done by the allotment policy. Collier, who had actually lived among the Zuni of New Mexico for a time, was one of the strongest champions of Native American rights to occupy such an influential administrative position in the federal government. It is significant to note, therefore, the correspondence between his views on Indian policy and the positions advanced by writers such as Eastman. In his annual report to Congress in 1934, Collier comments at length on the Wheeler-Howard Act (the Indian Reorganization Act), the bill he had largely designed and shepherded through Congress. In a particularly interesting section dealing with "spiritual rehabilitation," he notes the failure of the "individualization" policies of the preceding fifty years. Collier goes on to observe that "even before the passage of the Wheeler-Howard bill a great spiritual stirring had become noticeable throughout the Indian country. That awakening *of the racial spirit* must be sustained, if the rehabilitation of the Indian people is to be successfully carried through" [my emphasis] (qtd. in Prucha, *Documents* 227). This imperative for "spiritual" renewal buttresses many of Collier's other proposals for increased Indian sovereignty and self-determination (what he means by "rehabilitation"). That such a shift in policy was rooted in a new rhetoric stressing an essential Indian spiritual identity suggests that the literary struggles of allotment-era Indian writers (and the work of some early anthropologists) had finally begun to bear fruit. Even though the idea of a "racial spirit" is, itself, a kind of myth making, it is a more progressive myth, with important legal and political consequences.

The connections between administrative policy and Native American literature during the progressive era demand further study. (Robert Warrior's work on John Joseph Matthews in *Tribal Secrets* provides an excellent starting point here.) Similarly, it seems to me that an understanding of the historical relationship between legal models of self and the rhetoric of Indianness in Native autobiography might also help us better appreciate the complex performances of many writers of the subsequent Native American Renaissance. At the end of the disastrous (but thankfully short-lived) termination policy of the 1950s, U.S. Indian policy began to focus again (as it had in the 1930s) on greater acknowledgment of Native American sovereignty and the need to live up to extant treaty obligations. (There are, of course, significant exceptions, but the general tenor of Indian policy in recent decades has been more conciliatory.) The Commission on the Rights, Liberties, and Responsibilities of the American Indian (established in 1957) published an influential report in 1966 calling for greater attention to the views and desires of Native Americans in the creation of federal policy, and some of those concerns were incorporated into the Civil Rights Act of 1968. At the same time, lawsuits surrounding tribal status and the recognition of treaty rights has led to an intriguing ideological shift during the last thirty years. Rather than centering on strategies for incorporating Native Americans into mainstream America, the discourse of Indian law has focused increasingly on defining what constitutes "authentic" Indianness, what is a tribe, and who is entitled to claim rights and privileges laid out in past treaties. Reading the autobiographical writings of contemporary literary figures such as Gerald Vizenor and N. Scott Momaday against the background of this legal history reveals what may be a radically new phase in the history of colonial engagement.

Momaday's 1976 work *The Names* represents a drastic break with the kind of writing that had characterized Native American autobiography up to that point. He offers his readers a complex, difficult text, one that embodies the active role of the imagination in constituting a sense of Indian identity. What is particularly striking to me about Momaday's text, though, is the way he seems to reconfigure the idea of "salvaging" the past in a way that enables him to establish a "stable," authentic Indian self despite the disruptions of colonialism. In this respect, Momaday's autobiography can be read as a subtle entry into the complex legal debates about Indian identity after "assimilation" (debates like those that surrounded the Mashpee in the late 1970s). The dedication page of *The Names* establishes the book's complex rhetorical approach to issues of identity:

> My name is Tsoai-talee. I am, therefore, Tsoai-talee; therefore I am.
>   The storyteller Pohd-lokk gave me the name Tsoai-talee. He believed that a man's life proceeds from his name, in a way that a river proceeds from its source.
>
> In general my narrative is an autobiographical account. Specifically, it is an act of the imagination. When I turn my mind to my early life, it is the imaginative part of it that comes first and irresistibly into reach, and of that part I take hold. This is one way to tell a story. In this instance, it is my way, and it is the way of my people. When Pohd-lohk told a

story he began by being quiet. Then he said, Ah-keah-de, "They were camping," and said it every time. I have tried to write in the same way, in the same spirit. Imagine: they were camping.

In these passages, Momaday reveals his intention to subvert Western individualistic models of self (his clever reformulation of the Cartesian *cogito* setting the tone). Names are the essence of self, he tells us, and only through one's names does one truly exist. Yet for Momaday, a name is neither a rigid label nor something that one "possesses," per se. He tells us that his first name, Tsaoi-talee ("Rock Tree Boy"—a translation, interestingly enough, not offered the non-Indian reader), was given to him by a *storyteller*. In this respect it is both a communal gift and the start of a lifelong *process* of becoming through the act of narration. "A man's life proceeds from his name," he writes, in the same way that a story begins with an initial word before it exfoliates into something much larger and (for Momaday's Kiowa ancestors) collective. Having made that claim, Momaday then redefines the autobiographical act (much in line with recent autobiography theory) as an imaginative act of self-creation (of storytelling). In doing so, he suggests that autobiography can actually overcome gaps in memory (both personal and historical)—a point with great significance for contemporary Native Americans engaged in the process of reinvigorating cultural traditions interrupted by colonialism. And yet Momaday carefully defines this "way of telling a story" as specifically Indian ("it is the way of my people"). Implicitly, then, he frames his book as a claim regarding Native Americans' (perhaps unique) ability to collectively reimagine themselves. (This is central to his recurrent metaphor of "blood memory," which appears throughout his published work.) There is perhaps no more hopeful, and subtle, response than this to a period of U.S. Indian policy that sought to "terminate" tribal identity.

While Momaday's response to colonialism has been to celebrate the recreative power of the Indian imagination, Gerald Vizenor's project seems to be to overtly deconstruct the legal and academic discourses of Indianness. In both his fiction and autobiography, Vizenor's regular references to the courts, the BIA, and the university clearly establish the larger context for his work; like many Native American writers before him, he is deeply concerned with a variety of institutions and their discourses of self. Unlike the work of his predecessors, though, Vizenor's "trickster discourse" (the term he uses for his own writing) relentlessly mocks and undermines those institutions and their languages. An early passage from his first collection of autobiographical essays, *Interior Landscapes* (1990), offers a taste of Vizenor's typical rhetorical mode. In a chapter called

"Families of the Crane," he opens with the claim that tricksters, posing as humans at the beginning of the world, were the originators of the major Anishinaabe clans (including his own family clan, that of the crane). The crane, a central symbol of self for Vizenor, subsequently becomes a sign of contradiction, of comic randomness, and of playful imagination in the book. Vizenor explains that his familial and tribal line of descent "is celebrated here [in the book] in the autobiographical myths and metaphors of my imagination, my crossblood remembrance" (3).

Precisely what the preceding statement means is difficult to explain without immersing oneself deeply in the world of Vizenor's prose. Essentially, though, what Vizenor is suggesting is that his autobiographical acts "liberate the mind" (as he would say) by refusing to allow the reader a stable discursive position from which to "define" him (or his Indianness). Throughout *Interior Landscapes* (and in its "sequel," *Crossbloods*), Vizenor deploys his relentless irony against academic and legal language, commenting, for example, on how tribes were "amended" during the nineteenth century, and referring to himself as a "racial felon." His narratives also constantly circle back on and revise themselves. In a moving chapter called "Death Song of a Red Rodent," for example, Vizenor speaks of the grim lesson he learned when an "urban" Indian like himself "pretended to be a tribal hunter" (167). Later on in the book, he reveals the "Red Rodent" chapter to have been a fiction cobbled together from multiple sources and not a literal memory. The effect, then, is to leave the reader even more puzzled about the author's "true" self. Is he an "urban" Indian? A "tribal hunter"? A "Red Rodent"? A journalist with a vivid imagination? Or perhaps, as Vizenor prods us to consider, the subject of autobiography is not its author at all, but rather a combination of all the stories that could be used to define the self.

Generally speaking, what an autobiographical act like *Interior Landscapes* sets out to do is to foreground the radically postmodern notion that identity is essentially "fictive" and fluid. Vizenor mocks the discursive "fictions" (both legal and academic) that have been deployed to define the Indian. In this respect, his autobiographies are acts of refusal—a refusal to be "known" by colonial institutions. Vizenor's "positive" claims regarding himself center around the idea that his identity is that of a trickster. Like the protagonists in his short stories and novels, he thus becomes the hero of an ever-changing, comic language game. Toward the end of *Interior Landscapes* Vizenor offers the following complex observations:

> Survival is imagination, a verbal noun, a wild transitive word in my mixedblood autobiographies; genealogies, the measured lines in our time,

and place, are never the same in our personal memories . . . My memories and interior landscapes are untamed. (263)

My survival is mythic, an imaginative transition, an intellectual pre-dation, deconstructed as masks and metaphors at the water holes in autobiographies.

"Language is the main instrument of man's refusal to accept the world as it is," wrote George Steiner in *After Babel: Aspects of Language and Translation.* "Ours is the ability, the need, to gain-say or un-say the world, to image and speak it otherwise . . . To misinform, to utter less than the truth was to gain a vital edge of space or subsistence." (265)

Such remarks highlight both sides of Vizenor's trickster persona—the "liberated" writer who revels in the imaginative process of storytelling and shifting identity and the crossblood "translator" who refuses either to be interpreted by colonial institutions or to accept the world as it is. Vizenor engages colonialist discourse, then, in the way that a virus "en-gages" a cell. But he also refuses to allow his own writing and imagina-tion to become solely fixated on the tragic history of colonial contact. In this respect, Vizenor has found a path away from autoethnography and toward a more radical form of self-determination than that shown by the writers examined in this study.

Clearly, as such a brief precis would indicate, there is much to be said about the ongoing relationship between contemporary Native American autobiography and legal institutions. I am confident that the varied works of writers such as Momaday, Vizenor, and others can be appreciated in new ways when they are reconsidered in the contexts I have tried to establish in this book. For in many ways, the experiences and literary achievements of the earlier writers discussed here provide the foundation upon which the Native American Renaissance was built, even if critics have yet to fully appreciate that debt. As we move into the twenty-first century, Americans are only beginning to engage in the real work of writing a more definitive and inclusive history of our nation's internal imperialism. Similarly, as Robert Warrior, Craig Womack, and others have suggested, Native Americans are just beginning to fully grasp the rich intellectual heritage of the last two to three hundred years of Indian writing. Appreciating how the literary tradition of Native American auto-biography took shape during the nineteenth century should spur all of us to broaden our understanding of the ways that colonial institutions of self have functioned in the United States. At the same time, we can come to better see how Native Americans have wrestled with those institutions (and discourses) over time. In the end, we should recognize that Indian law has been built on a foundation of storytelling; its models of Indian identity and Indian rights are rooted in a wide range of legal fictions and narratives. Such a point helps foreground again the argument I have been making throughout this book. I have tried to show that autobiographical acts of storytelling have the potential to enable political resistance and lay a foundation for legal change. By rearticulating and disseminating new ways of conceptualizing Indian identity and Indian rights, these texts are an important part of the ongoing struggle for Native American sovereignty. The end of that story is yet to be written.

NOTES

Introduction

1. Throughout this book, the term "colonialism" is used to refer to the process whereby one group of people dominates and undermines the sovereignty of another, not merely at the political level but also at the level of individual identity. As Edward Said suggests, colonial domination can be achieved not only through military and economic power, but also through social or "cultural" means (9). Following the lead of Said and others, in recent years Americanists have demonstrated an increasing willingness to look at U.S. history and literature through the lens of postcolonialism. For a representative sampling of such "New Americanist" work, see Kaplan and Pease, as well as Moon and Davidson.

2. Georg Misch's two-volume *A History of Autobiography in Antiquity* is one of the classic examples of the latter approach. Misch's successor is Karl Joachim Weintraub, whose *The Value of the Individual* argues for a simultaneous historical emergence of the concept of "individuality" and the arrival of autobiography at its final "perfected" form. Both processes, in Weintraub's estimation, culminated during the nineteenth century. An interesting attempt to bring a more rigorous historical perspective to the study of autobiography is William Spengemann's *The Forms of Autobiography.* Spengemann seeks to clarify the relationship between changing conceptions of self and changes in the form of autobiographical writing. Though his periodization is probably too broad and schematic ("historical autobiography" is seen to dominate from the Middle Ages to the Enlightenment), Spengemann's approach provides a welcome corrective to the essentializations of Weintraub's book.

3. The phrasing is from Weintraub's essay "Autobiography and Historical Consciousness." While it is certainly not my intention to imply an imperialist agenda on Weintraub's part, it does seem important to point out the unfortunate connotations of his choice of language. It is also significant that his essay includes a subtle shift from a discussion of the historical "unfolding" of individualism to a more teleological treatment of its natural (evolutionary) "development." This kind of thinking has regularly been adapted as a justification for colonial domination.

4. See Carrithers, Collins, and Lukes.

5. The classic example of a "performative utterance" from Austin's book *How to Do Things with Words* would be "I do," a phrase that not only denotes the act of marriage, but actually effects the transition into a married state (as long as it is uttered in the proper context). Saying the words makes you married, in other

words. For a basic introduction to the concept of "performative language," see Austin (1–11).

6. Tracing Lejeune's career reveals a number of key paradigm shifts within the field of autobiography studies. In his early writings, Lejeune sought to avoid the dead-ends of genre criticism by blending formalist and reader-response approaches. He designated "autobiography" as a retrospective narrative focusing on an individual life, where the author, narrator, and protagonist are understood to be the same. This "identity," for Lejeune, was ratified by an "autobiographical pact" between author and reader, a generic "contract" of sorts presented on the very title page of the text. The value of Lejeune's approach was that it began to draw attention to a process of self-creation taking place within language and in a specific cultural setting (between speaking and hearing subjects). Where he erred in this early criticism, though, was in his assumption that there is a single linguistic and contractual model of self that applies universally. Significantly, in his later work (essays such as "Autobiography and Literary History," for instance) Lejeune acknowledges some of the limitations of his earlier theories. He raises the idea (drawn from reader-response critics like Iser and Jauss) that genre is not something inherent in the text itself; rather, it is an interpretive or communicative structure, if you will, which can change over time. What we recognize as "autobiography," then, is tied to a particular historical "horizon of expectations" (as Jauss would say) regarding what constitutes a "self," a "life," and a life story. Thus, where Lejeune's earlier work posited a normative definition of autobiography (a universal model of what constitutes the autobiographical pact) his later work aims to correct this imbalance by offering a descriptive one (centered on more historically particular claims). He even opens himself up to such unconventional formulations as the "autobiographies of those who do not write."

7. In his introduction to Lejeune's *On Autobiography*, Paul John Eakin makes a similar point. He suggests that "the locus of reference in autobiography" is "the autobiographical act, where the identity of author, narrator, and protagonist is textually postulated" (Eakin x). In other words, the "self" which is the subject of autobiography does not have a precise external referent. Rather, that self is constituted textually in the act of memory and narration. Eakin's other critical work further develops this crucial idea.

8. In *How Institutions Think*, Mary Douglas provides an intriguing discussion of the way cognition and categorization depend on institutional structures (55–90).

9. Mascuch provides the most recent in a series of persuasive arguments linking the rise of modern autobiography as a unified, retrospective, first-person narrative with broad range of cultural practices surrounding the emergence of modern individualism. Mascuch points out that the essential values of the individualist self include a notion of autonomy and self-direction, the importance of privacy and self-development, and a sense of agency inscribed in a consciousness of rights.

10. These debates have often focused on the meaning and interpretation of the Constitution. Issues facing literary critics, such as the role of authorial intent, the freedom of future readers to find "new" meaning in texts, and the need to historicize meaning, have obvious connections to central debates in American constitutional law and legal history. For a good introduction to the work being done in this area, see Levinson and Mailloux, and Levinson. For an interesting

example of the persistence of a belletristic interest in the connection between law and literature, and for an argument regarding the need to distinguish legal and literary interpretation, see Posner.

11. See Spivak, "Subaltern." See also Ashcroft, Griffiths, and Tiffin.

12. See Krupat, *For Those Who Come After* (28–54).

13. These terms are developed explicitly in *For Those Who Come After* (1–27). See also Krupat, The *Voice in the Margin* (96–131).

14. There is no consensus regarding which phrase ("Native American" or "American Indian") is more acceptable. Though there seems to be a broad move among non-Indian literary critics to use the term "Native American," many groups (the Pueblo peoples of New Mexico, for instance) explicitly prefer the designation "American Indian." Departing from Krupat, then, I refer to these kinds of texts alternately as Native American autobiography or American Indian autobiography. In cases where I am aware that an author prefers one or the other designation, I attempt to follow that preference. Otherwise, my choices are purely rhetorical. I confess that I am still seeking a wholly satisfactory term to designate the "as-told-to" or edited varieties of Indian lifewriting, though something like "collaborative Indian autobiography" might come close to the necessary precision.

15. In her otherwise useful discussion of *The Narrative of the Life of Black Hawk* in *Indian Nation,* for example, Cheryl Walker underestimates the role of editors and interpreters in shaping the final text (60–83).

16. According to Vizenor's postmodern sensibility, though, "inauthenticity" is not a problem to be solved or lamented. His form of autobiographical "trickster discourse" attempts to move beyond the signifier "Indian" (which he sees as wholly a product of colonialism) toward a liberated sense of identity built on play, irony, and subversive humor. Vizenor's essay "Postindian Autoinscriptions" offers his general position on the authenticity issue. The pieces collected in *Interior Landscapes* reveal his approach to autobiography.

17. For an introduction to recent discussions of "decolonizing methodologies" and the struggle for greater *intellectual* sovereignty being waged by Native American scholars in the academy, see Tuhiwai Smith and Mihesuah.

Chapter 1: The Discourse of Indian Law

1. Here I draw broadly on a sociolinguistic understanding of communication. See Hymes.

2. My use of the term "structure" here follows Barthes's formulation in his essay "Introduction to the Structural Analysis of Narratives." Barthes argues that the study of narrative discourse might begin by borrowing from linguistics the strategy of describing "utterances" on a variety of levels—looking at elements such as "syntax," "function," code manipulation, the construction of both a narrator and narratee, etc. The relationship between linguistics and narratology, in other words, is analogical; one discipline suggests a pattern of interpretive questions that might be developed in the other. My attempt to draw on speech-act theory here follows just such an analogical approach. See Barthes (79–124).

3. J. L. Austin's discussion of "felicitous" and "infelicitous" utterances foregrounds the importance of shared conventions (codes) and the interaction between

speaker(s) and hearer(s) in enabling a performative utterance to take effect. See Austin (12–24).

4. The fundamental weakness in the speech-act theory of ordinary language philosophers, of course, is that it tends to model communication as occurring between two persons, an untenable simplification of social interaction. Of course, there is no logical reason that such theories cannot be expanded in scope. Entering into a critical discussion of the debates surrounding speech-act theory goes well beyond the scope of the present study. For a brief introduction to the general issues, though, see Hymes (52–54).

5. See Strickland (vii). I use the term "Indian law" throughout this study to designate a broad range of jurisprudence. Cohen defines the term to mean the "body of jurisprudence created by treaties, statutes, executive orders, court decisions and administrative action defining and implementing relationships among the United States, Indian Tribes, Individuals and the States" (Strickland 1). Indian law is primarily federal law, owing to the peculiar status of Indian peoples in our constitutional system.

6. Scholars who have undertaken a study of such breadth have generally had to limit their inquiries either to a specific aspect of this discourse or to a smaller historical period. For a classic example of the former kind of scholarship, see Pearce. For a good discussion of a wider range of thinking about Indian identity during a more condensed historical period, see Sheehan.

7. My understanding of law, not just as a body of texts but as an active force integrating doctrines, institutions, formal procedure, and daily experience, follows the general tenor of arguments made by the so-called "legal realists" during the early decades of this century. The sociological work of the realists has been invaluable in opening up our understanding of the ways law directly impacts individual lives, and it provides the basis of the legal anthropology of today. Indeed, one of the most important works on Native American law, Karl L. Llewellyn's *The Cheyenne Way*, engages directly with realist assumptions. For a good overview of the "legal realist" movement, see Fisher.

8. If this definition of Indian law seems excessively broad to some, I would point out only that my approach is in line with much excellent legal scholarship currently being done in a number of areas. I have been particularly influenced by Michael Grossberg's work on family law in nineteenth-century America. Harold J. Berman's work on the formation of the Western legal tradition and Llewellyn's discussion of "law ways," have also been helpful in my thinking. For the definitions above, I am particularly indebted to Berman.

9. See Jennings, *Invasion* (228–53).

10. Admittedly, Eliot's overzealousness and the excessively repressive nature of the plantations under his supervision limited the effectiveness of his project. The basic point about the need for a legal superstructure to make religious models effective, though, is supported by the history of the more successful "South Sea Indian Plantation" on Cape Cod by Richard Bourne. For a discussion of Bourne's plantation and its legacy, see Clifford. For a general overview of the state-sponsored missionary work in early Massachusetts, see Kellaway.

11. For good, general overviews of Indian law, see Getches and Wilkinson, Pevar, and Strickland.

12. See also Williams, *The American Indian in Western Legal Thought*, and Getches and Wilkinson (34–36).

13. For another useful discussion of the international law roots of Indian law, see Falkowski. A brief but helpful overview of the early roots of U.S. Indian law also opens Deloria and Lytle's *American Indians, American Justice.*

14. Reflecting altered historical circumstances, U.S. Indian law now uses slightly different terminology, though the essential legal concepts remain constant. Today, Indians are seen to have "a perpetual right to remain on ancestral lands until such time as Congress decides to take this land for another purpose." This right is now referred to as a "possessory and not a property interest (that is, Indians have a right to possess their ancestral land but not to own it unless Congress gives them ownership rights)" (Pevar 25). See also Henderson.

15. Vattel's most pointed reference to these issues comes in Book I, Chapter VII of *The Law of Nations: Or Principles of the Law of Nature* (1758). In that chapter, titled "Of the cultivation of the earth," Vattel notes that the cultivation of the soil is "an obligation imposed by nature on mankind." This obligation, he asserts, renders lawful the colonization of the continent of North America since "the people of these vast countries rather over-ran than inhabited them."

16. Tellingly, at one point in "On the American Indians," Vitoria points out that assuming guardianship over a child does not deprive that child of legal rights. The fact that the Indians were born in sin and lacked "the use of reason to prompt them to seek baptism or the things necessary for salvation" thus provides no justification for their outright dispossession (Pagden and Lawrence 250). The European colonizer, though, does have an obligation to try to raise the Indian from this state of ignorance. According to Vitoria, the "barbarian" is obliged by natural law to listen to peaceful persuasion regarding the true religion and "to acquiesce with what they hear if it is reasonable" (271). On the trust relationship in U.S. Indian law, see Pevar (32–45).

17. A full survey of the development of English colonial theory is beyond the scope of the present discussion. The earliest texts that deal, albeit indirectly, with colonialism include John Rasell's *Interlude of the Four Elements* (1519) and Thomas More's *Utopia* (1516). In 1555, Richard Eden's preface to his 1555 translation of Peter Martyr's *De Novo Orbe* provides a brief commentary on the Spanish controversy over the legality of conquering the Indies. Eden embraced Sepulveda's Aristotelian argument asserting that the Indians were "natural slaves." A 1583 translation of Las Casas, though, rejected the conquest argument for colonization. Richard Hakluyt's *Principle Navigations* (1589), Robert Johnson's *Nova Britannia* (1609), William Strachey's *History and Travel into Virginia Bretania* (1618), and Samuel Purchas's *Purchas, His Pilgrimes* (1619) make up a core of early English texts on colonial policy and expansion. Overall, the tenor of these writings was much more aggressive than would characterize later English writings; they tended to apply the legal principle of discovery to justify seizure of lands. In time, though, such an approach gave way to the treaty-based system that dominated during the eighteenth century. For a good general overview of this early literature, see Cave.

18. The "Walking Purchase" involved the discovery by Thomas Penn of a treaty signed by three Delaware chiefs ceding lands around the forks of the Delaware River "as far as a man can go in a day and a half." The colonists selected three runners, who trained for nine days, and colonists cleared obstacles and brush from their path in anticipation of the "walk." Two of the three runners died from dehydration, but one covered sixty-five miles in a day and a half, securing about

1200 square miles of territory. The Delaware initially refused to move but were forced to acquiesce by the Iroquois.

19. For good discussions of the English treaty system, see Strickland (62–107) and Jones, *License*.

20. Before the Revolution, we are more likely to find a manifestly imperial and paternalistic strain of Indian law in individual colonies' internal legal codes dealing with Indians living within their borders. Tracing the history of the treatment of Indians in Massachusetts during the colonial period, for instance, we see a clear progression toward legal domination. While the English initially sought to extend their jurisdiction beyond their borders through treaties or similar agreements, in the years after King Philip's War, Massachusetts absorbed its Indian population. English common law was unilaterally extended to cover the Indians, who were also placed (sometimes individually and sometimes collectively—as in the case of various "praying towns" or "plantations") under white guardianship. By the beginning of the eighteenth century, specific laws regulating Indians as a distinct minority group were developed. For a detailed discussion of Indian law in Massachusetts, see Kawashima.

21. There is a certain irony (or perhaps political sophistication) in the fact that Washington was characterized during the nineteenth century by the various nations of the Iroquois League as a savior, unique in his fair dealings with his Indian "children." Lewis Henry Morgan's *The League of the Iroquois* (1851) included a discussion of Washington's placement within the "heaven" of the Iroquois, the only white man to occupy such a position. See Morgan (178–81).

22. Henry Knox, the official later primarily responsible for Indian affairs as Washington's secretary of war, also campaigned for the abandonment of an Indian policy based on conquest for one based on purchase and treaty relations. The Treaty of Grenville (1795), negotiated under Knox's tenure as war secretary, was a watershed in that it involved the U.S. relinquishing claims of absolute sovereignty over unceded lands north of the Ohio River, reserving instead the right of purchase under the law of discovery.

23. Admittedly, Locke was not the originator of many of the ideas he expresses that bear on Indian identity and colonialism. His theories of "waste" and the state of nature can be found in earlier Puritan writers (both New World colonizers and Old World theologians). Locke did, however, present many of these ideas in a larger theoretical context and was extremely influential in early American thought. For a discussion of which Locke texts should be seen as the most influential on Indian affairs, see Squadrito. Squadrito argues that Lockean epistemology (as expressed in the *Essay on Human Understanding*) was more influential than his political philosophy, but she does a thorough job drawing attention to the relevant ideas from both texts.

24. See Pearce (68, 89).

25. See also Getches and Wilkinson (37–42).

26. Kent's discussion of Indian title appears in the opening "lecture" in his discussion of the law of real property. In that lecture, he highlights the persistence of elements of feudal English law in the American legal system's dealings with issues of Indian property rights.

27. One of the principal differences between Indian law in antebellum American and later in the nineteenth century was the development of a powerful, central-

ized administrative colonial apparatus. The model of Indian identity remained broadly consistent throughout the nineteenth century (though the paternalistic discourse of the Indian-as-child became more dominant and complex after the Civil War). One of the main things that changed, though, were the strategies by which that model was brought to bear on *individual* Indian subjects. This shift to dealing with the Indian as an "individual" rather than as a cultural group was a function of the development of the allotment policy and the increasing bureaucratization of Indian law needed to administer such a policy. The ability to interpellate the Indian as an "individual" subject, though, also required a retreat from international law paradigms within the body of U.S. Indian law, culminating in the suspension of treaty negotiations with tribes. These issues will be explored in greater detail in chapter 5.

28. Historically, there has been a great deal of interest in the phenomenon of treaty making with Native Americans, ranging from eighteenth-century texts like Cadwallader Colden's *The History of the Five Indian Nations* to contemporary work by scholars like Francis Prucha (who has written voluminously on the subject) and Robert A. Williams Jr. Treaties have fascinated historians and other scholars for a variety of reasons: first, they continue to have legal force and bear on many contemporary disputes; second, they reveal a great deal about American history and the potential for a multicultural jurisprudence; and third, they also have been seen as possessing intrinsic dramatic and/or literary interest. For some early examples of "literary" discussions of treaties, see Wroth, and Drummond and Moody.

29. This, of course, helps explain why mourning rituals provided the ceremonial basis for Iroquois diplomacy. The Iroquois condolence ritual involved honoring a dead chief, naming his successor, and re-enacting the prophet Deganawidah's gift of a vision of solidarity—the gift that, according to tradition, originated the Iroquois League. A text of the condolence ritual can be found in Bierhorst (109–86).

30. What has shifted most over time is the interpretation of the balance of power and responsibility in these contractual relationships. As Pevar points out, during much of the nineteenth century "the trust doctrine was viewed as a source of federal power *over* Indians," while more recently the courts have seen the doctrine as "a source of federal responsibility *to* Indians" (33). It is the latter interpretation that Indian peoples have cannily, and consistently, asserted for more than two hundred years.

Chapter 2: Seneca Politics and the Rhetoric of Engagement

1. My understanding of predication and reference as facets of linguistic "performativity" draws heavily on Searle's *Speech Acts.*

2. It is worth noting here that, traditionally, Iroquoian nations did not understand treaties dealing with land as exchanges of property (as real estate transactions) in the Euro-American sense. As Robert A. Williams Jr. points out, for Indian peoples treaties granting land settlement rights were typically thought of as "a way for American Indians to harmonize their interests and create a relationship of trust with a stranger group" (*Linking Arms* 130).

3. For another example of Seneca political rhetoric from this time period, see

Konkle's discussion of the speeches of Red Jacket (233–36). Konkle's discussion emphasizes Red Jacket's resistance to what she refers to as the "theory of Indian difference, which holds that Indians cannot rise out of their state of nature because of their inherent moral failings, which are demonstrated in their inherent traits that exclude them from the universally human" (10).

4. Vine Deloria Jr. stresses Indian appreciation of the "contractual" nature of treaties. He notes that "treaties were originally viewed as contracts. Many treaties contain the phrase 'contracting parties' and specify that each party must agree to the terms of the treaty for it to be valid. It would have seemed that, if treaties were contracts, the United States was required under the impairments of contracts of due process clause to protect the rights of the Indian tribes. Or at least it seemed to the Cherokees, Choctaws, and other tribes who continually went to court to establish their property rights" (Deloria, *Custer* 35).

5. For an excellent historical discussions of the struggles of the Seneca after the Revolution, and of Cornplanter's complex position as a mediator figure, see Wallace (149–83).

6. During the antebellum period, state politicians often sought to sidestep federal Indian law and negotiate land sales with Indian tribes. These efforts were aided by the national push to develop large-scale transportation systems (the Erie Canal project, completed in 1825, provides one example) and to stimulate entrepreneurial energies throughout the country. On the complex and often illegal attempts by New York politicians to dispossess the Iroquois, see Hauptman, *Conspiracy.*

7. On the Gardeau sale, see Hauptman, *Conspiracy* (148–60).

8. The national emergence of Native American writers in the late nineteenth century was similarly rooted in a relatively small, educated elite. Individuals like Francis LaFlesche (Omaha), Zitkala-Sa and Charles Eastman (Sioux), Arthur Parker (Seneca), and Carlos Montezuma (Yavapai), formed the core of what might be called the first Native American Renaissance in letters. The next major explosion of Indian writings would begin in the 1960s and 1970s, with the rise to prominence of writers like Leslie Marmon Silko, N. Scott Momaday, and James Welsh.

9. The drafter of this document is listed as one Oliver Silverheels, though twelve other Seneca are designated as having been present at the writing.

10. The Society of Friends would continue to draw attention to such willingness to engage with the forms of "civilized" life in publications throughout the 1840s. In an 1849 collection of *Letters Concerning the New Form of Government Adopted by the Seneca Indians,* the Quakers included a letter submitted to the commissioner of Indian affairs lauding the Seneca for their efforts to apply themselves "to the cultivation and improvement of their forms and dwellings" (5). The letter also highlights the shift to a practice of keeping "written" records, described (interestingly enough) as a check on the authority of chiefs (who are represented as susceptible to bribery). In this respect, the emergence of Seneca writing is framed simultaneously as a sign of assimilation and an important example of legal engagement.

11. For an overview of Pierce's life and involvement in these controversies, see Vernon.

12. In his introduction to the 1962 reprint of *The League of the Iroquois,* Wil-

liam N. Fenton remarks that Morgan's classical education and legal training helped shape his approach to his subject matter (xii). Readers of the text may notice Morgan's considerable interest in issues of law and government and his subtle debts to writers like Montesquieu and Locke in his thinking about the role of Iroquois "legislators," the "spirit" of the League, and the transition from a hunter society into an oligarchic confederation. Fully half of Morgan's ethnographic text seeks to comprehend the Iroquois's cultural condition (relative to other Indian tribes and to "civilization") in terms of the progression of forms of government. Indeed, some of the tensions in Morgan's text may be attributable to its intellectual ambivalence—gesturing simultaneously toward legal models and a more modern ethnographic approach to comprehending Indian identity.

13. For a detailed discussion of Parker's life, see Armstrong.

14. This piece, and other Parker manuscripts not documented otherwise, can be found in the Ely S. Parker Papers at the Huntington Library in San Marino, Calif. Items in the manuscript collection will by cited as PP.

15. The full text of the autobiography appears in Arthur Parker, "Writings" (527–35).

16. This unpublished letter is found in the Parker Papers (PP).

Chapter 3: William Apess and the Constraints of Conversion

1. All of Apess's writings have been collected into a single edition by Barry O'Connell (*On Our Own Ground*). All future references to Apess's work are drawn from this volume. Occom's work appears in several sources. References in this chapter to "A Short Narrative of My Life" come from Peyer, *The Elders Wrote*.

2. Arnold Krupat has dealt extensively with his work, both in *The Voice in the Margin* and *For Those Who Come After*. Others critics, including David Murray, Randall Moon, Gordon Sayre, and A. LaVonne Brown Ruoff, have also turned their attention to his varied autobiographical acts. As a result of this body of scholarship, Apess's prominent place in the study of nineteenth-century autobiography has been secured.

3. A useful overview of the Pequot War can be found in Waldman (90–91). More detailed accounts appear in Cave, *The Pequot War*, and Jennings, *Invasion*. Dwight's seven-part neoclassical American epic was first published in 1794. In the Spenserian stanzas of Part IV, "The Destruction of the Pequods," Dwight clearly assumes that the Pequots had passed away into the pages of history.

4. For a good discussion of Pequot history after the War of 1636–37, see Campisi and De Forest. For two conflicting assessments of the widely discussed renaissance of the Mashantucket Pequots (owing to the development of Foxwood's Casino in Ledyard, Connecticut), see Benedict and Eisler.

5. Barry O'Connell continues to try to fill gaps in the biographical record. See O'Connell "Once More."

6. For a range of historical interpretations of Apess's work, see McQuaid, O'Connell, "Survival" and "Once More," Dannenberg, and Konkle. Some examples of scholarship focused on the religious components of Apess's writings would include Gustafson, Haynes, David Murray, and Warrior "William Apess."

7. Though "Experience" was not published until 1833, four years after the first

[1829] edition of *A Son of the Forest*, O'Connell has presented persuasive textual evidence that it was written before the latter, longer autobiography. In "The Experience of the Missionary," Apess makes reference to his intention to pen a longer work providing a more detailed account of his life. This text, presumably, was *A Son of the Forest*.

8. Occom's "A Short Narrative of My Life" has already been mentioned. Copway's "The Life of Kah-ge-ga-gah-bowh" was first published in 1847 (and is reprinted in Ruoff, et al. George Copway: *Life, Letters, and Speeches*). Jacobs's short autobiographical sketch "Peter Jacobs' History of Himself" appears at the beginning of his English-language journal that was first published in 1857. The text is reprinted in Peyer, *The Elders Wrote*. Peter Jones's personal journal was published in 1860.

9. Laura Murray's collection of the writings of Joseph Johnson (Mohegan) provides an excellent overview of this (largely unpublished) form of missionary discourse. See also McCallum. Some critics, most notably Hilary Wyss, see this material as evidence of a significant tradition of lifewriting flourishing well before published autobiographies like Apess's. In her view, letters, journal entries, and confessions embedded in published tracts of colonial missionaries represent sites of contest, where Indian converts struggled to attain literacy and define an Indian identity through writing. As in this study, Wyss's approach (which also highlights the problems inherent in the critical paradigm of authenticity) focuses on Native "engagement" with a specific form of colonial discourse. However, Wyss sees fewer limitations than I do for Native writers in this engagement with the discourse of conversion. Because her focus is on recovering a sense of Native agency, she places much less emphasis on institutional constraint than I will here.

10. See Bowden and Ronda.

11. For an overview of the genre of "dying Indian" speeches and their cultural function, see Bross.

12. I should note here that I am referring to *written* autobiographies that follow the conventions of Protestant spiritual autobiography. As recent scholarship has suggested, when we look at records of oral "confessions" by Praying Indians in early Massachusetts, we may see a slightly different picture. As Craig White has argued, the oral narratives embedded in a range of tracts published by John Eliot in the mid-seventeenth century reveal Indian converts engaged in a "symbolic dialogue" revealing their "commitment to adapt and survive by using a Puritan genre to maintain native oral traditions" (458). What is left out of White's discussion, of course, is a treatment of the fate of the Praying Indians (and the abandonment of Eliot's commitment to the work of conversion) in the wake of King Philip's War.

13. In her introduction to Joseph Johnson's writings, Laura Murray takes a somewhat different view. Discussing the importance of Richard Baxter's *The Saint's Everlasting Rest* (1650) on Johnson, she argues that while Baxter directs readers inward, his "language of physical exertion is so vivid that it may have served for more than one reader as a call to address earthly as well and heavenly goals" (17). I would agree that the *figurative* language used by Puritan writers often allowed for a form of conciliation between this-worldly and other-worldly striving. (See Carlson). I would also agree that in his private journal, Johnson may

demonstrate the kind of balance that Murray describes. In their published conversion narratives, though, Indian writers (such as Apess and Occom) were often more constrained by the form, a tension that is often recorded quite explicitly in their texts.

14. See Shea and Nussbaum.

15. Much recent criticism has focused on the "subversive" aspects of early Native American Christian writing. In general, though, such scholarship has not convincingly demonstrated the presence of such elements in *autobiographical* narratives from this period. In *That the People Might Live,* for example, Jace Weaver sees the works of Occom, Apess, and Jones as examples of a persistent "communitism" in Indian writing. While correctly noting the presence of a voice of protest in some of these writers' works, though, Weaver's insistence that Apess's texts, in general, "must be viewed as resistance literature, affirming Indian cultural and political identity over the dominant culture" strikes me as an overreading (55). There is relatively little close analysis of Apess's autobiographies in Weaver's study to support such a claim with respect to those works. Joanna Brooks, on the other hand, has argued that Samson Occom "discovered in Christianity . . . a venue for strengthening Indian communities and rearticulating tribal identities under siege by colonialism" (56). Her argument, however, focuses on Occom's composition of hymns and publication of his influential hymnal (published in 1774). In that text, Occom does seem to have been able, as Brooks argues, to escape from an excessive focus on "form" and "method" in Christian discourse, allowing him to open up space for representations of cultural difference. Yet even Brooks tacitly acknowledges that his autobiography (and published sermon) presents instead a picture of an "autoethnographic confessor" who was less able to evade such formal restrictions (74).

16. In an essay on Samson Occom, Keely McCarthy makes this same point, noting that "Protestant missionary tradition . . . held that religious conversion was complete only if accompanied by a cultural transformation (assimilation)" (354).

17. For a detailed discussion of the historical development of the split between secular and sacred law, see Berman (271–94).

18. For a general discussion of the Puritan consensus regarding the linkage of "civilization" policies and conversion, see Kellaway (5–8) and Love (9–14).

19. See McCarthy and Laura Murray.

20. As Konkle has suggested, Peter Jones's historical writings demonstrate a somewhat more nuanced rhetorical position vis-à-vis Ojibwe traditions. In his 1860 *History of the Ojebway Indians,* he accepts the need for the "improvement" of the Ojibwe people (largely through the civilizing influence of Christianity) while rejecting the political subordination of Indians. See Konkle (181–87).

21. For general information on the controversy and Occom's involvement, see Blodgett.

22. For a sampling of criticism on Occom's text, see Peyer, Nelson, and Elliott.

23. Several aspects of Occom's "Narrative" are wholly conventional. He draws explicitly on genre-specific terminology in discussing some of his experiences. Recalling that he had occasion to hear a number of "extraordinary ministers" preach during the Great Awakening, Occom notes that "after I was *awakened* and

converted, I went to all the meetings I could come at" [my emphasis] (13). At a point like this, he is explicitly invoking the stages of conversion codified within New England Protestantism. Later, when he refers to a moment at age seventeen when he had "a Discovery of the way of Salvation through Jesus Christ," Occom is doing the same thing.

24. See Laura Murray (50–54), and also Wheelock.

25. Nelson has written about the self-fracturing involved in Occom's role as a "colonized colonizer" (58).

26. For a good discussion of the Brotherton project, and Occom's role in it, see Wyss (123–55). Wyss argues that Occom sought to "simultaneously celebrate Native identity and reject Anglo-American colonial control by invoking a powerful rhetoric of Native manhood" (135). In her reading, Wyss also acknowledges the discursive pressure placed on Indian converts by Anglo-American religious discourse. Her discussion of Brotherton highlights Occom's increasing sense of the need for political separation if the Christianization of Indians were to take a truly egalitarian form in eighteenth-century America.

27. I would stress here that I am not suggesting that Christian conversion has *always* been understood to involve such a stark process of self-negation. Indeed, by the early twentieth century changes in the relationship between missionary work and state institutions—changes centering on an increased tolerance for and interest in Indian religiousness—signal the rise of a new dynamic. A large body of work, too large to be cited here, has been done looking at the fascinating conjunction between Catholicism and Native religious forms, especially among Plains tribes like the Lakota Sioux. (Nicholas Black Elk has been a central figure of interest in such studies.) Lakota Catholicism, like the blending of peyote use and Christian symbolism in the Native American Church, represents a different kind of cultural contact than we see in the experience of someone like Occom.

28. McCarthy notes that this statement also echoes 2 Corinthians 11:22–23, where Paul is lamenting the need to defend himself against those already inclined to pay undo heed to "false apostles." In this respect, Occom does manage to register an indirect protest against his mistreatment by fellow Christians. Yet even McCarthy acknowledges that in the context of the overall narrative, this critique is "subtle" (366).

29. The correspondence of Occom's son-in-law, Joseph Johnson, to Wheelock often reveals similar moments of "constraint." In a letter dated Sept. 27, 1768, for example, Johnson writes two paragraphs. The first laments the lack of financial support he is receiving, but he immediately shifts focus from these protestations to a second paragraph dominated by self-scrutiny. "I am fully Determined henceforth to leave myself to that Ever good God who has hitherto guided my doubtful paths," he writes (Murray 73). The balance of the paragraph traces his own moral blindness and backsliding. This rapid retreat from social criticism to self-scrutiny is typical of the writings of the early Christian Indians.

30. It is worth noting here that George Copway uses the same phrasing ("child of the forest") throughout his 1847 *Life.*

31. As Robert Warrior has noted, this is not surprising, "because of what it meant to be a Pequot person in the late eighteenth and early nineteenth centuries." In such a context, "Apess would have had access only to a social, religious, and political culture in constant crisis" ("William Apess" 191).

Chapter 4: William Apess and Indian Liberalism

1. For two other critical responses to Krupat's reading, both related in some respects to my own, see Sayre and Moon.

2. There are two published version of *A Son of the Forest*, one from 1829, and the second from 1831. The 1831 version, which appears in Barry O'Connell's edition of Apess's collected writings, differs from the original in that it offers a toned-down account of Apess's split with the Episcopal Methodists, has ten chapters instead of six, and is somewhat more polished in its writing. I will be quoting from the 1831 version throughout, as this seems to have been the final version preferred by Apess. For a thorough account of the textual variations between the two editions, see the "Textual Afterword" in O'Connell's *On Our Own Ground*.

3. For a different interpretation of this "error," see Velikova.

4. This kind of debt to non-Indian texts for his understanding of Indian identity persisted throughout his literary career during the 1830s. When he penned his 1836 "Eulogy on King Philip," Apess drew heavily (and without acknowledgment) on Washington Irving's essay "Philip of Pokanoket," from his 1819 *Sketchbook of Mr. Geoffrey Crayon, Gent.*

5. Elias Boudinot's text seems to have been particularly influential in shaping Apess's thinking. The primary purpose of his book was to reinforce the argument that the American Indians were one of the lost tribes of Israel, descendants of Jacob. As such, Boudinot saw the Indians as having been cut off from the mass of humanity as a result of past transgressions, but not altogether forsaken. He concedes that the poor opinion held by whites of Indian character has some justification, in that it is based on the "miserable hordes that infest our frontier" (vi). Yet Boudinot does not blame the Indian for such degeneracy. In his view, the Indian character is defined by the fact that the Indian's sensibilities are not as diffused as they are in the white man. As he puts it, they run in "steadier, deeper, channels." The Indian is more passionate than the white man, and more susceptible to the influence of both eloquence and superstition. Nevertheless, he has an innate store of virtue and nobility which might be brought out through Christian treatment. Indeed, the central argument of Boudinot's book is that these lost tribes are part of biblical history and its prophetic narrative. He argues that Christians have a divine mandate and responsibility to convert the Jews (the Indians are included in that category) and to prepare them for the return to the new Jerusalem, the kind of millennialist argument which drove a great deal of religious revivalism in antebellum America. He closes his text commenting, "who knows but God has raised up these United States in these latter days, for the very purpose of accomplishing his will in bringing his beloved people to their own land" (297). Thus, to the extent that conversion and civilization are linked endeavors (as we have seen), Boudinot provides a powerful religious argument for colonialism, in spite of his sympathy for the Indians. Further discussion of the Israelite thesis and other theories of Indian origin can be found in Huddleston.

6. In his note to the text, Barry O'Connell dismisses Apess's elision of the Pequot War and King Philip's War, noting that "he has just confused them" (4). Yet to treat a moment like this as a simple historical error, and to excuse Apess for it, is to miss something significant happening. The fact that Apess could make

such an "error" is telling, when we think of his autobiographical struggle to define himself as an Indian.

7. Where Apess's schooling took place is not a matter of record, though it is clear he did not attend an "Indian" school. Because of his legal status as a ward of white foster parents, Apess would have been educated in a traditional grammar school (or "academy," as they were called after the Revolution), not in a missionary school, a point which distinguishes him from many of his predecessors and contemporaries. What is most interesting about this is that regardless of how he was treated by peers or teachers, Apess would have been taught the same curriculum as a white child. Perhaps for this reason, his years in school seem to have contributed greatly to his subsequent fluency in the forms and assumptions of American civil society.

8. See Kaestle (3–29).

9. In addition to *An Essay on Human Understanding*, Locke's *Some Thoughts Concerning Education* and *Of the Conduct of the Understanding* (1693; 1695) stand as influential articulations of these ideas. In the latter text, in particular, Locke stresses a model of youth education centered around a process of habituation designed to produce virtuous (i.e., self-restrained) behavior.

10. In *Some Thoughts on Education* Locke stresses the counterproductivity of corporal punishment for children. Only in the case of willful "obstinance" does he allow that beating serves any useful purpose (54–57).

11. This incident contrasts directly with his memory of being wrongfully accused and punished on another occasion by Mr. Furman. In that incident, having been accused by a vindictive maidservant of having chased her with a knife, Apess is flogged by Mr. Furman, who only later "undertook to investigate the matter" and "found out his error" (12). At moments like this, we see Apess manipulating paternalistic discourse to argue for proper (i.e., effective) parenting and moral education on the part of adult guardians. It is possible to see him making some specific gestures regarding Indian law in this instance as well. He notes Furman's comment that he would teach his "Indian dog, how to chase people with a knife." At such a moment Apess points out that he was not seen by white society, represented here by his court-appointed parent, in the same way as a white child would have been. Thus, his commentary on education can be taken as an even more poignant attempt to engage with the paternalistic assumptions of Indian law—a plea for careful and compassionate guardianship.

12. On this point, Apess echoes Benjamin Rush. In his "Plan for the Establishment of Public Schools," Rush stresses the need for moral and religious education of the young. He notes that he dissents in this respect "from one of those paradoxical opinions with which modern times abound: that it is improper to fill the minds of youth with religious principles of any kind and that they should be left to choose their own principles after they have arrived at an age in which they are capable of judging for themselves." He concludes his point noting, "could we preserve the mind in childhood and youth a perfect blank, this plan of education would have more to recommend it, but we know this to be impossible" (qtd. in Rudolph 11).

13. In an odd paragraph in Chapter Two, Apess takes up the issue of "improper naming," demonstrating the ways in which self-definition through the autobiographical act was always a challenge for him:

I know of nothing so trying to a child as to be repeatedly called by an improper name. I thought it disgraceful to be called an Indian; it was considered as a slur upon an oppressed and scattered nation, and I have often been led to inquire where the whites received the word, which they so often threw as an opprobrious epithet at the sons of the forest. I could not find it in the Bible and therefore considered that it was a word imported for the special purpose of degrading us. At other times I thought it was derived from the term *in-gen-uity*. But the proper term which ought to be applied to our nation, to distinguish it from the rest of the human family is that of *"Natives"*—and I humbly conceive that the natives of this country are the only people under heaven who have a just title to the name, inasmuch as we are the only people who retain the original complexion of our Father Adam (10).

14. As O'Connell points out, for years Snelling was frequently assumed to have written the book, and he was listed as its author in some bibliographies. I would agree with O'Connell, though, that it is unlikely that Snelling was the primary author of the text. The aggressive tone of the book is quite out of keeping with the dispassionate "realism" that dominates Snelling's *Tales of the Northwest*. See O'Connell, *On Our Own Ground* (xlii).

15. See also Hutchens.

16. Literature on the Cherokee and on the removal crisis of the 1820s and 1830s is voluminous. The writings of Elias Boudinot (the editor of the first Native American newspaper, *The Cherokee Phoenix*, who took his name from the Jesuit writer of *A Star in the West*) provide interesting insights into the Cherokee's engagement with civilized forms and models of self. His "An Address to the Whites" (1826) attempts to provide evidence of the tribe's advancement, documenting the development of written language, a court system and a set of written laws, and other institutions, as well as providing statistical evidence of the rapid increase in the scope of agriculture and manufacturing. See Perdue, ed., *Cherokee Editor* 65–84. The "Cherokee Cases" include *Cherokee Nation v. Georgia* (1831) and *Worcester v. Georgia* (1832). John Marshall's ambiguous opinions in these cases stand as central texts in the body of U.S. Indian law, establishing a peculiar balance between paternalism and limited sovereignty.

17. For a good overview of these legal issues from the perspective of one of the leading participants in the crisis, see Calhoun.

18. The letter notes that "the Great Spirit . . . has raised up among you a brother of our own and has sent him to us that he might show us all the secret contrivances of the pale faces to deceive and defraud us" (166). The language here obliquely alludes to Apess as part of the line of "messianic" Indian leaders (whose ranks would include individuals like the Shawnee Prophet). It is easy to see how such language might be interpreted by those inclined to overreact to the "threat" of Indian uprisings. Certainly, images of the Indian as a violent and dangerous threat long outlasted any real risks (especially in the lands east of the Mississippi).

19. See Clifford (277–348).

Chapter 5: Charles Eastman and the Discourse of Allotment

1. The clarion call of Indian reform had begun in earnest in the 1850s, with texts like John Beeson's *A Plea for the Indian* (1858) and the appointment of the Episcopalian minister Henry B. Whipple to the Bishopric of Minnesota. Whipple was instrumental in bringing together a religious coalition (including Quakers and Episcopalians), which, in turn, shaped the development of Grant's Peace Policy.

2. John Marshall opens his opinion in *Cherokee Nation v. Georgia* with a similar acknowledgment (and disavowal) of the power of sympathy, noting that "if the courts were permitted to indulge their sympathies, a case better calculated to excite them can scarcely be imagined" (qtd. in Pevar 46). Interestingly, this attempt to quarantine law from the effects of the discourse of "sympathy" may explain the fact that Indian autobiographies by male writers have been historically more directly engaged with legal discourse. A different set of cultural and generic pressures has tended to lead Indian women writers, even those dealing with political issues, to draw more directly on the language of moral suasion and the rhetorical techniques of sentimental literature in speaking to the colonizing power.

3. For an excellent overview of Indian policy during this era, see Hoxie (41–82).

4. For a general overview of the rise of these and other Indian reform organizations, see Fritz.

5. Though there was no statutory or constitutional basis for the Courts of Indian Offenses, the Supreme Court upheld them in *United States v. Clapox* (1888) as a valid exercise of administrative power. The decision argued that the Indian courts were not "constitutional courts" but rather "educational and disciplinary instrumentalities." The reservation as a whole was imagined as a school. (qtd. in Prucha, *Documents* 161)

6. See Harring (110–11). For an illuminating discussion of the kinds of traditional Indian "law ways" being ignored by the courts and legislatures of this period, see Llewellyn and Hoebel.

7. The Major Crimes Act has been amended several times. Today it includes more than a dozen crimes. See Pevar (142–66).

8. For a further overview of the allotment policy and the Dawes Act, see Pevar (112–22).

9. For an excellent biographical overview of Winnemucca's life, see Karttunen (44–73).

10. For an overview of the conflict with Brown, see Wilson (67–81). Eastman provides his own version of events in his second autobiography in a chapter called "War with the Politicians." See Eastman, *From the Deep Woods to Civilization* (116–35).

11. Eastman's wife Elaine (who had her own history of political and legal activism on behalf of Native Americans and who had been a successful writer of poetic juvenilia) greatly influenced his decision to commence a writing career. Seething at the treatment they had received at the hands of the BIA (reflected in the publicity campaign she waged on their behalf in papers ranging from *The New York Post* to the *Omaha Daily Bee*), Elaine Goodale Eastman actively encouraged her

husband to try to publish the thoughts and reflections that he was beginning to pen, with her editorial assistance. See Wilson (73, 131) and also Elaine Goodale Eastman.

12. For an excellent biographical sketch of Eastman, focusing on his role as a mediator, see Karttunen (135–64).

13. On the dedication page for *Indian Boyhood*, Eastman characterizes the text as "the imperfect record of my boyish impressions and experiences up to the age of fifteen years." Elaine Goodale Eastman's foreword to *From the Deep Woods to Civilization* also describes the earlier work as one that "pictures the first of three distinct periods in the life of the writer of this book" (xvi).

14. See Wilson (33).

15. For a good overview of the pan-Indianism of the period, and the role of Native Americans such as Eastman in these movements, see Hertzberg.

16. See Brumble.

17. Three of Zitkala-Sa's autobiographical sketches ("Impressions of an Indian Childhood," "The School Days of an Indian Girl," and "An Indian Teacher Among Indians"), subsequently combined with other texts and published in 1921 in the volume *American Indian Stories*, were first published in the *Atlantic Monthly* in 1900. La Flesche's account of his experiences as a student at the Presbyterian mission school on the Omaha Reservation in Nebraska was also published in 1900 as *The Middle Five: Indian Schoolboys of the Omaha Tribe.*

18. See Jacobson (13).

19. See Wong (19). See also Krupat, *Ethnocriticism.*

20. See Lejeune (3–30).

21. See Wong (43–44).

22. For a more critical Indian perspective on the impact of allotment on Sioux families, see Ella Deloria (86–98).

23. On this topic, see DeMallie.

24. Dennis Tedlock's work on Zuni storytelling suggests that inconsistency and ambiguity is central to the way mythology often functions in American Indian cultures. See Tedlock, "The Spoken Word."

25. It is worth noting that in other early writings Eastman showed a willingness to strike a different rhetorical balance in his acts of cultural translation. For example, in his 1895 essay on "The Sioux Mythology," while characterizing "these people" (another act of distancing) as "uncivilized" and "untutored," Eastman nevertheless goes out of his way to foreground the rationality of traditional Sioux religion. "The human mind," he writes, "equipped with all its faculties, is capable even in an uncultured state of a logical process of reasoning" (88). The "nature-worship" of the Indian, in this respect, is a rational way of conceiving the relation between God and man, through analogy. Eastman's discussion of the "advent" of the white man (which, he notes, disabused the Sioux of the notion that the earth was flat and "suspended in a dark space") clearly shows his commitment to assimilation and "progress." However, this essay's more aggressive advocacy of traditional Sioux cultural practices only serves to highlight the comparative reticence of *Indian Boyhood.*

26. On the role of the agency physicians in opposing traditional "medicine men," see Prucha, *American Indian Policy in Crisis* (193–226).

27. See Brumble (147–64).

28. For a general overview of Morgan's ethnological theories and his attitudes about the proper pace of assimilation, see Beider (194–246).

29. The Lake Mohonk Conference of the Friends of the Indian was a loose-knit group of reformers interested in Indian affairs who met at Lake Mohonk, New York, from 1883 to 1916. The conferences were extremely influential in the formulation of federal Indian policy during those years. Eastman knew many of the members of the organization well and addressed the group on numerous occasions.

30. The opening of the book thus unquestionably allows non-Indian readers to experience safely the pleasures of what Philip Deloria calls "playing Indian," an act of cross-cultural mimicry whose particular significance varied historically, but which generally has been tied to the need of white Americans to buttress their sense of identity by appropriating Indianness. In the period during which Eastman was writing, Deloria describes the act of "playing Indian" in the proliferation of back-to-nature organizations (like the Boy Scouts), which are rooted in a range of anxieties about modernity. Eastman, it should be noted, was involved later in his life in the Boy Scout movement, and contributed pieces to *Boy's Life* magazine.

31. See Grossberg, *Governing the Hearth* (234–307).

32. The Supreme Court's decision in *Lone Wolf v. Hitchcock* (1903) fully established Congress's "plenary power" to abrogate treaty stipulations through statutes. This decision undermined the strongest remaining legal basis by which Native tribes could counter white encroachment on their territorial and cultural sovereignty.

Chapter 6: Charles Eastman and the Rights of Character

1. The emphasis on filiopiety here links Eastman's autobiography with Winnemucca's, though the conflict between father figures that characterized her text is largely absent in his.

2. For a general discussion of Sioux kinship structures, see Ella Deloria.

3. See Standing Bear (176–90).

4. See Wilson (67–78).

5. See Wilson (93).

6. An 1863 statute specified that special congressional legislation was required as a prerequisite before an Indian tribe could enter suit in the U.S. Court of Claims. Eastman's initial task, therefore, was to push Congress to pass such legislation. See Wilson (92).

7. On the distinction between a will theory and equity theory of contracts, see Horwitz (180–85).

8. Regrettably, both before and after 1924, the rights attendant to Indian citizenship were limited by a "sympathetic" judiciary. As Frederick Hoxie has pointed out, Indians' rights as citizens came into conflict with the government's ongoing paternalistic sense of responsibility over its Native wards. The rearticulation of principles of guardianship during the early twentieth century highlights the ongoing tensions between "partial" sovereignty and "full" citizenship. Many of the restrictions placed on Indian "citizens" at this time (surrounding issues such as voting rights) would remain in place until the 1960s and 1970s. While such limitations should not undermine our appreciation of the shift in Eastman's

discourse, they do foreground the need to continue to assess the "success" of his acts of legal engagement with a sense of historical context. Eastman's struggle remains part of a longer, historical narrative. On the limitations of citizenship rights during the early decades of the twentieth century, see Hoxie (211–38). For a good overview of the history of Indian civil rights, see Pevar (260–77) and Getches and Wilkinson (548–98).

9. A key decision was *United States v. Nice* (1916). In that case Justice Van Devanter notes explicitly that "[c]itizenship is not incompatible with tribal existence or continued guardianship, and so may be conferred without completely emancipating the Indians or placing them beyond the reach of congressional regulations adopted for their protection" (qtd. in Getches and Wilkinson 551). This basic assumption, that Indians can claim the rights of ordinary U.S. citizens while still occupying their unique semisovereign position as "domestic dependent nations," continues to be in effect in the U.S. court system. The result has been a unique blend of legal vulnerabilities and strengths.

10. Eastman's opposition to the peyote religion of what would become the Native American Church reveals that he did not see all Indian religious practices as legitimate, however. This opposition is one of the "perturbing" elements Warrior finds in Eastman's work.

11. See Eastman, *Scout Talks* (137–45).

12. See Wilson (172–73).

WORKS CITED

Althusser, Louis. "Ideology and Ideological State Apparatuses." *Lenin and Philosophy.* Trans. Ben Brewster. 127–86. New York: Monthly Review, 1971.

Aristotle. *The Politics.* Ed. Stephen Everson. Cambridge, Mass.: Cambridge University Press, 1988.

Armstrong, William H. *Warrior in Two Camps: Ely S. Parker, Union General and Seneca Chief.* Syracuse, N.Y.: Syracuse University Press, 1978.

Ashcroft, Bill, Gareth Griffiths, and Helen Tiffin. *The Empire Writes Back: Theory and Practice in Post-Colonial Literatures.* New York: Routledge, 1989.

Austin, J. L. *How to Do Things with Words.* Ed. J. O. Urmson and Marina Sbisa. Cambridge, Mass.: Harvard University Press, 1962.

Axtell, James. *The European and the Indian: Essays in the Ethnohistory of Colonial North America.* New York: Oxford University Press, 1981.

Barthes, Roland. "Introduction to the Structural Analysis of Narratives." *Image, Music, Text.* Trans. Stephen Heath. 79–124. New York: Hill and Wang, 1977.

Bataille, Gretchen M., and Kathleen Mullen Sands. *American Indian Women: Telling Their Lives.* Lincoln: University of Nebraska Press, 1984.

Beider, Robert F. *Science Encounters the Indian, 1820–1880: The Early Years of American Ethnology.* Norman: University of Oklahoma Press, 1986.

Benedict, Jeff. *Without Reservation: The Making of America's Most Powerful Indian Tribe and Foxwoods, the World's Largest Casino.* New York: Harper Collins, 2000.

Benveniste, Emile. *Problems in General Linguistics.* Trans. Mary Elizabeth Meek. Coral Gables, Fla.: University of Miami Press, 1971.

Berkovitch, Sacvan. *The American Jeremiad.* Madison: University of Wisconsin Press, 1978.

Berman, Harold J. *Law and Revolution: The Formation of the Western Legal Tradition.* Cambridge, Mass.: Harvard University Press, 1983.

Bierhorst, John, ed. *Four Masterworks of American Indian Literature.* Tucson: University of Arizona Press, 1974.

Blackstone, William. *Commentaries on the Laws of England.* 4 vols. 1765. Chicago: University of Chicago Press, 1979.

Blodgett, Harold. *Samson Occom.* Hanover, N.H.: Dartmouth College Publications, 1935.

Boudinot, Elias. *A Star in the West: A Humble Attempt to Discover the Long Lost Ten Tribes of Israel Preparatory to their Return to their Beloved City, Jerusalem.* Trenton, N.J.: D. Fenton, S. Hutchinson, and J. Dunham, 1816.

Bowden, Henry W., and James P. Ronda, ed. *John Eliot's Indian Dialogues: A Study in Cultural Interaction.* Westport, Conn.: Greenwood Press, 1980.

Brooks, Joanna. *American Lazarus: Religion and the Rise of African-American and Native American Literatures.* New York: Oxford University Press, 2003.

Bross, Kristina. *Dry Bones and Indian Sermons: Praying Indians in Colonial America.* Ithaca, N.Y.: Cornell University Press, 2004.

———. "Dying Saints, Vanishing Savages: 'Dying Indian Speeches' in Colonial New England Literature." *Early American Literature* 36.3 (2001): 325–52.

Brumble, H. David III. *American Indian Autobiography.* Los Angeles: University of California Press, 1988.

Bruss, Elizabeth W. *Autobiographical Acts: The Changing Situation of a Literary Genre.* Baltimore: Johns Hopkins University Press, 1976.

Butler, Judith. *The Psychic Life of Power.* Stanford, Calif.: Stanford University Press, 1997.

Calhoun. John. C. *A Disquisition on Government and Selections from the Discourse.* Ed. C. Gordon Post. New York: The Liberal Arts Press, 1953.

Campisi, Jack. "The Emergence of the Mashantucket Pequot Tribe, 1637–1975." *The Pequots in Southern New England: The Fall and Rise of an American Indian Nation.* Eds. Laurence M. Hauptman and James D. Wherry. 117–40. Norman: University of Oklahoma Press, 1990.

———. *The Mashpee Indians: Tribe on Trial.* Syracuse, N.Y.: Syracuse University Press, 1993.

Carlson, David. "Edward Taylor and Puritan Entrepreneurship." *Studies in Puritan American Spirituality.* Vol 7. (Winter 2001): 111–41.

Carrithers, Michael, Steven Collins, and Steven Lukes, eds. *The Category of the Person: Anthropology, Philosophy, History.* Cambridge, U.K.: Cambridge University Press, 1985.

Cave, Alfred E. "Canaanites in a Promised Land: The American Indian and the Providential Theory of Empire." *American Indian Quarterly* 12 (Fall 1988): 277–98.

———. *The Pequot War.* Amherst: University of Massachusetts Press, 1996.

Clifford, James. "Identity at Mashpee," *The Predicament of Culture.* Ed. James Clifford. 277–348. Cambridge, Mass.: Harvard University Press, 1988.

Cmiel, Kenneth. *Democratic Eloquence: The Fight over Popular Speech in Nineteenth-Century America.* Los Angeles: University of California Press, 1990.

Coleman, Earl M., ed. *The Case of the Seneca Indians in the State of New York, Printed for the Information of the Society of Friends.* (1840). New York: Earl M. Coleman, Publisher, 1970.

Cover, Robert M. *Justice Accused: Antislavery and the Judicial Process.* New Haven, Conn.: Yale University Press, 1975.

———. "Nomos and Narrative." *Narrative, Violence, and the Law: The Essays of Robert Cover.* Eds. Martha Minow et al. 95–172. Ann Arbor: University of Michigan Press, 1992.

de Crèvecouer, J. Hector St. John. *Letters from an American Farmer and Sketches of Eighteenth-Century America.* Ed. Albert E. Stone. New York: Penguin, 1981.

Dannenberg, Anne Marie. "'Where, then, shall we place the hero of the wilderness?': William Apess's Eulogy on King Philip and the Doctrines of Racial Destiny." *Early Native American Writing: New Critical Essays.* Ed. Helen Jaskoski. 66–82. New York: Cambridge University Press, 1996.

De Forest, John W. *History of the Indians of Connecticut, From the Earliest Known Period to the 1850s.* Hartford, Conn.: Wm. Jas. Hamersley, 1851.

Deloria, Ella. *Speaking of Indians.* 1944. Lincoln: University of Nebraska Press, 1998.

Deloria, Philip, J. *Playing Indian.* New Haven, Conn.: Yale University Press, 1998.

Deloria, Vine Jr. *Custer Died for Your Sins: An Indian Manifesto.* 2nd ed. Norman: University of Oklahoma Press, 1988.

Deloria, Vine Jr., and Clifford M. Lytle. *American Indians, American Justice.* Austin: University of Texas Press, 1983.

DeMallie, Raymond J. "Kinship and Biology in Sioux Culture." *North American Indian Anthropology: Essays on Society and Culture.* Ed. Raymond J. DeMallie and Alfonso Ortiz. 125–46. Norman: University of Oklahoma Press, 1994.

Douglas, Mary. *How Institutions Think.* Syracuse, N.Y.: Syracuse University Press, 1986.

Drummond, A. M. and Richard Moody, "Indian Treaties: The First American Dramas." *Quarterly Journal of Speech.* (Feb. 1953): 15–24.

Eakin, Paul John. *Fictions in Autobiography: Studies in the Art of Self-Invention.* Princeton, N.J.: Princeton University Press, 1985.

———. *Touching the World: Reference in Autobiography.* Princeton, N.J.: Princeton University Press, 1992.

Eastman, Charles. *From the Deep Woods to Civilization.* 1916. Lincoln: University of Nebraska Press, 1977.

———. "The Indian as Citizen," *Lippincott's Magazine,* (Jan. 1915), 70–76.

———. *Indian Boyhood.* 1902. New York: Dover Publications, 1971.

———. *Indian Scout Talks.* 1914. New York: Dover Publications, 1974.

———. *The Indian To-day: The Past and Future of the First American.* New York: Doubleday, Page, and Co., 1915

———. "The Sioux Mythology," *Popular Science Monthly,* (Nov. 1894–April 1895), 88–91.

———. *The Soul of Indian: An Interpretation.* 1911. Lincoln: University of Nebraska Press, 1980.

Eastman, Elaine Goodale. *Sister to the Sioux.* Lincoln: University of Nebraska Press, 1978.

Eberwein, Jane Donahue, ed. *Early American Poetry.* Madison: University of Wisconsin Press, 1978.

Eisler, Kim Isaac. *Revenge of the Pequots: How a Small Native American Tribe Created the World's Most Profitable Casino.* Lincoln: University of Nebraska Press, 2002.

Elliott. Michael. "'This Indian Bait': Samson Occom and the Voice of Liminality." *Early American Literature.* 29.3 (1994): 233–53.

Elrod, Eileen Razzari. "'I Did Not Make Myself So . . .': Samson Occom and Religious Autobiography." *Christian Encounters with the Other.* Ed. John C. Rawley. 135–49. New York: New York University Press, 1998:

Falkowski, James E. *Indian Law/Race Law: A Five Hundred Year History.* New York: Praeger Publishers, 1992.

Fisher, William W., et al., eds. *American Legal Realism.* New York: Oxford University Press, 1993.

Foucault, Michel. *The Archaeology of Knowledge and The Discourse on Language.* Trans. A. M. Sheridan Smith. New York: Pantheon Books, 1972.

Franklin, Benjamin. *The Autobiography of Benjamin Franklin.* Ed. Leonard W. Labaree, et al. New Haven, Conn.: Yale University Press, 1964.

Fritz, Henry E. *The Movement for Indian Assimilation, 1860–1890.* Philadelphia: University of Pennsylvania Press, 1963.

Fuller, Lon L. *The Morality of Law.* 2nd ed. New Haven, Conn.: Yale University Press, 1964.

Geertz, Clifford. *The Interpretation of Cultures.* New York: Harper Collins, 1973.

Getches, David, and Charles Wilkinson. *Federal Indian Law: Cases and Materials.* St. Paul, Minn.: West Publishing Co., 1986.

Glendon, Mary Ann. *Rights Talk: The Impoverishment of Political Discourse.* New York: The Free Press, 1991.

Grossberg, Michael. *Governing the Hearth: Law and the Family in Nineteenth-Century America.* Chapel Hill: University of North Carolina Press, 1985.

———. *A Judgment for Solomon.* New York: Cambridge University Press, 1996.

Gustafson, Sandra. "Nation of Israelites: Prophecy and Cultural Autonomy in the Writings of William Apess." *Religion and Literature.* 26.1 (1994): 31–54.

Harring, Sidney L. *Crow Dog's Case: American Indian Sovereignty, Tribal Law, and United States Law in the Nineteenth Century.* Cambridge: Cambridge University Press, 1994.

Hauptman, Laurence M. *Conspiracy of Interests: Iroquois Dispossession and the Rise of New York State.* Syracuse: Syracuse University Press, 1999.

———. "The Pequot War and Its Legacies." *The Pequots in Southern New England.* Ed. Laurence M. Hauptman and James D. Wherry. Norman: University of Oklahoma Press, 1990.

Haynes, Carolyn. "A Mark for Them All to . . . Hiss At": The Formation of Methodist and Pequot Identity in the Conversion Narrative of William Apess." *Early American Literature.* 31.1 (1996): 25–44.

Henderson, J. Y. "Unravelling the Riddle of Aboriginal Title," 5 *American Indian Law Review* 75 (1977).

Hertzberg, Hazel W. *The Search for an American Indian Identity: Modern Pan-Indian Movements.* Syracuse, N.Y.: Syracuse University Press, 1971.

Horwitz, Morton J. *The Transformation of American Law 1780–1860.* Cambridge, Mass.: Harvard University Press, 1977.

Hoxie, Frederick E. *A Final Promise: The Campaign to Assimilate the Indians, 1880–1920.* Lincoln: University of Nebraska Press, 1984.

Huddleston, Lee Eldridge. *Origins of the American Indians: European Concepts, 1492–1729.* Austin: University of Texas Press, 1967.

Hutchens, Francis. G. *Mashpee: The Story of Cape Cod's Indian Town.* West Franklin, N.H.: Amarta Press, 1979.

Hymes, Dell. *Foundations in Sociolinguistics: An Ethnographic Approach.* Philadelphia: University of Pennsylvania Press, 1974.

Irving, Washington. *The Sketchbook of Geoffrey Crayon, Gent.* 1819. Ed. William L. Hedges. New York: Penguin Books, 1988.

Jacobson, Marcia. *Being a Boy Again: Autobiography and the American Boy Book.* Tuscaloosa: University of Alabama Press, 1994.

JanMohamed, Abdul. "Negating the Negation as a Form of Affirmation in Minority Discourse: The Construction of Richard Wrights as Subject." *Cultural Critique* 7 (1987): 245–66.

Jefferson, Thomas. *Notes on the State of Virginia.* 1785. Ed. William Peden. New York: W. W. Norton, 1982.

Jennings, Francis. *The Ambiguous Iroquois Empire: The Covenant Chain Confederation of Indian Tribes with English Colonies.* New York: W. W. Norton and Co., 1984.

———. *The Invasion of America: Indians, Colonialism, and the Cant of Conquest.* New York: W. W. Norton and Co., 1975.

Jones, Dorothy V. *License for Empire: Colonialism by Treaty in Early America.* Chicago: University of Chicago Press, 1982.

Kaestle, Carl F. *Pillars of the Republic: Common Schools and American Society, 1780–1860.* New York: Hill and Wang, 1983.

Karttunen, Frances. *Between Worlds: Interpreters, Guides, Survivors.* New Brunswick, N.J.: Rutgers University Press, 1994.

Kaplan, Amy, and Donald Pease, eds. *Cultures of United States Imperialism.* Durham, N.C.: Duke University Press, 1993.

Kawashima, Yasuhide. *Puritan Justice and the Indian: White Man's Law in Massachusetts, 1630–1763.* Middletown, Conn.: Wesleyan University Press, 1986.

Kellaway, William. *The New England Company 1649–1776: Missionary Society to the American Indians.* New York: Barnes and Noble, 1961.

Kent, James. *Commentaries on American Law.* 4 vols. 1826–1830. New York: Da Capo Press, 1971.

Konkle, Maureen. *Writing Indian Nations: Native American Intellectuals and the Politics of Historiography, 1827–1863.* Chapel Hill: University of North Carolina Press, 2004.

Krupat, Arnold. *Ethnocriticism: Ethnography, History, Literature.* Berkeley: University of California Press, 1992.

———. *For Those Who Come After: A Study of Native American Autobiography.* Berkeley: University of California Press, 1985.

———. *The Voice in the Margin: Native American Literature and the Canon.* Berkeley: University of California Press, 1989.

La Flesche, Francis. *The Middle Five: Indian Schoolboys of the Omaha Tribe.* 1900. Madison: University of Wisconsin Press, 1963.

Lauter, Paul, ed. *The Heath Anthology of American Literature.* Vol. 1, 3rd ed. Boston: Houghton Mifflin, 2000.

Lejeune, Philippe. *On Autobiography.* Trans. Katherine Leary. Minneapolis: University of Minnesota Press, 1989.

Levinson, Sanford. *Constitutional Faith.* Princeton, N.J.: Princeton University Press, 1988.

Levinson, Sanford, and Steven Mailloux, eds. *Interpreting Law and Literature: A Hermeneutic Reader.* Evanston, Ill.: Northwestern University Press, 1988.

Lionnet, Francoise. *Autobiographical Voices: Race, Gender, Self-Portraiture.* Ithaca, N.Y.: Cornell University Press, 1989.

Littlefield, Daniel F., Jr. "'They Ought to Enjoy the Home of Their Fathers': The Treaty of 1838, Seneca Intellectuals, and Literary Genesis." *Early Native American Writing: New Critical Essays.* Ed. Helen Jaskoski. 83–103. Cambridge: Cambridge University Press, 1996.

Llewellyn, K. N., and E. Adamson Hoebel. *The Cheyenne Way: Conflict and Case Law in Primitive Jurisprudence.* Norman: University of Oklahoma Press, 1941.

Locke, John. *A Letter Concerning Toleration.* Buffalo: Prometheus Books, 1990.

———. *Some Thoughts Concerning Education and of the Conduct of the Understanding.* Ed. Ruth W. Grant and Nathan Tarcov. Indianapolis, Ind.: Hackett Publ., 1996.

———. *Two Treatises of Government.* Ed. Peter Laslett. Cambridge, U.K.: Cambridge University Press, 1988.

Love, W. DeLoss. *Samson Occom and the Christian Indians of New England.* Boston: The Pilgrim Press, 1899.

Lyotard, Jean-Francois. *The Differend: Phrases in Dispute.* Minneapolis: University of Minnesota Press, 1988.

Lyotard, Jean-Francois, and Jean-Loup Thebaud. *Just Gaming.* Minneapolis: University of Minnesota Press, 1985.

Macpherson, C. B. *The Political Theory of Possessive Individualism.* Oxford: Oxford University Press, 1962.

Mascuch, Michael. *Origins of the Individualist Self: Autobiography and Self-Identity in England, 1591–1791.* Stanford, Calif.: Stanford University Press, 1996.

McCallum, James Dow. *The Letters of Eleazer Wheelock's Indians.* Hanover, N.H.: Dartmouth University Press, 1932.

McCarthy, Keely. "Conversion, Identity, and the Indian Missionary." *Early American Literature.* 36.3 (2001): 353–70.

McQuaid, Kim. "William Apess, Pequot: An Indian Reformer in the Jackson Era." *New England Quarterly.* 50.4 (1977): 605–25.

Memmi, Albert. *The Colonizer and the Colonized.* New York: The Orion Press, 1965.

Michaelsen, Scott. "Resketching Anglo-Amerindian Identity Politics." *Border Theory: The Limits of Cultural Politics.* Eds. Scott Michealsen and David E. Johnson. 221–52. Minneapolis: University of Minnesota Press, 1997.

Mihesuah, Devon A., ed. *Natives and Academics: Researching and Writing about American Indians.* Lincoln: University of Nebraska Press, 1998.

Momaday, N. Scott. *The Names: A Memoir.* Tucson: University of Arizona Press, 1976.

Montesquieu. *The Spirit of the Laws.* Trans. and Ed. Anne M. Cohler, Basia Carolyn Liller, and Harold Samuel Stone. Cambridge, U.K.: Cambridge University Press, 1989.

Moon, Michael, and Cathy N. Davidson, eds. *Subject and Citizen: Nation, Race, and Gender from Oroonoko to Anita Hill.* Durham, N.C.: Duke University Press, 1995.

Moon, Randall. "William Apess and Writing White." *Studies in American Indian Literatures.* 2nd series. 5.4 (1993): 45–54.

Morgan, Lewis Henry. *The League of the Iroquois.* Ed. William N. Fenton. 1851. Secaucus, N.J.: Citadel Press, 1996.

Murray, David. *Forked Tongues: Speech, Writing, and Representation in North American Indian Texts.* London: Pinter Publishers, 1991.

Murray, Laura. *To Do Good to My Indian Brethren: The Writings of Joseph Johnson, 1751–1776.* Amherst: University of Massachusetts Press, 1998.

Nelson, Dana D. "'(I Speak Like a Fool but I Am Constrained)': Samson Occom's Short Narrative and Economies of the Racial Self." *Early Native American Writing: New Critical Essays.* Ed. Helen Jaskoski. 42–65. Cambridge, U.K.: Cambridge University Press, 1996.

Nielsen, Donald. "The Mashpee Indian Revolt of 1833." *New England Quarterly.* 58 (1985): 400–420.

Nussbaum, Felicity A. *The Autobiographical Subject: Gender and Ideology in Eighteenth-Century England.* Baltimore: Johns Hopkins University Press, 1989.

O'Connell, Barry. "'Once More Let Us Consider': William Apess in the Writing of New England Native American History." *After King Philip's War: Presence and Persistence in Indian New England.* Ed. Colin G. Calloway. 162–77. Hanover, N.H.: University Press of New England, 1997.

———, ed. *On Our Own Ground: The Complete Writings of William Apess, a Pequot.* Amherst: University of Massachusetts Press, 1992.

———. "William Apess and the Survival of the Pequot People." *Algonkians of New England: Past and Present.* Ed. Peter Benes. 89–100. Boston: Boston University Press, 1993.

Olney, James. *Metaphors of Self.* Princeton, N.J.: Princeton University Press, 1972.

Pagden, Anthony, and Jeremy Lawrence, eds. *Francisco de Vitoria: Political Writings.* New York: Cambridge University Press, 1991.

Parker, Arthur C. *The Indian How Book.* 1927. New York: Dover Publications, 1975.

———, ed. "Writings of General Parker." *Proceedings of the Buffalo Historical Society* 8 (1905): 520–36.

Pascal, Roy. *Design and Truth in Autobiography.* New York: Garland Press, 1960.

Pearce, Roy Harvey. *Savagism and Civilization: A Study of the Indian and the American Mind.* Berkeley: University of California Press, 1988.

Pease, Donald, ed. *National Identities and Post-Americanist Narratives.* Durham, N.C.: Duke University Press, 1994.

Perdue, Theda, ed. *Cherokee Editor: The Writings of Elias Boudinot.* Knoxville: University of Tennessee Press, 1983.

Peterson, Erik. "An Indian, An American: Ethnicity, Assimilation and Balance in Charles Eastman's *From the Deep Woods to Civilization,*" *SAIL* (Summer/Fall 1992): 145–60.

Pevar, Stephen L. *The Rights of Indians and Tribes.* Carbondale: Southern Illinois University Press, 2002.

Peyer, Bernd. "Samson Occum: Mohegan Missionary and Writer of the 18th Century." *American Indian Quarterly.* 6.3–4 (1982): 208–17.

———, ed. *The Elders Wrote: An Anthology of Early Prose by North American Indians 1768–1931.* Berlin: Deitrich Reimer Verlag, 1982.

Pierce, Maris B. "Address on the Present Conditions and Prospects of the Aboriginal Inhabitants of North America." *The Elders Wrote: An Anthology of Early Prose by North American Indians 1768–1931.* Ed. Bernd Peyer. 56–65. Berlin: Deitrich Reimer Verlag, 1982.

Posner, Richard. *Law and Literature: A Misunderstood Relation.* Cambridge, Mass.: Harvard University Press, 1988.

Pratt, Mary Louise. "Arts of the Contact Zone." *Profession* 91 (1991): 33–40

———. *Imperial Eyes: Travel Writing and Transculturation.* New York: Routledge, 1992.

Prucha, Francis. *American Indian Policy in Crisis: Christian Reformers and the Indian, 1865–1900.* Norman: University of Oklahoma Press, 1976.

———. *American Indian Treaties: The History of a Political Anomaly.* Berkeley: University of California Press, 1994.

———. *Documents of United States Indian Policy.* 2nd ed. Lincoln: University of Nebraska Press, 1990.

Radin, Paul. *The Autobiography of a Winnebago Indian: Life, Ways, Acculturation, and the Peyote Cult.* 1920. New York: Dover Publications, 1963.

Reed, John Philip. *Constitutional History of the American Revolution.* Madison: University of Wisconsin Press, 1986.

Rose, Mark. *Authors and Owners: The Invention of Copyright.* Cambridge, Mass.: Harvard University Press, 1993.

Rudolph, Frederick, ed. *Essays on Education in the Early Republic.* Cambridge: Harvard University Press, 1965.

Ruoff, A. LaVonne Brown. "Three Nineteenth-Century American Indian Autobiographers." *Redefining American Literary History.* Eds. A. LaVonne Brown Ruoff and Jerry W. Ward Jr. 251–69. New York: The Modern Language Association, 1990.

Ruoff, A. LaVonne Brown, and Donald B. Smith, eds. *George Copway: Life Letters and Speeches.* Lincoln: University of Nebraska Press, 1997.

Said, Edward W. *Culture and Imperialism.* New York: Random House, 1993.

Sarris, Greg. "American Indian Lives and Others' Selves." *Thinking Bodies.* Ed. Juliet Flower MacCannell and Laura Zakarin. 142–48. Stanford, Calif.: Stanford University Press, 1994.

Saunders, David. *Authorship and Copyright.* New York: Routledge, 1992.

de Saussure, Ferdinand. *Course in General Linguistics.* Trans. Wade Baskin. New York: McGraw-Hill, 1959.

Sayre, Gordon. "Defying Assimilation, Confounding Authenticity: The Case of William Apess." *a/b: Auto/Biography Studies.* 11.1 (1996): 1–18.

Searle, John R. *The Social Construction of Reality.* New York: The Free Press, 1995.

———. *Speech Acts: An Essay in the Philosophy of Language.* Cambridge, U.K.: Cambridge University Press, 1969.

Seaver, James. *A Narrative of the Life of Mrs. Mary Jemison.* 1824. Norman: University of Oklahoma Press, 1992.

Shea, Daniel B. Jr. *Spiritual Autobiography in Early America.* Princeton, N.J.: Princeton University Press, 1968.

Sheehan, Bernard W. *Seeds of Extinction: Jeffersonian Philanthropy and the American Indian.* Chapel Hill: University of North Carolina Press, 1973.

Smith, Donald. "Kahgegahgahbowh: Canada's First Literary Celebrity in the United States." In *George Copway: Life Letters and Speeches.* Eds. A. LaVonne Brown Ruoff and Donald B. Smith. 23–60. Lincoln: University of Nebraska Press, 1997.

Smith, Linda Tuhiwai. *Decolonizing Methodologies: Research and Indigenous Peoples.* New York: Zed Books, 2002.

Society of Friends. *Letters Concerning the New Form of Government Adopted by the Seneca Indians.* 1849.

———. *Proceedings of an Indian Council, Held at the Buffalo Creek Reservation, State of New York, Fourth Month, 1842.* Baltimore: Wooddy, 1842.

Sollors, Werner. *Beyond Ethnicity: Consent and Descent in American Culture.* New York: Oxford University Press, 1986.

Spengemann, William C. *The Forms of Autobiography: Episodes in the History of a Literary Genre.* New Haven, Conn.: Yale University Press, 1980.

Spivak, Gayatri Chakravorty. "Can the Subaltern Speak?" *Wedge,* 7–8 (1985): 271–313.

———. *A Critique of Postcolonial Reason: Toward a History of the Vanishing Present.* Cambridge, Mass.: Harvard University Press, 1999.

Squadrito, Kathy. "Locke and the Dispossession of the American Indian." *American Indian Culture and Research Journal* 20:4 (1996): 145–81.

Standing Bear, Luther. *My People the Sioux.* 1928. Lincoln: University of Nebraska Press, 1975.

Strickland, Rennard, et al., eds. *Felix S. Cohen's Handbook of Federal Indian Law.* Charlottesville, Va.: The Michie Company, 1982.

Strong, Nathaniel T. *Appeal to the Christian Community on the Condition and Prospects of the New York Indians, in Answer to a Book, Entitled the Case of the New-York Indians, and Other Publications of the Society of Friends.* New York: E. B. Clayton, 1841.

Stuart, Paul. *The Indian Office: Growth and Development of an American Institution 1865–1900.* Ann Arbor, Mich.: UMI, 1978.

Szasz, Margaret. *Indian Education in the American Colonies, 1607–1783.* Albuquerque: University of New Mexico Press, 1988.

Tedlock, Dennis. "The Spoken Word and the Work of Interpretation." *Traditional Literatures of the American Indian: Texts and Interpretations.* Ed. Karl Kroeber. 68–87. Lincoln: University of Nebraska Press, 1997.

Thomas, Brook. *Cross-Examination of Law and Literature: Cooper, Hawthorne, Stowe, and Melville.* New York: Cambridge University Press 1987.

de Tocqueville, Alexis. *Democracy in America.* 1835. Ed. Phillips Bradley. 2 vols. New York: Vintage Books, 1945.

Trachtenberg, Alan. *The Incorporation of America: Culture and Society in the Gilded Age.* New York: Hill and Wang, 1982.

United States ex rel. Standing Bear v. Crook. 25 f. Cas 695; 1879 U.S. App. LEXIS 1667; 5 Dill. 453.

Vattel, Emmerich de. The *Law of Nations: Or Principles of the Law of Nature.* Northampton: Simeon Butler, 1820.

Velikova, Roumiana. "'Philip, King of the Pequots': The History of an Error." *Early American Literature* 37.2 (2002): 311–36.

Vernon, H. A. "Maris Bryant Pierce: The Making of a Seneca Leader." *Indian Lives: Essays on Nineteenth- and Twentieth-Century Native American Lead-*

ers. Eds L. G. Moses and Raymond Wilson. 19–42. Albuquerque: University of New Mexico Press, 1985.

Vizenor, Gerald. *Interior Landscapes: Autobiographical Myths and Metaphors.* Minneapolis: University of Minnesota Press, 1990.

———. "Postindian Autoinscriptions: The Origins of Essentialism and Pluralism in Descriptive Tribal Names." *Cultural Difference and the Literary Text: Pluralism and the Limits of Authenticity in North American Literatures.* Eds. Winfried Siemerling and Katrin Schwenk. 29–39. Iowa City: University of Iowa Press, 1996.

Waldman, Carl. *Atlas of the North American Indian.* New York: Facts on File, 1985.

Walker, Cheryl. *Indian Nation: Native American Literature and Nineteenth-Century Nationalisms.* Durham, N.C.: Duke University Press, 1997.

Wallace, Anthony F. C. *The Death and Rebirth of the Seneca.* New York: Vintage Books, 1972.

Warrior, Robert Allen. *Tribal Secrets: Recovering American Indian Intellectual Traditions.* Minneapolis: University of Minnesota Press, 1995.

———. "William Apess: A Pequot and a Methodist under the Sign of Modernity." *Liberation Theologies, Postmodernity, and the Americas.* Eds. David Batstone, et al. New York: Routledge, 1997.

Weaver, Jace. *That the People Might Live: Native American Literature and Native American Community.* New York: Oxford University Press, 1997.

Weintraub, Karl Joachim. "Autobiography and Historical Consciousness." *Critical Inquiry* (June 1975): 821–48.

———. *The Value of the Individual: Self and Circumstance in Autobiography.* Chicago: University of Chicago Press, 1978.

Wheelock, Eleazar. *A Plain and Faithful Narrative of the Original Design, Rise, Progress, and Present State of the Indian Charity School at Lebanon, in Connecticut.* Boston. 1763.

White, Craig. "The Praying Indians' Speeches as Texts of Massachusetts Oral Culture." *Early American Literature.* 38.3 (2003): 437–67.

White, James Boyd. *When Words Lose Their Meaning: Constitutions and Re-constitutions of Language, Character, and Community.* Chicago: University of Chicago Press, 1984.

Williams, Robert A. Jr. *The American Indian in Western Legal Thought: The Discourses of Conquest.* Oxford: Oxford University Press, 1993.

———. *Linking Arms Together: American Indian Treaty Visions of Law and Peace 1600–1800.* New York: Routledge, 1999.

———. "The Medieval Discourse of Crusade." *Native American Law and Colonialism Before 1776 to 1903.* Ed. John R. Wander. New York: Garland Publishing, 1996. 77–122.

Wilson, Raymond. *Ohiyesa: Charles Eastman, Santee Sioux.* Chicago: University of Illinois Press, 1983.

Winnemucca Hopkins, Sarah. *Life among the Piutes.* 1883. Las Vegas: University of Nevada Press, 1994.

Wong, Hertha Dawn. *Sending My Heart Back across the Years: Tradition and Innovation in Native American Autobiography.* New York: Oxford University Press, 1992.

Womack, Craig S. *Red on Red: Native American Literary Separatism.* Minneapolis: University of Minnesota Press, 1999.

Wroth, Lawrence C. "The Indian Treaty as Literature" *Yale Review.* 17 (1928): 748–66.

Wyss, Hilary E. *Writing Indians: Literacy, Christianity, and Native Community in Early America.* Amherst: University of Massachusetts Press, 2000.

INDEX

DAVID J. CARLSON is an assistant professor of English at California State University, San Bernardino.

The University of Illinois Press
is a founding member of the
Association of American University Presses.

Composed in 9.5/12.5 Trump Mediaeval
by Jim Proefrock
at the University of Illinois Press
Manufactured by Versa Press, Inc.

University of Illinois Press
1325 South Oak Street
Champaign, IL 61820-6903
www.press.uillinois.edu